READING AND WRITING CHINESE

READING AND WRITING

CHINESE

A Guide to the Chinese Writing System:
The Student's 1,020 List
The Official 2,000 List

by

WILLIAM MCNAUGHTON

CHARLES E. TUTTLE COMPANY
Rutland · Vermont : Tokyo · Japan

Published by the Charles E. Tuttle Company, Inc.
of Rutland, Vermont & Tokyo, Japan
with editorial offices at
Suido 1-chome, 2-6, Bunkyo-ku, Tokyo

Copyright in Japan, 1979
by Charles E. Tuttle Co., Inc.

Library of Congress Catalog Card No. 77-77699
International Standard Book No. 0-8048-1583-6

First printing, 1979
First softcover edition, 1989
Tenth printing, 1997

PRINTED IN SINGAPORE

TABLE OF CONTENTS

PREFACE

Learning to read and write modern Chinese with reasonable fluency has in recent years become much less of a chore than it used to be. Any student interested in learning to read and write simple everyday Chinese or in using a knowledge of everyday Chinese as the foundation for later study can now reach that goal with less strain on his or her time, attention, and memory. Among American teachers of Chinese, a consensus has developed as to the 1,020 characters most useful for the student to learn first. In addition, an official list of 2,000 characters has been published in mainland China for the purpose of adult education.* I have prepared *Reading and Writing Chinese* to help students master both these lists as rapidly and easily as possible.†

In selecting and arranging the materials in this book, I have been guided by the following principles:

1. To teach the student the most useful characters, as determined by the "Yale 1,020 List" and the official "2,000 List"

2. To present the characters in the order in which they are likely to be most useful; that is, to begin with the most frequently seen characters and to proceed to the less frequently seen ones

* See George A. Kennedy, ed., *Minimum Vocabularies of Written Chinese* (New Haven: Far Eastern Publications, 1954).
† *A Guide to Reading and Writing Japanese*, ed. Florence Sakade (Tokyo and Rutland, Vt.: Charles E. Tuttle Co., revised edition, 1961), has played a similar role in the study of Japanese for years.

3. To teach the elements of the writing system—the 214 radicals and the "phonetics" (sound components) students will find most valuable in their study of the lists mentioned above

4. To break down the subject matter (the characters that make up the two lists) into units of information based on the most recent developments in programed instruction and to arrange these units in order of growing difficulty

5. To help students master the problem of "look-alike" characters; through juxtaposition and cross-reference, I have tried to clarify the three main causes of the problem: look-alike radicals, look-alike characters, and different forms of the same radical*

The characters are presented in two groups. The first group presents the basic characters for adult students of Chinese and the elements of the writing system from which these basic characters are made. These are the characters which students, using almost any elementary textbook, will be expected to learn in the first year, or in some cases the first two years, of study. The Yale guidelines, which have become standard in teaching Chinese in the United States, are followed here.

The second group of characters contains the rest of the characters on the "Yale 1,020 list" and the rest of the 2,000 characters on the officially published China list. In all, this gives the student the 1,500 characters that George A. Kennedy has described as "a good foundation for the Western student of modern Chinese," plus 500 characters officially designated in China as being of most frequent occurrence. It should be noted that another list of 421 characters has been promulgated in China to cover technical terms used by the workers; this list has not been included in the present volume, however, because it is of only slight value to the foreigner studying modern Chinese.

I have used earlier versions of this book side by side with the Yale Mirror Series textbooks to teach my Chinese language classes at

* See Henry C. Fenn, ed., *Chinese Characters Easily Confused* (New Haven: Far Eastern Publications, 1953).

Oberlin College. Teachers should find it quite easy to use this book with any of the other textbooks now popular in the United States, however, for the logic of the writing system is always the same and the vocabulary in the various series of elementary and intermediate textbooks is virtually identical.

When I teach, I assign six or seven characters a night as homework. We spend almost all our class time with the spoken Chinese and grammar text, since the format of this character book enables the students to learn on their own. I generally quiz students every day or so on new characters so as to enforce regular study habits. These quizzes do not usually take up more than five minutes of regular class time.

Working steadily at this rate, a class can cover all the material in the first character group in two sixteen-week semesters. The class will then know all the characters through *Read Chinese II* and *Read About China,* as well as the frequently seen component radicals and phonetics. More advanced students who have used this book in their first year of Chinese will have a tremendous advantage when they begin to study the characters in the second group. Quite clearly, their knowledge of basic character components will help speed their acquisition of this group, since the presentation here uses these components in programed sequences.

It has been my experience that students can be safely given *Reading and Writing Chinese* on their first day of Chinese study. Far from discouraging students, the characters and the writing system seem to stimulate enthusiasm and to increase motivation.

The work of preparing handwritten characters for the text, indexes, and charts used in this book was shared by Tseng Li-yü of the Chinese Literature Faculty of Tunghai University, Taichung, Taiwan, and by Chou Chih-p'ing of the Chinese Literature Faculty of Oberlin College. For valuable help I am indebted to various editors of the Charles E. Tuttle Company. I have incurred innumerable debts to students who used these texts in earlier forms for many years in my Chinese language classes at Oberlin College, but Howard Spendelow and John Dove deserve special mention for the amount and quality of their contributions. I am also indebted to colleagues who have suggested changes and improvements in the earlier versions. I should acknowledge the importance to this work of *Minimum Vocabularies of Written Chinese,* edited by George A. Kennedy (New Haven: Far Eastern Publications, 1954), and of *Jianhuazi Zongbiao Jianzi* (Peking: Wenzi Gaige Chubanshe, 1965).

—WILLIAM MCNAUGHTON

STUDENT'S GUIDE

The Writing System

The basis of the Chinese writing system is 214 elements often referred to as "radicals." These radicals are used either independently or as parts of more complex characters. The Chinese also use radicals to organize their dictionaries, from one-stroke radicals in the beginning to a seventeen-stroke radical at the very end. Dictionary makers take every character which is not itself a radical, determine which of the radicals within it is logically the most important, and then classify the character in the dictionary under that radical.

Every time a new character was created to represent some word of the spoken language, the character was formed according to one of six principles. Classifying Chinese writing according to these principles, we can say that six—and only six—kinds of character exist: (1) pictures, (2) symbols, (3) sound-loans, (4) sound-meaning compounds, (5) meaning-meaning compounds, and (6) reclarified compounds.

If we understand these six principles, we will be able to see *why* every new character we study means what it does. Instead, then, of seeming a capricious aggregation of strokes set down by an equally capricious pen, the character will reflect a logical system for representing words and concepts: each new character will be a combination of familiar elements.

Let us look at each of the six kinds of Chinese character.

1. *Pictures.* Some Chinese characters are mere pictures of things. The character for "man" is a simple stick drawing of a man 人. The

character for "child" or "baby" is a drawing of an infant with open
fontanel 兒. Sometimes, though, the modern character is a very styl-
ized picture of what it represents. We then have to look into the
history of the character before we can really see the resemblance
clearly. The character for "moon" 月 used to look like this 𝄐 ; the
character for "eye" 目 like this ⟁ .

2. *Symbols.* Some Chinese characters are symbols—some more,
some less arbitrary—for the concept to which they refer. Some examples of symbols are: 上 "above," 下 "below," 一 "one," 二 "two,"
三 "three."

3. *Sound-loans.* Some Chinese characters stand for a word which
is, or once was, pronounced the same as another but with a different
meaning, like "feet" and "feat." This type of character, a picture or
symbol for one of two homonyms, was borrowed to represent the
companion homonym, too; the context was relied on to make the
meaning clear. For example, the words for "scorpion" and "10,000"
were once homonyms. The character 萬, now used to write "10,000,"
originally meant "scorpion" but was borrowed for "10,000" since
there was little danger of confusing the two meanings in context. You
can probably see that it would have been inconvenient to write
"10,000" in the same symbolic notation used to write the numbers
"one," "two," and "three."

4. *Sound-meaning compounds.* Sometimes one part of a Chinese
character gives a hint about the meaning, and another, a hint about
the pronunciation. For example, the character 包 "to wrap" is pronounced *bau-1*. (The pronunciation of the romanization and tone
markings used here is explained in the section beginning on page 21.)
If this character is combined with the character 魚 "fish," the result
is a new character 鮑 "salted fish," pronounced *bau-4*. The "fish"
component suggests the meaning, and the "wrap" component (*bau-1*)
suggests the sound.

5. *Meaning-meaning compounds.* Sometimes two characters are
put together to form a new character whose meaning derives from
some logic in the juxtaposition of the two component characters.
The character 女 "woman" beside the character 子 "child" forms
好, a character that means "to love" or "to be lovable, to be likable,
to be good." Although the logic in such juxtapositions is usually not

obvious enough to allow you to figure out the meaning of a new character, it is usually a great help when trying to remember a character you have seen only once.

6. *Reclarified compounds.* At various times in the history of the written language, a scribe has wanted to better "control" the meaning of a character he was using, either because the character—by sound-loan, perhaps—had come to stand for a number of different words or because the word the character represented had a number of different meanings. In doing this, the scribe could add to the existing character either to clarify the word to which it referred or to pinpoint the meaning intended in the particular context. For example, the character for "scorpion" 萬, which we saw above, was later reclarified when it was used to represent "scorpion" (rather than "10,000") by adding the "bug" radical 虫 to produce a new character 蠆 that always meant "scorpion" and only "scorpion." The character 廷 *ting-2* stood for "court"—whether it was the king's court or the court in someone's front yard. Eventually someone added the "lean-to" radical 广, which is a picture of a roof and wall, to distinguish the king's court (庭 *ting-2*) from the ordinary citizen's front yard (廷 *ting-2*). Some of these reclarified compounds will in their new guise be simple sound-meaning compounds, and some of them— if the reclarified character itself was already a sound-meaning compound—will be sound-meaning compounds with one component to suggest the sound and two components to suggest the meaning.*

Explanatory Notes

On the following page there appears an annotated character entry. It has been slightly modified from the actual entry in this book to show the full range of information provided for characters in the first character group.

---

* Bernhard Karlgren identifies dozens of such characters in *Analytic Dictionary of Chinese and Sino-Japanese* (Paris: Paul Geuthner, 1923). Chao Yuen Ren treats reclarified compounds as a subclass of sound-meaning compounds: see *Mandarin Primer* (Cambridge: Harvard University Press, 1961), pp. 61–63. Traditionally, the sixth of the six principles was something called *chuan chu,* and whether or not this had anything to do with reclarified compounds is uncertain, since there is a great deal of dispute about the correct interpretation and reference of *chuan chu.*

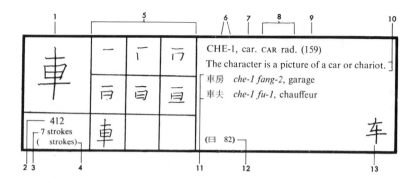

KEY:

1 the character
2 character serial number
3 stroke count
4 If there is a difference between the actual number of strokes as written by hand and the official number of strokes used in dictionaries, the official number will appear in parentheses here. See the discussion of stroke and form discrepancy on page 15.
5 stroke-order diagram
6 pronunciation and tone
7 character definition
8 radical information
9 radical number
10 character explanation
11 character combinations with pronunciation and meaning
12 Since characters may have more than nine strokes, it has sometimes been necessary to add *in toto* to the stroke-order diagram of the main character an element that is itself a character. (The element and serial number shown in this sample are provided only to show how a reference to an element added *in toto* will appear.) If such a reference is missing, either that element's stroke order is obvious or it can be found in one of the two preceding character entries.
13 simplified character

UNDERSTANDING THE ENTRIES. You should try to keep in mind that a Chinese character is not what we think of as a word in English, and that Chinese words for which the characters stand are often subject to different kinds of syntactic restriction. In fact, what we consider nouns, verbs, adjectives, and adverbs in English are, in classical Chinese, all considered one part of speech—any noun can be a verb, adjective, or adverb. Owing to the unavoidable use in this book of English articles, infinitives, suffixes, and the like, you may be misled into too narrow an interpretation of a character. These explicit definitions are provided for clarity, but you should always be aware that they really represent only the most basic outline of a character's "meaning."

Most of the punctuation marks used in the characters' explanatory blocks are grammatically logical. However, I have also adopted a few rules of my own to help you study. Semicolons are used to distinguish meaning "groups." Semicolons are also used after a character's romanized reading when a character's usage rather than meaning is given. In addition to their occasional use around slang terms or for clarity, quotation marks are used around character-compound definitions that are contextually proper in English but which cannot be derived from the characters themselves. For example, the Chinese use a character for "red" 紅 and the character for "tea" 茶 to write what in English we call "black tea." Since the more literal definition "red tea" would be meaningless, I have used quotation marks in the definition of the character combination as follows: 紅茶 *hung-2 cha-2,* "black" tea.

STROKE AND FORM DISCREPANCY. Each character has a traditional stroke count based on the character's placement in Chinese dictionaries. Small discrepancies—almost always of one stroke—sometimes exist between this traditional stroke count and the actual count used when the character is handwritten. Such discrepancies are indicated in parentheses throughout the presentation of the first group of characters. The most devastating problem for beginning students, however, is a change in shape and stroke count that occurs when a radical or character is used as an element to form a more complex character. I have therefore treated as entirely separate elements those characters whose shape changes may pose an identification problem. This treatment reflects more accurately the true nature of the writing system and has only resulted in about 40 characters being added to the text.*

For example, the radical 阜, when used as an element of another character, becomes 阝, a combining form that appears separately in this text as character 76. Appearing in the small box below the character is "3 strokes (8 strokes)." This means that though this form of the radical is actually written with three strokes, its independent form takes eight strokes; thus, all characters with 阝 as the radical component will appear among the eight-stroke radicals in a Chinese dictionary.

The radical chart on the back endpapers has been prepared with this in mind. Generally, the chart follows by stroke count the official list of 214 radicals. But where a discrepancy exists between a radical's independent and combining forms, the combining form will appear not only under its official stroke count but under its actual one as well. Thus, character 76 阝, above, will appear among the eight-stroke radicals alongside its independent form 阜 and also at the very end of the listing of three-stroke radicals.

Problems of correct character identification also result from the fact that typeset forms often differ from the handwritten forms that are usually learned first. Always compare a character in a typeset compound with its handwritten counterpart as you work through this book. The typeset list below provides the most common of these variant forms. Numbers refer to the serial number of characters in the first group; page numbers are for characters in the second group.

忄	67	令	284	昷	924
八	88	直	301	肖	939
入	152	眞	302	僉	974
辶	171	罒	338	掃	p.257
艹	192	示	480	歟	p.262
靑	198	冫	564	卽	p.277

* Also, twenty-two characters are identified as "heavenly stems" or "earthly branches." These "stems" and "branches" are characters which the Chinese use in various special ways in reckoning, calculation, and enumeration. The student who delves into Chinese history will need to know these twenty-two characters, because the traditional way of giving dates makes use of them.

CHARACTER COMBINATIONS. Individual characters themselves—each of which in general represents a single syllable of the spoken language—may occur in combination with other characters to denote Chinese words and expressions of two or more syllables. For example, a common expression for "woman" in the modern spoken language is the two-syllable *nyu-3 ren-2,* written with the characters for "woman" 女 (*nyu-3*) and "person" 人 (*ren-2*). Many of these common combinations are given in this book so that you will get used to seeing the characters within important expressions and words. Learning the combinations in which a character occurs can be a valuable aid to understanding that character. Moreover, since the characters used in these combinations are restricted to those that have already been presented in the text, these combinations provide review as well as new usage examples.

SIMPLIFIED CHARACTERS. In attempting to deal with the need for adult education and the complexity of the Chinese writing system, the mainland government has simplified many of the characters used for centuries. Traditional principles for making characters have been retained in making up new short forms. For example, in the short form 牺 *syi-1* "sacrifice," the traditional form 犧 has been shortened by simply replacing the complicated sound-component 羲 by the simple sound-component 西. The "cow" radical 牛 appears in both the short and traditional forms because the original meaning of the character was "sacrificial animal." Likewise, the traditional character 廳 *ting-1* "room, hall" has been simplified to 厅 mainly by substituting for the complicated sound-component 聽 the simpler sound-component 丁. Students who understand the logic of the traditional writing system and who have mastered the components of its characters will find that they attain mastery of the short forms much more easily.

I have used the unsimplified forms (most of which are still in use—in mainland China, too) as the basis for this book's presentation. I have included officially adopted simplified forms since students who want to read what is now published on the mainland will have to learn them sooner or later. To learn only these short forms, however, is a great mistake. In so doing students effectively cut themselves off from all the traditional Chinese literary and historical material as well as from most of the Chinese books available in Western libraries, which were written (and printed) before the process of simplification began. Students who can read only short forms will be able to read what Mao Tse-tung wrote, but they will be unable to read what Mao himself read—and that certainly is essential to any effort to understand modern China.

PHONETIC SERIES. When a certain character has been used to give the sound in a number of sound-meaning compounds, a group of characters emerges, each of which has a different meaning but contains the same sound-component. The different meanings are established, of course, by using a different meaning-component in each character. Such a group of characters is called a phonetic series, and students have often found that learning becomes more rapid when they study such character groups. In the second group of characters I have therefore introduced common characters as part of a phonetic series— if the characters belong to an important series. For example, the character "wrap" 包 (*bau-1*), mentioned above, is the sound-component for a number of common characters that appear in this book: 飽, 抱, 袍, 泡, 砲.

PHONETIC SYMBOLS. On page 295 is a key to the phonetic symbols (derived from abbreviated Chinese characters) used in recent dictionaries and in a considerable amount of teaching material published under the auspices of the present Taiwan government. These symbols are written vertically and as a group are referred to by the name *bwo, pwo, mwo, fwo*. For some examples of their use, see page 298.

STUDY METHODS. Each radical introduced in this book is assigned a number in parentheses. This is its radical number and indicates where the radical occurs within the sequence of 214 radicals used to organize Chinese dictionaries. Every effort you make to memorize this number will pay off in time saved after you have begun to use such a dictionary. You are also advised, when first learning a character, to be conscious of all the radicals that appear within it.

Say aloud the component radicals while writing a new character. For example, say "knight-eye-cowrie" while writing 賣 "sell" (character 135), or "grass-mouth-mouth-dove-yawn" while writing 歡 "be pleased" (character 194). Such incantations may be of considerable help in recalling characters to memory three or four days after first encountering them.

You should read the explanations of the sources of new characters, but you need not formally study these explanations unless (as sometimes happens) you become fascinated by the written Chinese character itself. In that case you may want to learn all the explanations given and even to carry your studies afield into the various books which present such explanations in greater, and sometimes fanciful, detail.

You can easily use *Reading and Writing Chinese* as a programed textbook. Cover the character with a blank piece of paper placed along the vertical line that separates the character from the box containing its pronunciation and meaning. Then try to write down the character, and immediately after doing so pull the answer sheet away and compare the character you have written with the character in the book. If you have written the character incorrectly, take note of the error or errors and write the character correctly several times before proceeding to the next one. After working to the bottom of a page in this way, reverse the procedure and try to write down the pronunciation and meaning while looking only at the character. Immediately check your work against the correct pronunciation and meaning that appear in the text.

How to Write the Characters

The Chinese learn to write characters by an easy and effective method. The essential ingredient of this method is the fixed order in which the strokes of a character are written. Although Chinese occasionally disagree among themselves about minor details, the method has been worked out and perfected through centuries of experience. Follow the stroke-order diagrams presented in this book in order to acquire the proper habits early and remember to keep your characters uniform in size. The rules below explain the method in general.

19

1. Top to bottom:

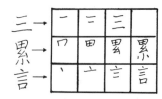

2. Left to right:

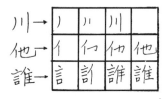

3. Upper left corner to lower right corner:

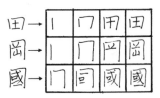

4. Outside to inside:

5. When two or more strokes cross, horizontal strokes before perpendicular strokes:

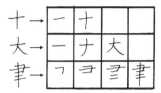

6. Slanting stroke to the left before slanting stroke to the right:

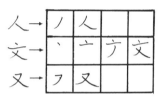

7. Center stroke before symmetrical wings:

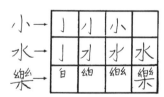

The Pronunciation of Chinese

The Yale romanization is used in *Reading and Writing Chinese* (except for tone notation) because it is the easiest romanization for a native speaker of English to learn and because it is the romanization that is most widely used in other elementary and intermediate Chinese language textbooks, including the Yale Mirror Series, the Yale University Press *Speak Mandarin* texts, and the Cornell University texts by Harriet Mills. Because the mainland romanization, *pinyin*, is so similar to the Yale romanization (and in fact was derived from it), students and teachers using the popular DeFrancis series of texts will not find it difficult to adjust to this book. A table on page 299 can be used to convert *pinyin* to Yale romanization.

1. The following letters are pronounced like their English equivalents: *f, k, l, m, n, p, s* (except *s* before *y;* see 7 below), *t, w,* and *y.*

2. The following letters are pronounced like the English sounds indicated: *a* (except as described in 8 below), as in *father; i,* as in *machine; o,* as in *worn; ai,* as in *aisle;* and *ei,* as in *eight.*

3. The following letters are pronounced like the English sounds indicated: *au,* like *ow* in *how; ou,* like *o* in *so;* and *e* (except *e* after *y;* see 8 below), like *o* in *done.*

4. The following letters are pronounced as explained: *b,* like *p* in *spy; d,* like *t* in *sty;* and *g,* like *k* in *sky;* that is, like English *p, t,* and *k* but with less aspiration (cp. 1, above).

5. The following letters are pronounced as described: *h,* with more friction than the English *h; u* (except *u* after *y;* see 8 below), like *oo* in *moon* but with the lips rounded and the tongue back; *dz,* like *ds* in *cads;* and *ts,* like *ts* in *it's hot.*

6. The following letters are pronounced as described: *sh,* as in *shred,* tongue very far back; *j* (except *j* before *i* or *y;* see 7 below), tongue flat against roof of mouth, very far back; *ch* (except *ch* before *i* or *y;* see 7 below), like *j* just described except with more breath; and *r,* tongue flat against roof of mouth, far back—like a *j* and *r* pronounced together.

7. The following letters are pronounced as described: *j* before *i* or *y,* like English *j* but with tongue tip forward where teeth meet; *ch* before *i* or *y,* like *j* just described but with more breath; and *s* before *y,* tongue tip against back of lower teeth (a lisping *s*).

8. The following letters are pronounced as described: *e* after *y,* as in *yet; u* after *y,* round the lips to say *oo* as in *moon* but try to pronounce instead *i* as in *machine; ywe,* like *yu* just described plus English *e* in *yet; a* after *y* and before *n* (but not before *ng*), like *e* in *yet;* and *a* after *yw* and before *n,* like *e* in *yet.*

TONE. In addition to its vowels and consonants, a word in modern Chinese has a characteristic "tone." The tone of a word is very important because it allows the Chinese ear to discriminate among words which have the same vowels and consonants. Tones result from changes in pitch which the speaker produces with the vocal chords while pronouncing the vowels and consonants. The difficulty of learning these tones has been much exaggerated. In fact, the system of tones in the National Language is actually one of the simplest in all Chinese dialects.

There are four tones, which this book identifies by the symbols −*1*, −*2*, −*3*, and −*4* attached to the spelling of each word (a modification of the Yale symbols ¯, ´, ˇ, and `, respectively, written over the syllable like the accent in French). Thus, *mau-1* is *m* + *au* (as described above) pronounced in the first tone, *mau-2* is *m* + *au* pronounced in the second tone, and so on. The way in which the speaker uses the vocal chords to change the pitch can be written on a musical staff, as below. Note that it is only the contour of the pitch which determines the tone; thus, a man's normal first tone will be a bit lower than a woman's. Pitch will normally be somewhere near the center of the speaking voice and will vary according to the individual and to his or her mood.*

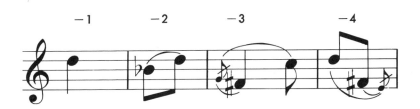

The description of tones given here is the simplest and is the one most often presented in texts. It is intended only to enable the student to pronounce words in isolation. In normal speech the tone may dis-

* The musical diagram is from Chao Yuen Ren, *A Grammar of Spoken Chinese* (Berkeley: University of California Press, 1968), p. 26.

appear from a word, and the word will be pronounced in a "neutral" or "zero" tone. In such cases in this book, the tone numbers have been omitted. In the case of two third tones in succession, native speakers change the first of them to a second tone: *hen-3 hau-3,* for example, becomes *hen-2 hau-3.* I have indicated such changes in this book if and only if the expression is a very common one. Many of the most common words change their tones all the time depending on the tone of the following word, and in these cases I have used the tone appropriate to each expression. Problems of words in discourse are, however, more properly a subject for a textbook of modern spoken Chinese, which you are urged to consult for more specific information.

1,062 BASIC CHARACTERS

and

Elements of the Writing System

				PYE-3, left stroke. LEFT rad. (4)
1 1 stroke				

				REN-2, man. MAN rad. (9) *Ren-2* is a picture—a rough stick drawing of a man. It occurs independently as a character and means "man" or "person." Learn to distinguish the "man" rad. from the "enter" rad. 入 (152, below).
2 2 strokes				

				GWUN-3, downstroke. DOWN rad. (2) Learn to distinguish from the "hook" rad. 亅 (13, below).
3 1 stroke				

				REN-2, man. MAN rad. (9) This form of the "man" rad. does not occur by itself as a character; it only occurs, in combination with other rads. or with sound-components, as a part of a character. To distinguish between it and the other form of the "man" rad. (2, above), we can call this form the "side-man."
4 2 strokes				

5 1 stroke				YI-3, twist; the second "heavenly stem." TWIST rad. (5) *Yi-3* occurs in early texts and means "fish guts." The character may originally have been a picture. Note that the character itself is bent and twisted.
6 3 strokes				YE-3, also Note that *ye-3* has "down" and "twist" in it. The other stroke is not a rad. (You need to learn how to write it but not to learn a name or number for it.) The history of *ye-3* involves the confusion of at least three different characters.
7 5 strokes				TA-1, he, him *Ta-1* is a sound-meaning compound. The "man" rad. (here, "side-man") suggests the meaning; the right half, *ye-3* (6, above), at one time suggested the sound, but now it is not such a good phonetic. Compare with 12 and 16, below.
8 1 stroke				YI-1, one. ONE rad. (1) *Yi-1* "one," *er-4* "two" (9, below), and *san-1* "three" (10, below) are probably the three simplest symbol-characters in the language.
9 2 strokes				ER-4, two. TWO rad. (7)

三	一	二	三	SAN-1, three
10 3 strokes				
女	く	女	女	NYU-3, woman. WOMAN rad. (38) *Nyu-3* is a picture—a rough stick drawing of a woman. It occurs independently as a character and means "woman." 女人　*nyu-3 ren-2*, woman
11 3 strokes				
她	く	女	女	TA-1, she, her This character is a sound-meaning compound. The "woman" rad. suggests the meaning, and *ye-3*, as in *ta-1* (7, above), once suggested the sound. Note the logic in the writing system: the "man" rad. occurs in the character for "he"; the "woman" rad. occurs in the character for "she."
她	女フ	女�┐	她	
12 6 strokes				
亅	亅			JYWE-2, hook. HOOK rad. (6) Note that the "hook" rad. has a little hook on the bottom of it. Do not confuse the "hook" rad. with the "down" rad. ｜ (3, above). The "down" rad. has no little hook on it.
13 1 stroke				
扌	一	扌	扌	SHOU-3, hand. HAND rad. (64) This form of the "hand" rad. does not occur by itself; it only occurs as a part of characters. We can call it the "side-hand." Compare "hand" (41, below). Don't confuse "side-hand" with "thumb" 寸 (186, below) or with "then" 才 (596, below).
14 3 strokes (4 strokes)				

27

牛 (15) 4 strokes	ノ ⺊ 牛 牛			NYOU-2, cow. cow rad. (93) *Nyou-2* is a picture. In older forms of the character, it is easy to see a cow with horns drawn from the front. This form of the "cow" rad. occurs only as a part of characters; another form 牛 (260, below) occurs as an independent character.
牪也 (16) 7 strokes	⺊ 牛 牛 牪 牪 牪也			TA-1, it The student should compare *ta-1* with *ta-1* "he" (7, above) and with *ta-1* "she" (12, above). *Ta-1* "it" has the "cow" rad. for meaning; as in "he" and "she," the sound of *ta-1* "it" once was suggested by *ye-3* (6, above).
了 (17) 2 strokes	⁊ 了			LE; a particle that goes after verbs or after sentences: *le* basically means "changed status" or "completed action"; LYAU-3, to finish, to conclude
子 (18) 3 strokes	⁊ 了 子			DZ-3, child. CHILD rad. (39) *Dz-3* is a picture. In older forms, it quite clearly resembles a child. *Dz-3* occurs often as an independent character and as a suffix to many nouns.
好 (19) 6 strokes	く ⼥ 女 女ˀ 奵 好			HAU-3, be good, be well *Hau-3* is a meaning-meaning compound. "Woman" beside "child" suggests "goodness, well-being, something desirable." This character may also be pronounced *hau-4*, in which case it means "to consider good, to like, to love."

	｜	冂		JYUNG-1, borders. BORDERS rad. (13)
20 2 strokes				
	｜	冂	囗	WEI-2, to surround. SURROUND rad. (31)
21 3 strokes				
	一	十		SHR-2, ten. TEN rad. (24) The "ten" rad. is simply an arbitrary symbol for the number "ten."
22 2 strokes				
	｜	冂	冎	TYAN-2, field. FIELD rad. (102) The "field" rad. is a picture of the typical Chinese (and East Asian) field—a large field divided by raised paths into small paddies.
	田	田		
23 5 strokes				
	ㄥ	ㄙ		SZ-1, be selfish, be private. COCOON rad. (28) The rad. originally was a picture of a tightly wound silk cocoon. Note that it appears also in several characters related to silk (25 and 28, below).
24 2 strokes				

29

么	ㄥ	幺	幺	**YAU-1, coil. COIL rad. (52)** The "coil" rad. originally was a picture of a coil of silk thread. Learn to distinguish "coil" from the "cocoon" rad. 厶 (24, above), from the "silk" rad. 糸 (28, below), and from the "dark" rad. 玄 (p. 242).
25 3 strokes				

ノ ＼	ノ	ノ ＼		**BA-1, eight. EIGHT rad. (12)** The history of this character is problematical. Memorize it as an arbitrary symbol. Note that there are other forms of the "eight" rad.: ` ´` and 八 (88 and 98, below).
26 2 strokes				

小	亅	´亅	´亅＼	**SYAU-3, be small, be little. SMALL rad. (42)** Originally, this rad. was three small dots to suggest "small." Two of the dots remain, but the center dot has been replaced by a "hook" rad.
27 3 strokes				

糸	ㄑ	幺	幺	**SZ-1, silk. SILK rad. (120)** The "silk" rad. was a drawing of silk thread. Note that the modern form includes the "coil" rad.
	糸	糸	糸	
28 6 strokes				

累	ㅣ	冂	甲	**LEI-4, be tired** In ancient China, the men's main work was in the fields; the women's main work was sericulture (silk farming). *Lei-4* may be a meaning-meaning compound to suggest everybody's work, whence "be tired."
	田	罒	罢	
29 11 strokes	罢	累	累	

彳 **30** 3 strokes	ノ	ク	彳	CHR-4, step. STEP rad. (60) Note that the "step" rad. includes the "side-man" (4, above), to which a stroke has been added. The added stroke is supposed to suggest movement, a step taken. The "step" rad. occurs often in characters for action or movement.

艮 **31** 6 strokes	コ ⊐	ヨ 月	ヨ 艮	GEN-4. STUBBORN rad. (138) In early texts, the "stubborn" rad. was used as an independent character and stood for a word that meant "stubborn." The character is originally supposed to have been a picture of a man with a big, staring eye—an obstinate type.

很 **32** 9 strokes	ノ 彳⁊ 彳艮	ク 彳ヨ 很	彳 彳艮 很	HEN-3, very This character is a sound-loan for hen-3 "very." Originally, it stood for a word that meant "to act stubborn, to resist"—a word that probably was cognate with gen-4 (31, above). The "stubborn" rad. was reclarified with the "step" rad., and sometime later the character was borrowed for hen-3.

口 **33** 3 strokes	丶	冂	口	KOU-3, mouth. MOUTH rad. (30) The "mouth" radical also occurs as an independent character and means "mouth." It is a picture. 人口 ren-2 kou-3, population 三口人 san-1 kou-3 ren-2, three people

ノ ㆍ ㆍ 丶 **34** 4 strokes	ノ ノ ㆍ ㆍ 丶	ㆍㆍ	ㆍㆍㆍ	HWO-3, fire. FIRE rad. (86) This is supposed to be a picture of the fire burning on the ground. This form of the "fire" rad. occurs only as a part of characters. It is called "fire dots." Compare the other form 火 (414, below).

馬	一	二	三	**MA-3, horse. HORSE rad. (187)** This character is a picture. The resemblance to a horse was clearer in older forms of the character. 馬子 *ma-2 dz-3*, commode (for a chamber pot)
	手	馬	馬	
35 10 strokes	馬	馬	馬	马

嗎	丶	冂	口	**MA; a particle added to statements to convert them to questions** This character is a sound-meaning compound. *Ma-3* (35, above) suggests the sound; the "mouth" rad. warns, as it often does, that the character is important for its sound usage as a grammatical particle.
	口一	口三	口手	
36 13 strokes	嗎	嗎	嗎	吗

亠	丶	亠		**TOU-2. LID rad. (8)** This character is a picture of the lid of a Chinese (or Japanese) kettle. Learn to distinguish between the "lid" rad., the "roof" rad. 宀 (127, below), and the "crown" rad. 冖 (47, below).
37 2 strokes				

言	丶	亠	士	**YAN-2, words. WORDS rad. (149)** Notice the "mouth" in "words." You may think of the other lines as words pouring from the mouth, or as "motion lines" that suggest the mouth moving. The character often occurs independently and means "words, speech."
	士	言	言	
38 7 strokes	言			

佳	丿	亻	亻	**JWEI-1, dove. DOVE rad. (172)** Dictionaries often define *jwei-1* as "short-tailed bird." In some ancient texts it specifically means "dove." The older forms of the character were clearly pictures of a bird.
	亻	亻	信	
39 8 strokes	佳	佳		

誰	丶	言	言	SHEI-2, who? whom?
	言	言	訂	This character is probably a sound-meaning compound. *Jwei-1* (39, above) is supposed to suggest the sound.
40 15 strokes	訂	誰	誰	谁

				SHOU-3, hand. HAND rad. (64)
手	ノ	二	三	The "hand" rad. looks like this when it occurs as an independent character meaning "hand." This form can sometimes occur as a part of characters. Compare the other form 扌 (14, above) which always occurs in combination.
41 4 strokes	手			

				YI-4, dart. DART rad. (56)
弋	一	弋	弋	The "dart" rad. is a picture. Compare the "lance" rad. (43, below) and learn to distinguish "lance" from "dart."
42 3 strokes				

				GE-1, lance. LANCE rad. (62)
戈	一	弋	戈	The "lance" rad. is a picture. Note that "lance" has one more stroke than "dart," at the bottom. In museums you can see that the old Chinese weapon called *ge-1* had a blade like this at the lower end. The weapon is also sometimes called a "dagger-axe."
43 4 strokes	戈			

				WO-3, I, me
我	ノ	二	千	The student should learn to distinguish *wo-3* from *jau-3* "look for" 找 (508, below). *Wo-3* is "hand" + "lance"; *jau-3* is "side-hand" + "lance."
	手	扐	我	
44 7 strokes	我			

33

門	丨	冂	冋	**MEN-2, gate.** GATE rad. (169)
	冋	冋	門	This character is a picture. It occurs often as an independent character and means "gate, door, entrance." Note that it resembles the swinging saloon doors in old Westerns.
45 8 strokes	門	門		門口 *men-2 kou-3*, doorway, area by an entrance 门

們	丿	亻	彳	**MEN-2;** a suffix for pronouns and for certain nouns: *men-2* pluralizes the noun or pronoun
	伩	伊	伊	A sound-meaning compound, *men-2* is used only with nouns and pronouns referring to people, so that the "man" rad. gives the meaning; *men-2* (45, above) gives the sound.
46 10 strokes	們	們	們	们

冖	丿	冖		**MI-4, crown.** CROWN rad. (14)
				This rad. appears at the top of a character or at the top of a part of a character. Learn to distinguish "crown" from the "lid" rad. 亠 (37, above) and from the "roof" rad. 宀 (127, below).
47 2 strokes				

尔	丿	冖	𠂇	**ER-3, you**
	尔	尔		This character came to mean "you" by sound-loan. The history of the character is too complicated to go into here.
48 5 strokes				

你	亻	伩	伩	**NI-3, you**
	你	你	你	*Ni-3* and *er-3* (48, above) almost certainly are cognate words; *ni-3* is *er-3* reclarified with the "man" rad. *Er-3* is very seldom seen in modern writing.
49 7 strokes				

大	一	ナ	大	DA-4, be big. BIG rad. (37)
				This character looks like a man with his arms extended; the extended arms perhaps are intended to suggest "big."
				大人　*da-4 ren-2*, adult
50 3 strokes				大小　*da-4 syau-3*, size

夫	一	二	夫	FU-1, husband, "big man"
	夫			大夫　*dai-4 fu-1*, medical doctor (note that *da-4* "big" is pronounced *dai-4* in this expression)
51 4 strokes				

天	一	二	于	TYAN-1, heaven; day
	天			The ancient Chinese recognized heaven as a deity. This character is supposed to be a picture of "an anthropomorphic deity."
52 4 strokes				天天　*tyan-1 tyan-1*, every day

夭	ノ	⺈	千	YAU-1, be tender, be gentle
	夭			Learn to distinguish *yau-1* from "heaven; day" (52, above). The clue: is there a "one" rad. or a "left" rad. across the top?
53 4 strokes				

竹	ノ	⺊	个	JU-2, bamboo. BAMBOO rad. (118)
	个ノ	竹	竹	This character is a good picture of the slender, drooping leaves of the bamboo.
54 6 strokes				

竹竹	ノ	⼂	⼓	JU-2, bamboo. BAMBOO rad. (118)
	⼓ノ	⼓⼂	⼓⼓	This form of the "bamboo" rad. only occurs as a part of characters. Compare the independent form that you just learned (54, above).
55 6 strokes				

笑	ノ	⼂	⼓	SYAU-4, to laugh
	⼓⼂	竹竹	竹	One scholar says, "When bamboo takes the wind, it leans back gently like a man who laughs." That explanation is probably more useful as a mnemonic for the character than it is as a real explanation.
56 10 strokes	竺	笁	笑	

儿	ノ	儿	REN-2, legs. LEGS rad. (10)
			Learn to distinguish the "legs" rad. from the character wu-4 "man with amputated foot" (58, below) and from the "table" rad. 几 (645, below).
57 2 strokes			

兀	一	丆	兀
			WU-4, man with amputated foot or feet
58 3 strokes			

尢	一	尢	尢
			WANG-1, be lame. LAME rad. (43)
			The character is a picture of two legs, one of which is shorter than the other to suggest lameness. The horizontal stroke serves to emphasize the unequal length of the two legs. Learn to tell this character from "lack" 无 (60, below) and from "big" 大 (50, above).
59 3 strokes			

无 60 4 strokes	一 二 チ 无	WU-2, to lack; not (a negator of verbs). LACK rad. (71) There is no satisfactory explanation for this character. The student must simply learn it. It should be distinguished from "lame" 尢 (59, above) and from "first" 元 (72, below). Variant form 无.
丶 61 1 stroke	丶	JU-3, dot. DOT rad. (3)
玉 62 5 strokes	一 二 チ 王 玉	YU-4, jade. JADE rad. (96) Originally this character was a picture of three discs of jade (the horizontal strokes) strung together on a string (the vertical stroke). The dot may have been added to distinguish "jade" from "king" 王 (92, below).
矢 63 5 strokes	ノ ノー 仁 午 矢	SHR-3, arrow. ARROW rad. (111) The character is a picture. The point of the arrow is at the top, and the feathers and notch are at the bottom.
木 64 4 strokes	一 十 才 木	MU-4, tree. TREE rad. (75) The "tree" rad. is a picture of a tree. As a rad., it often occurs as a part of characters for objects that are made of wood. The student should distinguish it from "grain" 禾 (65, below), "rice" 米 (101, below), and "sift" 釆 (516, below).

37

禾	ノ	ニ	千	**HE-2, grain. GRAIN rad. (115)** Note the similarity between "grain" and "tree" 木 (64, above). "Grain" has the left stroke across the top to represent the head of ripened grain. Distinguish "grain" from "sift" 釆 (516, below).
65 5 strokes	禾	禾		

矮	ノ	ﾉ	ﾄ	**AI-3, be short (not tall)** *Ai-3* is composed of "arrow" + "grain" + "woman." It may help you remember the character if you think that the rads. all represent things which, within their classes, are shorter: arrows are shorter than spears, grain than trees, women than men.
	午	矢	矫	
66 13 strokes	矫	矮	矮	

忄	ノ	ﾉ一	忄	**SYIN-1, heart. HEART rad. (61)** This form of the "heart" rad. does not occur as an independent character; it occurs only as a part of characters. When printed, it often takes the form 忄. Compare the other form of "heart" (70, below).
67 3 strokes (4 strokes)				

亡	`	亠	亡	**WANG-2, to die** There is no satisfactory explanation for the modern form of this character. It is classified in dictionaries under the "lid" rad. (37, above).
68 3 strokes				

忙	ノ	ﾉ一	忄	**MANG-2, be busy** *Mang-2* is supposed to be a sound-meaning compound. *Wang-2* (68, above) supposedly suggests the sound, and "heart" suggests the meaning.
	忄	忙	忙	
69 6 strokes				

心	`	㇃	心	**SYIN-1, heart. HEART rad. (61)** In the old forms of this character, it is easy to see that it is a picture. In this form, the "heart" rad. occurs as an independent character and as an element at the bottom of characters. Compare 67, above. 小心 *syau-3 syin-1*, Be careful!
	心			
70 4 strokes				

您	ノ	亻	亻′	**NIN-2, you** *Nin-2* is deferential, used to address elders and superiors. Note that the top half of this character is *ni-3* "you" (49, above).
	亻ク	亻尔	亻尔	
71 11 strokes	你	您	您	

元	一	二	丁	**YWAN-2, first** The "legs" rad. at the bottom of this character represents a man; the "two" rad. at the top is supposed to represent his head. From "head" comes the idea of "primary"; thus, "first."
	元			
72 4 strokes				

不	一	丆	亣	**BU-4; a negative prefix for verbs and adverbs** 不好 *bu-4 hau-3*, It's not good; No good! 不很 *bu-4 hen-3*, not very . . . 很不 *hen-3 bu-4*, very un- . . .
	不			
73 4 strokes				

太	一	ナ	大	**TAI-4, extremely** 太忙 *tai-4 mang-2*, be too busy 太太 *tai-4 tai-4*, married lady, wife, Mrs.
	太			
74 4 strokes				

高	、	亠	亠	GAU-1, be tall; to tower. TALL rad. (189) *Gau-1* is a picture of a tall building or tower.
	亠	古	高	
75 10 strokes	高	高	高	
阝	ㄱ	㇌	阝	FU-4, mound. MOUND rad. (170) *Fu-4* originally was a picture of stairs leading down from the mound. In form, "mound" is identical to the "city" rad. 阝 (136, below); you tell them apart by their position in the compound character. "City" always appears at the far right; "mound" never appears there. (This character doesn't occur independently.)
76 3 strokes (8 strokes)				
可	一	丁	口	KE-3, may, can; to suit; certainly The origin of this character is unclear. 可笑 *ke-3 syau-4*, be laughable 可口 *ke-3 kou-3*, to taste good 不可 *bu-4 ke-3*, should not
	可	可		
77 5 strokes				
阿可	ㄱ	㇌	阝	A-4; a prefix for people's names This character originally meant "slope." The "mound" rad. suggested the meaning, and *ke-3* (77, above) suggested the sound. As a prefix, it is used by sound-loan.
	阝一	阝丁	阝口	
78 8 strokes	阝口	阝可		
口阝可	丨	冂	口	A-1; a sentence-final particle A sound-loan: the "mouth" rad. reclarifies the fact that the character is being used for sound.
	口ㄱ	口㇌	口阝	
79 11 strokes	口阝丁	口阝丁	口阝可	

40

	ㄱ	ㅋ	ㅋ
80 3 strokes			

JI-4, pig's head. PIG'S HEAD rad. (58)

The character originally was a picture. This form of it does not occur independently (cp. 997, below). Certain older forms of the "hand" rad. look so much like this that even Chinese had trouble telling them apart.

	ㄱ	ㅋ	ㅋ
	ㅋ	ㅋ	聿
81 6 strokes			

YU-4, brush. BRUSH rad. (129)

Yu-4 is a picture of a hand holding a brush.

	ㅣ	冂	日
	日		
82 4 strokes			

YWE-1, to say. SAY rad. (73)

Ywe-1 has a stroke inside a mouth, perhaps to suggest the tongue moving. Learn to tell "say" 曰 from "sun" 日 (160, below). In "say" (but never in "sun") the inner stroke is usually incomplete. Also, "say" is usually shorter and fatter than "sun."

	ㄱ	ㅋ	ㅋ
	ㅋ	ㅋ	聿
	書	書	書
83 10 strokes			

SHU-1, book

"Brush" + "say" = "book." (Although this explanation is not accurate historically, it can help you remember the character.)

书

	ㄱ	卩	
84 2 strokes			

JYE-2, seal (as in "seal ring"). SEAL rad. (26)

Learn to tell "seal" from "mound" 阝 (76, above) and from "city" 阝 (136, below).

41

又 85 2 strokes	フ	又		YOU-4, again. RIGHT HAND rad. (29) The character is a drawing of a right hand (cp. "left hand," 179, below). It means "again" by sound-loan. 又不 *you-4 bu-4*, not at all . . .
土 86 3 strokes	一	十	土	TU-3, earth. EARTH rad. (32) Note that the "earth" rad. is a picture of a cross stuck into the earth. Some scholars connect it with the "axis mundi." The "earth" rad. often occurs as an independent character and means "earth, soil."
干 87 3 strokes	一	二	干	GAN-1, shield. SHIELD rad. (51) The "shield" rad. is a picture.
ヽノ 88 2 strokes	ヽ	ヽノ		BA-1, eight. EIGHT rad. (12) This is the second form of the "eight" rad. that the student has learned. In printed characters the form of this rad. given as 26, above, is often used instead of this form. Compare 286, below.
幸 89 8 strokes	一 ⼟ 坴	十 寺 幸	土 圭	SYING-4, be lucky The student should learn to tell *sying-4* from the "bitter" rad. 辛 (549, below). "Be lucky" has "earth" on top; the "bitter" rad. has "lid" on top.

報 90 12 strokes	土	耂	耂
	彗	幸	幸卩
	𡙛	報	報

BAU-4, to announce; newspaper; to requite

The old form of this character meant "to requite" because it was a picture of a kneeling man with manacles and a hand to mete out the punishment. It stands for "announce" by sound-loan. It will have to be memorized as "lucky" + "seal" + "right hand." 报

筆 91 12 strokes	丿	𠂉	⺮
	⺮⺮	𥫱	笁
	笁	筀	筆

BI-3, brush, writing instrument

Bi-3 is a meaning-meaning compound: "bamboo" + "brush" = the traditional Chinese writing instrument, a brush made of bamboo. 笔

| 王 92 4 strokes | 一 | 二 | 于 |
| | 王 | | |

WANG-2, king; a common surname

Wang-2 is classified in dictionaries under the "jade" rad. 玉 (62, above), although wang-2 has one less stroke. Characters in which the rad. seems to be wang-2 also will be found under "jade" in the dictionary.

玩 93 8 strokes	一	二	于
	王	𤣩	𤣩
	玗	玩	

WAN-2, to play, to amuse oneself

A sound-meaning compound. Ywan-2 (72, above) suggests the sound. The "jade" rad. is supposed to help with the meaning, perhaps because toys often were made of jade; "toys" suggests "to play."

金 94 8 strokes	丿	人	人
	合	仐	全
	余	金	

JIN-1, gold, metals. GOLD rad. (167)

The "gold" rad. occurs as an independent character and means "gold" or "metals." You also will often see it as a part of characters for various specific metals or objects made of metal.

43

山	丨	丄	山	SHAN-1, mountain. MOUNTAIN rad. (46)
				Shan-1 is a picture. In the old form it is clearly three peaks sticking up. The "mountain" rad. often occurs independently as a character and means "mountain" or "hill."
95 3 strokes				

岡	丨	冂	冂	GANG-1, ridge
	冈	冈	罔	Notice the "mountain" rad. in the center of *gang-1*: it suggests the meaning. The rest of *gang-1* is from an old character which gave the sound.
96 8 strokes	岡	岡		冈

鋼	丿	人	合	GANG-1, steel
	今	午	金	This character is a sound-meaning compound: the "gold" rad. for meaning, *gang-1* (96, above) for sound.
97 16 strokes	金	釘	鋼	钢

八	丿	八		BA-1, eight. EIGHT rad. (12)
				The student should compare this form of the "eight" rad. to the other forms he has learned (26 and 88, above). This is the form which is usually seen as an independent character.
98 2 strokes				

合	八	公	合	YAN-3, marsh
	合			
99 5 strokes				

鉛	ノ	〈	𠆢
	金	金	釒
100 13 strokes	釒八	鉛	鉛

CHYAN-1, lead (the metal)

鉛筆　*chyan-1 bi-3*, pencil

鉛

米	丶	⸲⸲	⸲⸲
	半	米	米
101 6 strokes			

MI-3, rice. RICE rad. (119)

The "rice" rad. was originally a picture of rice growing in a paddy. The horizontal stroke represented the water that stands in paddies. Distinguish "rice" from "sift" 釆 (516, below), from "grain" 禾 (65, above), and from "tree" 木 (64, above).

刀	コ	刀	
102 2 strokes			

DAU-1, knife. KNIFE rad. (18)

Dau-1 is a picture of a knife. Distinguish "knife" from the "strength" rad. 力 (206, below).

刀子　*dau-1 dz-3*, knife

分	ノ	八	分
	分		
103 4 strokes			

FEN-1, to divide

The "eight" rad. at the top is actually a picture of something being cut in two by the knife below.

分子　*fen-1 dz-3*, numerator; molecule

粉	丶	⸲⸲	半
	半	米	米丶
104 10 strokes	米八	粉	粉

FEN-3, dust, powder

Face powder in China was made of rice. *Fen-3* is a sound-meaning compound: "rice" for meaning, *fen-1* (103, above) to suggest the sound.

米粉　*mi-2 fen-3*, rice flour

立	、	亠	宀
	亣	立	
105 5 strokes			

LI-4, to stand. STAND rad. (117)

Li-4 is a picture: a man standing with feet planted firmly on the ground.

里	丶	冂	日
	日	旦	甲
106 7 strokes	里		

LI-3, village. VILLAGE rad. (166)

A meaning-meaning compound: "field" + "earth" = "village." A Chinese commentator says, "Where there's land by fields, you build a village." This character is also used by sound-loan for a *li*, that is, a unit of distance (= 1/3 English mile).

童	丶	亠	亡
	立	产	音
107 12 strokes	音	童	童

TUNG-2, child, children

童女 *tung-2 nyu-3*, virgin, maiden

童心 *tung-2 syin-1*, childish disposition

鐘	丿	人	合
	全	金	釒
108 20 strokes	鉙	錇	鐘

JUNG-1, clock

The "gold" rad. here signifies "some object made of metal," and the character *tung-2* (107, above) suggests the sound.

钟

衣	丶	亠	宀
	亣	衣	衣
109 6 strokes			

YI-4, gown. GOWN rad. (145)

This character is a picture. The gown's sleeves and skirt can be seen clearly in older forms. As a part of other characters, this rad. often means "clothing."

大衣 *da-4 yi-4*, overcoat

衣子 *yi-4 dz-3*, covering

表	一	二	主
	主	丰	表
110 8 strokes	表	表	

BYAU-3, to show

It is a little difficult to see the "gown" rad. in *byau-3*, but *byau-3* is classified under "gown" 衣 (109, above) in dictionaries. *Byau-3* originally meant "overcoat." It may have come to mean "to show" by sound-loan, or else "overcoat" and "to show" were cognate words.

錶	丿	人	仝
	仝	全	金
111 16 strokes	金	釒	錶

BYAU-3, wristwatch, watch

The word for which this character stands may be cognate with *byau-3* "to show." If so, this character is reclarified with the "gold" rad. This character may, however, be a simple sound-meaning compound.

表

中	丶	口	口
	中		
112 4 strokes			

JUNG-1, middle

The downstroke through the center of the rectangle suggests "middle."

中心 *jung-1 syin-1*, center, core

或	一	一	口
	口	豆	或
113 8 strokes	或	或	

HWO-4, perhaps

This character is a sound-loan. Originally it meant "nation" (see 114, below). As "nation," it was a combination of meanings: "lance" (for the army) + "mouth" (for a language) + "earth." "Earth" has been corrupted into "one" in the modern form.

國	丨	冂	冂
	同	或	或
114 11 strokes	國	國	國

GWO-2, nation

Gwo-2 is 113, above, reclarified with the "surround" rad. to suggest the national boundaries.

中國 *jung-1 gwo-2*, China

国

羊	`	` `	丷
	丷	兰	羊
115 **6 strokes**			

YANG-2, sheep. SHEEP rad. (123)

Yang-2 is a picture. The "eight" rad. at the top represents the horns.

美	`	` `	丷
	丷	兰	羊
	羊	美	美
116 **9 strokes**			

MEI-3, be beautiful

Supposed to be a meaning-meaning compound; one dictionary says, "If the sheep is big, it will be fat and beautiful." Chinese consider plumpness in women beautiful.

美國 *mei-3 gwo-2*, America, U.S.A.

夕	ノ	ク	夕
117 **3 strokes**			

SYI-4, dusk. DUSK rad. (36)

The character is a drawing of the moon, to suggest "dusk." Learn to tell "dusk" from the "chip" rad. 歹 (727, below).

卜	｜	卜	
118 **2 strokes**			

BU-3, to divine. DIVINE rad. (25)

In the Shang Dynasty (1751–1122 B.C.), the Chinese kings divined by scratching messages on tortoise shells. A professional diviner applied heat to the shell until it cracked, then read the cracks to divine. The "divine" rad. is supposed to represent the divination cracks in the shell.

外	ノ	ク	夕
	夕	外	
119 **5 strokes**			

WAI-4, outside

Bernhard Karlgren says, ". . . 'Moon' [dusk] and 'divine'. . . . Moon may be phonetic . . . and the oracle cracks appeared on the outside . . . of the shell when the inside was singed."

外國 *wai-4 gwo-2*, foreign

目	丨	冂	冃	**MU-4, eye. EYE rad. (109)**
	月	目		This character is a picture. The student should learn to distinguish the "eye" rad. from the "small nose" rad. 自 (515, below).
120 **5 strokes**				

看	ノ	二	三	**KAN-4, to look at**
	手	手	看	A meaning-meaning compound: "hand" over "eye" to suggest "to look at." Note that the "hand" rad. (41, above) is slightly altered in form in this character. Distinguish "look at" from 着 (476, below).
121 **9 strokes**	看	看	看	

襾	一	冂	冖	**SYA-4, cover. COVER rad. (146)**
	襾	襾	襾	This rad. is a picture.
122 **6 strokes**				

貝	丨	冂	月	**BEI-4, cowrie. COWRIE rad. (154)**
	月	貝	貝	A cowrie is a small, yellowish white shell "with a fine gloss, used by various peoples as money" (*Century Dictionary*). The Chinese used cowries as money. We find the "cowrie" rad. in characters for value, money, business transactions, etc.
123 **7 strokes**				贝

貴	丨	冖	口	**GWEI-4, be expensive, be precious**
	中	虫	貴	*Gwei-4* is a sound-meaning compound. The top part, no longer used as an independent character, gave the sound, and "cowrie" suggested the meaning.
124 **12 strokes**	貴	貴	貴	貴

更	一	厂	厅
	百	百	更
125 7 strokes	更		

GENG-4, still more

The modern character is too much changed to make the explanation helpful.

更好 *geng-4 hau-3*, be better; even more

便	ノ	イ	仁
	仁	何	佢
126 9 strokes	便	便	

BYAN-4, convenient, **PYAN-2**, the first syllable of *pyan-2 yi*, be inexpensive

小便 *syau-3 byan-4*, to piss, a piss

大便 *da-4 byan-4*, to shit, defecation

宀	丶	宀	宀
127 3 strokes			

MYAN-1, roof. ROOF rad. (40)

The character is a picture. The top stroke may represent a chimney. The student will want to distinguish "roof" from "lid" 亠 (37, above) and from "crown" 冖 (47, above).

且	丨	冂	月
	月	且	
128 5 strokes			

CHYE-3, further

The character is a drawing of the ancestral tablet. Originally it stood for the word for ancestor or grandfather. Now it is used by sound-loan.

宜	丶	宀	宀
	宀	宀	宜
129 8 strokes	宜	宜	

YI-2, be appropriate

The character is a picture of "the sacred pole of the altar to the soil, behung with . . . meat." It meant "sacrifice to the earth-god." It is used for "be appropriate" by sound-loan.

便宜 *pyan-2 yi*, be inexpensive

西	一	厂	冂
	丙	两	西
130 6 strokes			

SYI-1, west

The character is a picture of a bird in a nest and originally meant "to nest." It is used for *syi-1* "west" by sound-loan. Characters in which *syi-1* seems to be the rad. will be found under the "cover" rad. 襾 (122, above). Distinguish "west" from the "wine" rad. 酉 (363, below).

要	一	厂	冖
	襾	襾	西
131 9 strokes	要	要	要

YAU-4, to want; to ask for

要人 *yau-4 ren-2*, important person (usually a government official)

目	㇏	冂	冂
	冂	目	
132 5 strokes			

MU-4, eye. EYE rad. (109)

This form of the "eye" rad. occurs only as a part of characters (cp. 120, above). In form, it is identical to a form of the "net" rad. (637, below). Sometimes you will have to look a character up under both rads. before you can find it in the dictionary.

買	冂	冂	冂
	四	罒	罒
133 12 strokes	罒	買	買

MAI-3, to buy

Mai-3 is a meaning-meaning compound. The eye is watching over the cowries (remember that the Chinese used cowries for money).

买

士	一	十	士
134 3 strokes			

SHR-4, knight. KNIGHT rad. (33)

According to some scholars, to act as a *shr-4* meant to get things organized for your lord—take ten things and organize them into one. Thus, "ten" 十 over "one" 一 became *shr-4*. Distinguish "knight" from "earth" 土 (86, above).

賣	一	十	士	**MAI-4**, to sell 買賣 *mai-3 mai-4*, business
	士	声	吉	
135 15 strokes	青	膏	賣	卖

阝	ㄱ	阝	阝	**YI-4**, city. CITY rad. (163) Learn to tell the "city" rad. from the "mound" rad. 阝 (76, above). They look exactly alike, but when the form occurs *far right* in a character, it is always "city." Review: at the right, it's "city"; elsewhere, it's "mound."
136 3 strokes (7 strokes)				

ヒ	レ	ヒ		**BI-3**, ladle. LADLE rad. (21) This character is a picture.
137 2 strokes				

老	一	十	土	**LAU-3**, be old. OLD rad. (125) *Lau-3* is a picture of an old man with long hair and a cane, according to the dictionaries. The modern form is very stylized. Note that you can analyze the form of the modern character into "earth-left-ladle."
	耂	尹	老	
138 6 strokes				老二 *lau-3 er-4*, second son or daughter; second brother or sister

者	一	十	土	**JE-3**; a suffix to verbs: verb + *je-3* means "a person who . . ." Compare English suffix "-er." Although it may be hard to see in *je-3* the "old" rad., we know it is there because *je-3* is classified in the dictionaries under rad. 125, the "old" rad. 老.
	耂	者	者	
139 9 strokes	者	者	者	

都	一	十	耂	**DOU-1**, all; **DU-1**, metropolis, capital In the sense of "metropolis," this character is a sound-meaning compound; "city" gives the meaning, and *je-3* (139, above) once gave the sound. In the sense of "all," it is used by sound-loan.
140 11 strokes (12 strokes)	耂	者	者	
	者丁	者阝	都	

廾	一	𠃌	廾	**GUNG-3**, clasped hands. CLASP rad. (55) A picture, now very stylized, of two clasped hands. Distinguish "clasp" from the form ⺾ of the "grass" rad. (192, below). The vertical strokes in "clasp" are longer than in "grass." Distinguish also from 142, below.
141 3 strokes				

廿	一	十	廿	**NYAN-4**, twenty The character is formed of two "ten" rads. written together. Note that sometimes *nyan-4* is written 卄.
142 3 strokes				

匚	一	匚		**FANG-1**, basket. BASKET rad. (22) The character is a picture. The student should learn to distinguish the "basket" rad. from the "box" rad. 匸 (145, below). The two are almost identical.
143 2 strokes				

甘	一	十	廿	**GAN-1**, to taste sweet. SWEET rad. (99) *Gan-1* is a picture of a mouth with something in it; something you would want to hold in your mouth is something "sweet."
144 5 strokes	甘	甘		

				SYI-4, box. BOX rad. (23)

SYI-4, box. BOX rad. (23)

The character is a picture. Note that, unless we assume the box is tipped on its side, the right-hand side of the box is not drawn in.

145
2 strokes

PI-1, PI-3, mate, one-half a pair

There is no satisfactory explanation for the form of this character.

一匹馬　*yi-2 pi-1 ma-3*, a horse

146
4 strokes

SZ-4, four

This is an arbitrary symbol; memorize it.

147
5 strokes

WU-3, five

148
4 strokes

LYOU-4, six

149
4 strokes

七	一	七	
150 2 strokes			

CHI-1, seven

The student will want to distinguish *chi-1* from the "ladle" rad. 匕 (137, above).

九	丿	九	
151 2 strokes			

JYOU-3, nine

入	丿	入	
152 2 strokes			

RU-4, to enter. ENTER rad. (11)

Learn to distinguish the "enter" rad. from the "man" rad. 人 (2, above).

入口 *ru-4 kou-3*, entrance

入門 *ru-4 men-2*, to make a good start; primer

甚	一	十	廿
	廿	甘	苴
153 9 strokes	甚	甚	甚

SHEN-2; the first syllable of *shem-2 ma*, what? SHEN-4, very

Originally this character stood for a word meaning "peace and happiness." It was a meaning-meaning compound: "sweet" + "mate." Now the character is used by sound-loan.

厂	一	厂	
154 2 strokes			

HAN-3, slope, cliff. SLOPE rad. (27)

Han-3 is a picture of a slope.

广	丶	亠	广	YAN-3, lean-to. LEAN-TO rad. (53) The character is a picture. Learn to distinguish "lean-to" from the "slope" rad. 厂 (154, above) and from the "sick" rad. 疒 (531, below).
155 3 strokes				

林	一	十	才	LIN-2, forest Lin-2 is a meaning-meaning compound: "tree" beside "tree" = "forest, woods."
	木	杧	村	
156 8 strokes	村	林		

麻	丶	亠	广	MA-2, hemp. HEMP rad. (200) The old form was a picture of plants growing beside a curved line, perhaps on the inside of a river curve (hemp grows well in such damp grounds). The curved line is corrupted into "lean-to" in the modern form.
	广	庁	庁	
157 11 strokes	府	麻	麻	

么	ノ	厶	么	YAU-1, puny; one (in dice-games) Variant 幺. Compare 25, above.
158 3 strokes				

麼	丶	亠	广	MA; the second syllable of shem-2 ma, what? This character was originally a sound-meaning compound. It meant "thin, puny," and "puny" gave the meaning, ma-2 (157, above) the sound. Now it is used by sound-loan.
	庁	床	麻	
159 14 strokes	麻	麼	麼	么

56

日	丨	冂	日	**R-4, sun. SUN rad. (72)**
	日			*R-4* is a picture. Learn to tell "sun" from the "say" rad. 曰 (82, above) will be taller and thinner, or (2) the inner line in "say" will be incomplete, or (3) the two will be indistinguishable and you will have to look a character up under both rads. before you find it in the dictionary.
160 4 strokes				

杲	丨	冂	日	**GAU-3, to shine**
	日	旦	杲	This character is a meaning-meaning compound: "sun" above "tree" suggests "to shine."
161 8 strokes	杲	杲		

桌	丨	卜	卜	**JWO-1, table**
	占	占	占	The "tree" rad. at the bottom of this character gives you a hint that it refers to some object made of wood.
	卓	卓	桌	桌子 *jwo-1 dz-3*, table
162 10 strokes				

奇	一	ナ	大	**CHI-2, be weird**
	去	夻	夻	*Chi-2* is said to be a meaning-meaning compound, but it is not clear why "big" + "be able" should suggest "be weird."
163 8 strokes	奇	奇		

椅	一	十	才	**YI-3, chair**
	木	木	杦	*Yi-3* is supposed to be a sound-meaning compound. The "tree" rad. helps with the meaning, and *chi-2* (163, above) is supposed to help with the sound.
	杍	柠	椅	椅子 *yi-2 dz-3*, chair
164 12 strokes				

DUNG-1, east

Lexicographers now explain *dung-1* as a meaning-meaning compound; "the sun tangled in the branches of a tree" is supposed to suggest "sunrise" and, therefore, "east." Actually the character originally meant "bundle" and was a picture. "East" is by sound-loan.

165
8 strokes

JYAN-1, be thin

Jyan-1 originally meant "be fierce; be cruel." It was a meaning-meaning compound: two lances to suggest "fierce." It is "thin" by sound-loan.

166
8 strokes

CHYAN-2, money

The "gold" rad. gives the meaning, and *jyan-1* (166, above) suggests the sound in this sound-meaning compound.

九分錢　*jyou-3 fen-1 chyan-2*, nine cents
筆錢　*bi-3 chyan-2*, fund

167
16 strokes

GU-3, ancient

According to the usual explanation, *gu-3* is a meaning-meaning compound. "Ten" + "mouth" suggests something which has been passed through ten generations of mouths (people); therefore, "ancient."

168
5 strokes

GU-4, be hard, be strong

Gu-3 (168, above) helps give the sound. There is no satisfactory explanation for the "surround" rad.

169
8 strokes

個	ノ	イ	们	GE-4; a measure used to enumerate nouns in the construction "number + *ge* + noun."
	们	佣	佣	三個　*san-1 ge-4*, three
				個人　*ge-4 ren-2*, oneself; personal
170 10 strokes	佣	個	個	個子　*ge-4 dz-3*, size　　　　個

辶	﹀	氵	辶	CHWO-4, to halt. HALT rad. (162)
				The character was a picture of a foot halted at a crossroads. This form of the "halt" rad. does not occur as an independent character but only as a part of characters. The independent form appears as 983, below. Its printed form is 辶. (Sometimes counted as four strokes.)
171 3 strokes (7 strokes)				

這	丶	二	言	JEI-4, JE-4, this
	言	言	言	這個　*jei-4 ge-4*, this one
				這麼　*je-4 ma*, this, these; in this way
172 10 strokes	言	言	這	这

那	コ	ヨ	弓	NEI-4, NA-4, NE-4, that
	那	那	那	那個　*nei-4 ge-4*, that one
				那麼　*ne-4 ma*, in that way; in that case; so much
173 7 strokes	那			

糸	く	幺	幺	SZ-1, silk. SILK rad. (120)
	幺	幺	幺	This is another way to write 糸 (28, above). The student should learn to recognize both forms as the "silk" rad.
174 6 strokes				

	丿	入	亼	JI-2, to get together, to come together
亼				The character is explained as "three things gathered around a single space."
175 **3 strokes**				

	丿	入	亼	HE-2, to join
合	今	合	合	The root meaning of *he-2* is "to join or close," as one would two panels of a double door. Early dictionaries call this character a meaning-meaning compound and say, "to close, like the mouth."
176 **6 strokes**				

	乙	幺	幺	GEI-3, to give; to allow; for (someone). . .; JI-3, to supply
給	幺	幺	幺	給我書 *gei-3 wo-3 shu-1*, gives me books
	糺	給	給	給我看 *gei-3 wo-3 kan-4*, let me look
177 **12 strokes**				給我買 *gei-3 wo-3 mai-3*, buy for me

給

	丿	冂	月	YWE-4, moon. MOON rad. (74)
月	月			The "moon" rad. is a picture. When you see this form as part of a character, you cannot be sure whether it is the "moon" rad. or the "meat" rad. 月 (326, below). You may have to try the dictionary under both rads. before you find the character. Note that "meat" has a different independent form (928, below).
178 **4 strokes**				

	一	尹		DZWO-3, left hand
尹				This is a picture of a left hand. Compare the right hand (85, above).
179 **2 strokes**				

有	一	ナ	冇	YOU-3, to have; there is, there are
	冇	有	有	The earliest forms show a hand taking hold of a piece of meat. Later lexicographers lost sight of it, so *you-3* now is classified under "moon" 月.
180 6 strokes				

氵	丶	冫	氵	SHWEI-3, water. WATER rad. (85)
✓				To distinguish this form of the "water" rad. from the other form 水 (362, below), the Chinese call this form "three-dots-water." It often appears in the characters for various liquids and fluids.
181 3 strokes (4 strokes)				

汗	丶	冫	氵	HAN-4, sweat
	汇	汇	汗	*Han-4* is a sound-meaning compound. The "three-dots water" rad. suggests the meaning; *gan-1* (87, above) suggests the sound.
182 6 strokes				

几	丿	几	殳	SHU-1, club, to club. CLUB rad. (79)
又	殳			*Shu-1* is a picture: a right hand holds the club. Distinguish "club" from these characters: "branch" 支 (271, below), "knock" 攵 (384), "pattern" 文 (360), "follow" 夂 (319), and "slow" 夊 (337).
183 4 strokes				

沒	丶	冫	氵	MWO-4, to inundate. MEI-2; the negator of *you-3* (180, above)
	氿	汈	沒	The function as "the negator of *you-3*" is by sound-loan. This character is sometimes written "three-dots-water" + "club" (183, above) instead of "three-dots-water" + "knife" + "right hand."
184 7 strokes	沒			沒有 *mei-2 you-3*, there isn't, there aren't; doesn't have

61

身	ノ	イ	冂	**SHEN-1, torso. TORSO rad. (158)** *Shen-1* is a picture of a person in which the torso is the most prominent part. It also means "self." 可身 *ke-3 shen-1*, to fit well (clothes) 身分 *shen-1 fen-1*, position, rank
	甸	自	身	
185 7 strokes	身			
寸	一	丁	寸	**TSWUN-4, thumb; inch. THUMB rad. (41)** The "thumb" rad. is a picture of a hand, with the dot added to indicate the thumb. Learn to distinguish "thumb," "side-hand" 扌 (14, above), and "then" 才 (596, below).
186 3 strokes				
射	ノ	勹	自	**SHE-4, to shoot** The character has been corrupted through time. Originally, the "torso" was a picture of an arrow on a bow, and the "thumb" was a hand drawing the bow, whence "to shoot."
	身	身	身-	
187 10 strokes	射	射		
謝	丶	亠	三	**SYE-4, thanks, to thank** *Sye-4* is a sound-meaning compound; the "words" rad. gives the meaning, and *she-4* (187, above) suggests the sound. 謝謝 *sye-4 sye-4*, thank you
	言	訁	訂	
188 17 strokes	訥	謝	謝	谢
吉	一	十	士	**JI-2, lucky** An early dictionary says the character is a meaning-meaning compound: "scholar" (or "knight") + "mouth" = "lucky."
	吉 亅	吉	吉	
189 6 strokes				

喜 190 12 strokes	一	十	士
	吉	吉	吉
	直	喜	喜

SYI-3, to enjoy

The top part of this, what is now "knight-mouth-eight-one," used to be a picture of a drum. *Syi-3* was a meaning-meaning compound: "drum" + "mouth" = "to sing and play drums, to enjoy yourself."

| 欠 191 4 strokes | 丿 | 𠂉 | 𠂊 |
| | 欠 | | |

CHYAN-4, yawn; to owe; to lack. YAWN rad. (76)

Note that the lower part of this character is the "man" rad. If it helps you remember the character, think of the upper part as his hand covering his mouth as he yawns.

| 艹 192 4 strokes (6 strokes) | 一 | 十 | 十一 |
| | 艹 | | |

TSAU-3, grass. GRASS rad. (140)

This is a picture of two little shoots of grass breaking through the soil. This form of the "grass" rad. only occurs as a part of characters. The student should distinguish this form of the "grass" rad. from "clasp" 廾 (141, above). Printed 艹.

雚 193 18 strokes	十	艹	吉十
	吉吉	莇	莃
	藋	雚	雚

GWAN-4, heron

(口 33)

歡 194 22 strokes	艹	吉吉	莃
	雚	雚	雚
	雚	歡	歡

HWAN-1, be pleased

In this character, *gwan-4* (193, above) suggests the sound. The "yawn" rad. is supposed to suggest the meaning, perhaps as a mouth open to smile or to laugh rather than to yawn.

喜歡 *syi-3 hwan-1*, to like

欢

止	丨	⺊	𫟃
	止		
195 4 strokes			

JR-3, toe; to stop. TOE rad. (77)

The "toe" rad. is a picture.

不止三個 *bu-4 jr-3 san-1 ge-4*, not stopping at three, not only three

足	丶	𠆢	口
	𠂊	𠯣	𠯣
196 7 strokes	足		

DZU-2, foot; be sufficient. FOOT rad. (157)

The bottom part of this character is, in fact, the "toe" rad. (195, above). See 197, below, in which the "foot" rad. appears as part of a character, and note that in the form used in compounds, the "toe" can be clearly seen. The character is a picture.

跟	口	𠯣	𧾷
	足	𧾷⁊	𧾷ヨ
197 13 strokes	跟	跟	跟

GEN-1, heel; to follow, to go with; with

Gen-1 is a sound-meaning compound; the "foot" rad. gives the meaning; *gen-4* (31, above) gives the sound.

青	一	二	丰
	主	圭	青
198 8 strokes	青	青	

CHING-1, be green. GREEN rad. (174)

Note that the bottom half of "green" resembles "moon." *Ching-1* by itself is, however, recognized as a radical. The character also occurs independently and means "green" and sometimes other "colors of nature," like azure, or even greenish black or gray. Often printed 青.

請	丶	亠	圡
	圥	訁	言
199 15 strokes	言丰	言圭	請

CHING-3, to invite; please . . .

This character is a sound-meaning compound; "words" gives the meaning, and *ching-1* (198, above) gives the sound.

誰請 *shei-2 ching-3*, Who's paying?

请

問	丨	冂	冃	WEN-4, to ask (for information)
				"Mouth" gives the meaning and *men-2* (45, above) once gave the sound in this sound-meaning compound.
	冃	冃丨	門	
				請問 *ching-3 wen-4*, Would you please tell me . . . ?
200	門	門	問	
11 strokes				(口 33)

問

耳	一	丆	冂	ER-3, ear. EAR rad. (128)
				The "ear" rad. is a picture.
	刄	耳	耳	耳子 *er-2 dz-3*, handle (as on a pot)
				木耳 *mu-4 er-3*, edible tree-fungus
201				
6 strokes				

聞	丨	冂	冃	WEN-2, to hear
				Notice that *men-2* (45, above) functions here, as in 200, above, to suggest the sound *wen*. In *wen-2* "to hear," the meaning is given by the "ear" rad.
	冃	冃丨	門	
				聞人 *wen-2 ren-2*, famous man
202	門	門	聞	
14 strokes				

聞

閒	丨	冃	冃丨	SYAN-2, leisure
				This character originally stood for a word that meant "crack, break"; it shows the moon shining through a crack in a gate (cp. 204, below). The sense "leisure" may be simply an extension of the root meaning, just as in English we call a rest "a break."
	門	門	閒	
203	閒	閒	閒	
12 strokes				

閒

間	丨	冃	冃丨	JYAN-1, space; a measure for rooms
				This character at first was just another way to write *syan-2* (203, above).
	門	門	間	
204	門	間	間	
12 strokes				

間

				DAU-1, knife. KNIFE rad. (18)
刂	丨	刂		This form of the "knife" rad. occurs only as a part of characters. Compare the independent form 刀 (102, above).
205 2 strokes				

				LI-4, strength. STRENGTH rad. (19)
力	丁	力		The student should distinguish "strength" from the "knife" rad. 刀 (102, above). 四匹馬力 *sz-4 pi-1 ma-3 li-4*, four horse-power
206 2 strokes				

				LING-4, separately
另	丨	冂	口	另外 *ling-4 wai-4*, in addition
	马	另		
207 5 strokes				

				BYE-2, to separate, to part; Don't . . . !
別	丨	冂	口	分別 *fen-1 bye-2*, difference 別人 *bye-2 ren-2*, other people 別買 *bye-2 mai-3*, Don't buy it!
	尸	另	別	
208 7 strokes	別			

				PENG-2, friend
朋	丿	几	月	The character originally stood for a fabulous bird and was a picture of the wing of that bird. It means "friend" by sound-loan. The character is now classified under the "moon" rad. 月 (178, above).
	月	朋	朋	
209 8 strokes	朋	朋		

友 **210** 4 strokes	一 友	广	方	**YOU-3, friend** A meaning-meaning compound: "left hand" + "right hand" = "friend." The character perhaps is supposed to suggest the Chinese gesture of parting from friends: clasping your own hands in front of you and bowing over them. 朋友 *peng-2 you-3*, friend
父 **211** 4 strokes	' 父	八	父	**FU-4, father. FATHER rad. (88)**
毋 **212** 4 strokes	ㄥ 毋	勺	毋	**WU-2, Don't! DON'T rad. (80)** The character is supposed to be the picture of a woman in irons. The relation of that to its present meaning is unclear. Learn to distinguish the "don't" rad. from "mother" 母 (216, below).
亲 **213** 9 strokes	` 六 辛	亠 立 亲	亠 立 亲	**JEN-1, hazel tree**
見 **214** 7 strokes	l 月 見	冂 目	月 見	**JYAN-4, to see; to perceive. SEE radical (147)** The modern form of "see" = "eye" over "legs." It comes from a drawing of a man in which the eye was drawn large to suggest "to see; to perceive." 见

67

親

215
16 strokes

CHIN-1, relatives; be attached to

The sound is suggested by *jen-1* (213, above). The "eye" rad. is supposed to help with the meaning.

父親 *fu-4 chin-1*, father

亲

母

216
5 strokes

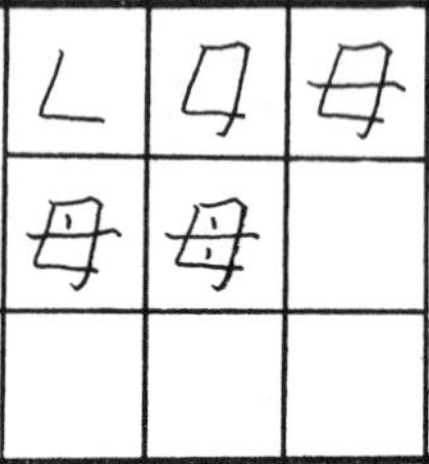

MU-3, mother

Mu-3 is a picture of a woman with two dots to emphasize the breasts. Learn to distinguish "mother" from the "don't" rad. 毋 (212, above).

母親 *mu-3 chin-1*, mother

哥

217
10 strokes

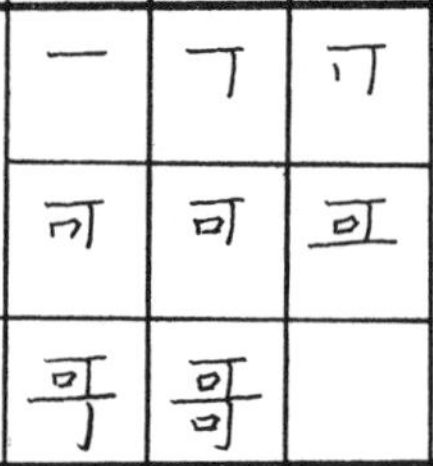

GE-1, older brother

哥哥 *ge-1 ge-1*, older brother

大哥 *da-4 ge-1*, oldest brother

表哥 *byau-3 ge-1*, older male cousin on the maternal side or on the paternal aunt's side

弓

218
3 strokes

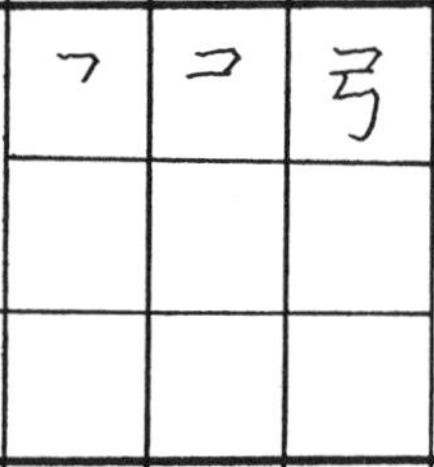

GUNG-1, bow. BOW rad. (57)

The "bow" rad. is a picture of a bow.

弓子 *gung-1 dz-3*, bow (e.g., a violin bow)

弔

219
4 strokes

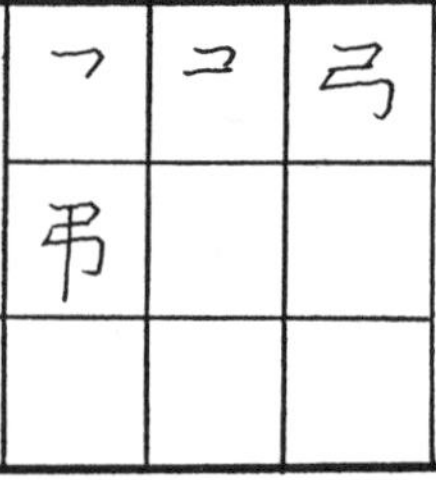

DYAU-4, to pity

This character is supposed to be a picture of an arrow stayed on the bow, hence "to pity."

弟	丶	⳾	⳾	DI-4, younger brother
	当	当	弟	弟弟 *di-4 di-4*, younger brother; younger male cousin
220 7 strokes	弟			二弟 *er-2 di-4*, second younger brother

姐	𡿨	𡿨	女	JYE-3, older sister
	如	如	妒	姐姐 *jye-3 jye*, older sister
				大姐 *da-4 jye-3*, oldest sister
221 8 strokes	姐	姐		小姐 *syau-2 jye-3*, Miss

未	一	二	于	WEI-4, not yet; the eighth "earthly branch"
	才	未		Distinguish "not yet" from *mwo-4* 末 (p. 294).
222 5 strokes				

妹	𡿨	𡿨	女	MEI-4, kid sister
	女	女	好	妹妹 *mei-4 mei*, younger sister
				姐妹 *jye-3 mei-4*, sisters
223 8 strokes	妹	妹		妹夫 *mei-4 fu-1*, brother-in-law (younger sister's husband)

氏	丿	𠂆	𠄌	SHR-4, clan. CLAN rad. (83)
	氏			The student may find it difficult to remember how to write rads. which, like the "clan" rad., do not make a clear picture of anything. But the number of such non-representational rads. is small, and the student will find that a little extra work solves the problem.
224 4 strokes				

紙	ㄥ	幺	幺	**JR-3**, paper
	幺	糸	糸	A sound-meaning compound. The "silk" rad. gives the meaning; *shr-4* (224, above) suggests the sound.
225 10 strokes	紅	紙	紙	纸

長	丨	厂	厂	**CHANG-2**, be long; **JANG-3**, to grow; senior. LONG rad. (168)
	厔	镸	長	The character is a drawing of a man with very long hair.
				長大 *jang-3 da-4*, to grow up
				長子 *jang-2 dz-3*, eldest son
226 8 strokes	長	長		长

張	弓	引	弸	**JANG-1**, to open out, to open up; a measure for objects coming in sheets
	弸	張	張	張手 *jang-1 shou-3*, to open the hand
				三張紙 *san-1 jang-1 jr-3*, three sheets of paper
227 11 strokes	張			(弓 218)
				张

畫	ㄱ	𢎒	圭	**HWA-4**, a painting
	圭	圭	聿	一張畫 *yi-4 jang-1 hwa-4*, a painting
				畫報 *hwa-4 bau-4*, illustrated magazine
228 12 strokes	書	畫	畫	(田 23)
				画

臼	丿	𠂉	𠂊	**JYOU-4**, mortar. MORTAR rad. (134)
	臼	臼	臼	*Jyou-4* is the drawing of a mortar (a vessel in which to grind things up).
229 6 strokes				

兒 230 8 strokes	ノ 彡	イ 彐	イ7 臼	ER-2, son, child; R; a noun-suffix This character is said to be a picture of a a child with open fontanel. 兒子 *er-2 dz-3*, son 女兒 *nyu-3 er-2*, daughter 兒童 *er-2 tung-2*, child 儿
白 231 5 strokes	ノ 白	イ 白	白	BAI-2, be white. WHITE rad. (106) The student should distinguish "white" from the "sun" rad. 日 (160, above). 白天 *bai-2 tyan-1*, in the daytime 白給 *bai-2 gei-3*, to give free of charge
勹 232 2 strokes	ノ	勹		BAU-1, to wrap. WRAP rad. (20) The character is a picture of a wrapper. As part of a character, the "wrap" rad. usually appears wrapped around other rads. or parts of the character.
勺 233 3 strokes	ノ	勹	勺	SHAU-2, spoon; frying pan 勺子 *shau-2 dz-3*, spoon 木勺 *mu-4 shau-2*, wooden ladle
的 234 8 strokes	ノ 白 的	イ 白 的	白 白′	DE; a suffix to nouns and pronouns; a grammatical particle; DI-4, bull's-eye 我的 *wo-3 de*, my, mine 有的 *you-3 de*, some 目的 *mu-4 di-4*, aim, purpose

71

本	一	十	才	**BEN-3**, root; volume; a measure for books
	木	本		*Ben-3* is a picture of a tree with a horizontal stroke at the bottom to signify that the meaning is "root."
235 5 strokes				日本　*r-4 ben-3*, Japan

對	丨	丨丨	丄丨	**DWEI-4**, to face, facing; to match; be correct
	丄丨	业	半	對了　*dwei-4 le*, That's right!
				對手　*dwei-4 shou-3*, opponent
				對鐘　*dwei-4 jung-1*, to set a clock
236 14 strokes	半	坣	對	对

兄	丨	冂	口	**SYUNG-1**, older brother
	尸	兄		兄弟　*syung-1 di-4*, brothers
237 5 strokes				

兌	丶	丷	丷	**DWEI-4**, to hand over
	兯	兯	炉	兌給　*dwei-4 gei-3*, to pay to
238 7 strokes	兌			

稅	丿	二	千	**SHWEI-4**, tax
	矛	禾	禾	The peasantry in China traditionally paid their taxes in grain, so "to hand over" + "grain" was a good meaning-meaning compound for "tax."
239 12 strokes	稻	稅	稅	

説	⟋	⟋	⟋	SHWO-1, to speak This is a sound-meaning compound: the "word" rad. for meaning, *dwei-4* (238, above) for sound. (When the character was first invented, *dwei-4* gave the sound more accurately than it does now.)
	言	言	訳	
240 14 strokes	説	説	説	说

千	⟋	二	千	CHYAN-1, one thousand The "ten" rad. gives a clue that the character stands for a number. 千里　*chyan-1 li-3*, many miles; long journey
241 3 strokes				

重	⟋	二	千	JUNG-4, be heavy; CHUNG-2, over again, to repeat by mistake, to duplicate 重要　*jung-4 yau-4*, be important 買重　*mai-3 chung-2*, to buy an extra one (one too many) 重了　*chung-2 le*, done twice
	白	白	白	
242 9 strokes	重	重		

董	一	十	十一	DUNG-3, to correct, to supervise
	十十	土	苗	
243 13 strokes	苗	董	董	

懂	⟋	⟍	忄	DUNG-3, to understand This character may stand for the same word as 243, above: "be correct (in the mind) about, to understand." Note that in form it is identical to 243, with the addition of the "heart" rad.
	忄	忄十	忄土	
244 16 strokes	懂	懂	懂	

疋	一	丁	下	PI-3, bolt (of cloth). BOLT rad. (103)
	疋	疋		
245 5 strokes				

是	丨	冂	日	SHR-4, am, is, are; be right 不是 *bu-2 shr-4*, "No"; a fault 是的 *shr-4 de*, "Yes" 可是 *ke-3 shr-4*, but
	日	旦	早	
246 9 strokes	早	昆	是	

先	丿	宀	壮	SYAN-1, to precede; late (deceased) 先父 *syan-1 fu-4*, my late father 先夫 *syan-1 fu-1*, my late husband
	生	牛	先	
247 6 strokes				

生	丿	宀	仁	SHENG-1, to bear (give birth to). BIRTH rad. (100) 先生 *syan-1 sheng-1*, "Mr."; teacher 生女兒 *sheng-1 nyu-3 er-2*, to bear a daughter 女生 *nyu-3 sheng-1*, a coed
	牛	生		
248 5 strokes				

李	一	十	才	LI-3, plum tree; a surname 李子 *li-2 dz-3*, plum 李先生 *li-3 syan-1 sheng-1*, Mr. Li
	木	杢	李	
249 7 strokes	李			

亥	`丶`	`亠`	`宀`	HAI-4, the twelfth "earthly branch" This character was originally a picture of a boar. It still is similar in form to the "pig" rad. 豕 (389, below). The boar is the symbolical animal of the twelfth category in the "earthly branches" cycle.
	`歺`	`亥`	`亥`	
250 6 strokes				

孩	`フ`	`了`	`子`	HAI-2, child The "child" rad. gives the meaning; *hai-4* (250, above) gives the sound. 孩子 *hai-2 dz-3*, child 孩童 *hai-2 tung-2*, children
	`子`	`子亠`	`孖`	
251 9 strokes	`孖`	`孩`	`孩`	

爻	`ノ`	`乂`	`乂丶`	YAU-2, crisscross. CRISSCROSS rad. (89)
	`爻`			
252 4 strokes				

學	`ノ`	`亻`	`千`	SYWE-2, to study, to learn 學生 *sywe-2 sheng-1*, student 學問 *sywe-2 wen-2*, learning 大學 *da-4 sywe-2*, university
	`乍`	`𦥯`	`𦥑`	
253 16 strokes	`𦥯`	`學`	`學`	(子 18) 学

男	`丨`	`冂`	`𠃌`	NAN-2, male 男人 *nan-2 ren-2*, man 男生 *nan-2 sheng-1*, male student 長男 *jang-3 nan*, eldest son
	`田`	`田`	`男`	
254 7 strokes	`男`			

75

姓

255
8 strokes

SYING-4, surname, be surnamed

您貴姓 *nin-2 gwei-4 sying-4*, What is your name? (polite)

我姓李 *wo-3 sying-4 li-3*, My (sur)name is Li.

名

256
6 strokes

MING-2, name

Ancient Chinese dictionaries say that *ming-2* is a meaning-meaning compound: "dusk" (117, above) + "mouth." In the "dark" you can't see someone, so you "mouth" (call) his name.

姓名 *sying-4 ming-2*, full name

有名 *you-3 ming-2*, be famous

字

257
6 strokes

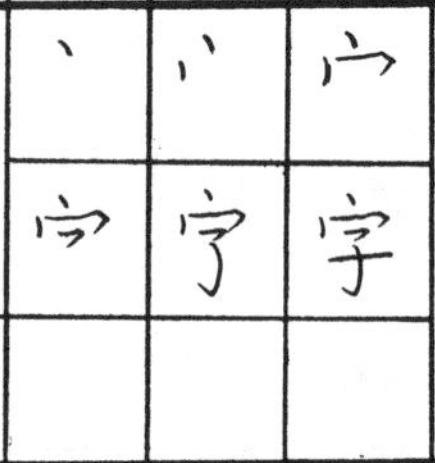

DZ-4, written character

The original meaning is "bring up, cherish," and the character is meaning-meaning: "a child under your roof." The character means "written character" by sound-loan.

名字 *ming-2 dz-4*, name

字母 *dz-4 mu-3*, alphabet; letter

丩

258
2 strokes

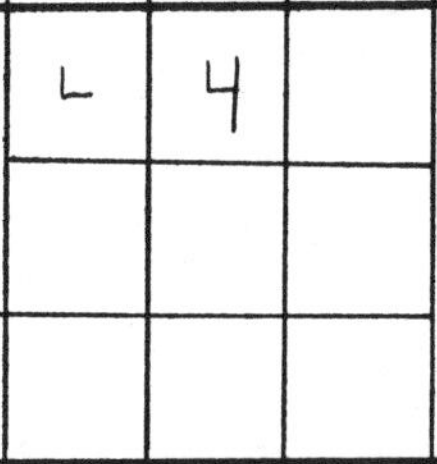

JYOU-1, to connect

叫

259
5 strokes

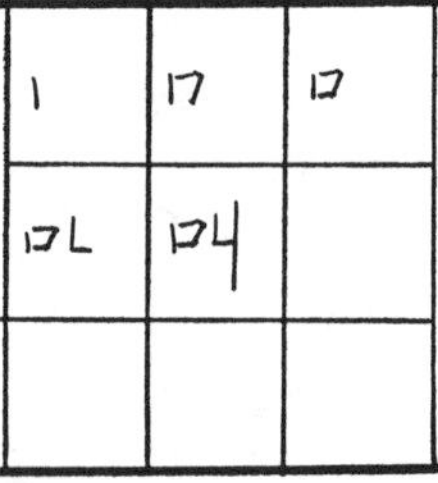

JYAU-4, to call, be called; to order a person to do something

"Mouth" gives the meaning; *jyou-1* (258, above) gives the sound.

叫甚麼 *jyau-4 shem-2 ma*, What's it called (named)?

馬叫 *ma-3 jyau-4*, The horse neighs.

牛	ノ	⊢	仁	**NYOU-2, cow. cow rad. (93)** This character is a picture (cp. 15, above). This form occurs as a part of characters and also as an independent character. Learn to distinguish "cow" from *wu-3* "noon" 午 (594, below).
	牛			
260 4 strokes				

告	ノ	⊢	牛	**GAU-4, to inform** The original meaning of this character was "muzzle for cows." The character was a meaning-meaning compound: "cow" + "mouth" suggested the device. It is used by sound-loan to mean "to inform."
	屮	告	告	
261 7 strokes	告			

斤	ノ	亻	斤	**JIN-1, axe. AXE rad. (69)** The "axe" rad. is a picture. The character now stands also for a measure of weight, a *jin* or "catty," which equals 1⅓ pounds.
	斤			
262 4 strokes				

斥	ノ	亻	斤	**CHR-4, to scold**
	斤	斥		
263 5 strokes				

訴	、	亠	言	**SU-4, SUNG-4, to inform** 告訴　*gau-4 su-4*, to inform; to accuse 告訴人　*gau-4 su-4 ren-2*, accuser
	言	言	言	
264 12 strokes	訂	訴	訴	訴

77

知口	ノ	ﾉー	仁
	午	矢	矢ı
265 8 strokes	知口	知	

JR-1, to know

The early lexicographers pretty much agree that this is a meaning-meaning compound—"arrow" (63, above) + "mouth"—"because when you know, your mouth is sharp and far-reaching, like an arrow."

知心 *jr-1 syin-1*, to understand each other

首	丶	ﾉﾉ	丷
	丷	丷	丷
266 9 strokes	首	首	首

SHOU-3, chief; the head. CHIEF rad. (185)

The student should distinguish the "chief" rad. from the "head" rad. 頁 (333, below) and from the "face" rad. 面 (610, below). "Chief" was originally a picture of a head with horns or some big headdress.

道	丶	丷	丷
	丷	首	首
267 12 strokes	首	道	道

DAU-4, road; to say; the Way

知道 *jr-1 dau-4*, to know

道謝 *dau-4 sye-4*, to thank

道喜 *dau-4 syi-3*, to congratulate

此匕	⏐	⌐	止
	止	此匕	此匕
268 6 strokes			

TSZ-3, this

The form of the character can be analyzed as "toe" + "ladle," but the meaning cannot be explained on that basis. The student will just have to memorize it.

些	⌐	止	此匕
	此匕	些	些
269 8 strokes			

SYE-1, few

好些   *hau-3 sye-1*, quite a few

這一些書 *jei-4 yi-4 sye-1 shu-1*, this lot of books

大些   *da-4 sye-1*, be a bit larger

位	ノ	イ	亻
	伫	侊	位
270 7 strokes	位		

WEI-4, position, standpoint; seat; a polite measure for persons

三位小姐 *san-1 wei-4 syau-2 jye-3*, three young ladies

位子 *wei-4 dz-3*, seat

學位 *sywe-2 wei-4*, academic degree

支	一	十	丈
	支		
271 4 strokes			

JR-1, branch. BRANCH rad. (65)

The student will need to distinguish the "branch" rad. from "club" 殳 (183, above), "knock" 攵 (384, below), "pattern" 文 (360), "follow" 夊 (319), "slow" 夂 (337), and the 攴 form of "knock" (p. 270).

枝	一	十	才
	木	朾	朾
272 8 strokes	枋	枝	

JR-1, branch; a measure for pens, pencils, chalk, etc.

In this character, 271, above, has been re-clarified with the "tree" rad.

枝子 *jr-1 dz-3*, (tree) branch

一枝筆 *yi-4 jr-1 bi-3*, pen

己	㇇	㇆	己
273 3 strokes			

JI-3, self; the sixth "heavenly stem." SELF rad. (49)

As a cyclical character ("heavenly stem"), this was probably a symbol. The meaning "self" is probably by sound-loan. Learn to tell "self" from "already" 已 (274, below), from *sz-4* 巳 (275), and from "seal" 卩 (760).

已	㇇	㇆	已
274 3 strokes			

YI-3, already

See the note under 273, above, for characters with which *yi-3* is likely to be confused.

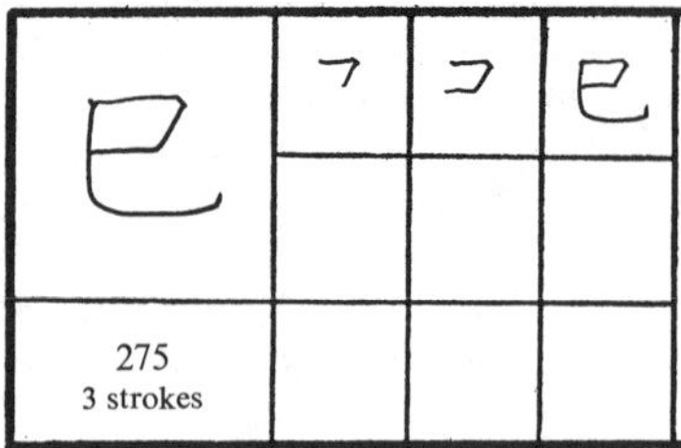

275
3 strokes

SZ-4, the sixth "earthly branch"

Sz-4 is supposed originally to have been a drawing of a fetus, with large head and curled-up lower part. The student should learn to distinguish *sz-4* from 273 and 274, above.

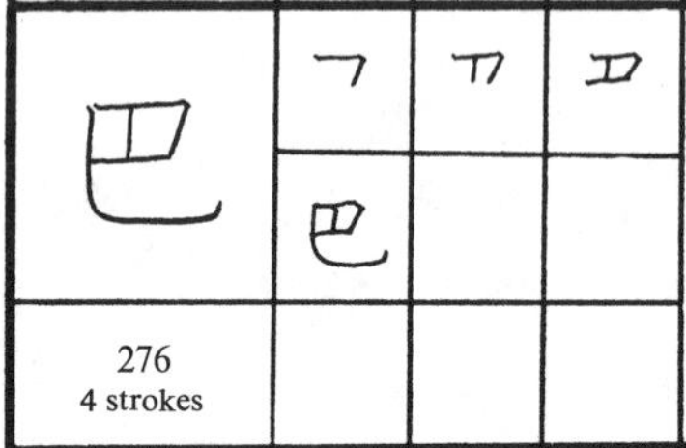

276
4 strokes

BA-1, open hand, palm; to stick to

In ancient texts, this character meant python—as the dictionaries call it, "the elephant snake"—and it was a picture. It came to mean "open hand" by sound-loan.

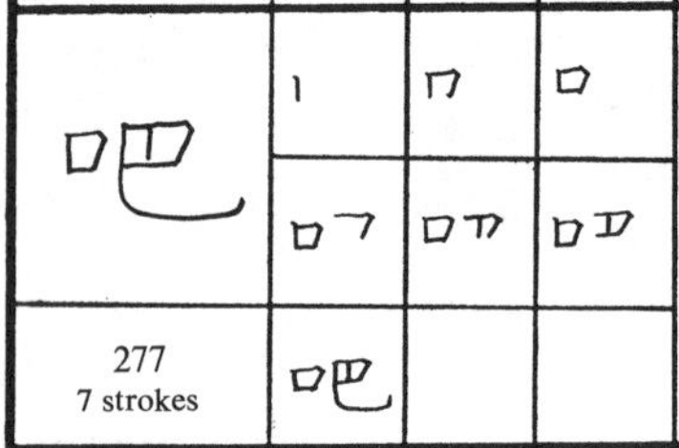

277
7 strokes

BA; a sentence-final particle

This character is a sound-meaning compound.

好吧　*hau-3 ba*, Okay! Fine! Bravo!

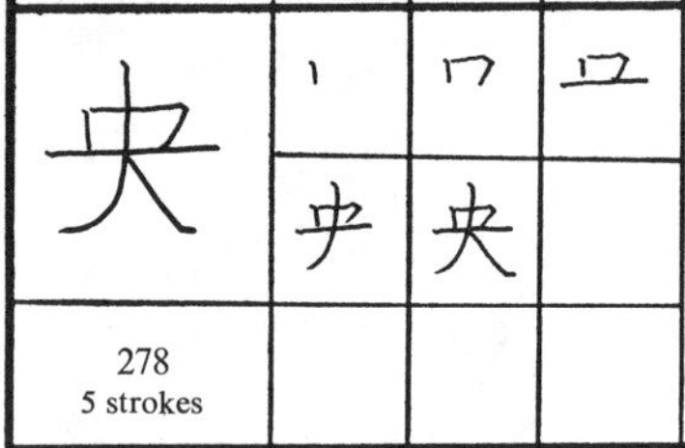

278
5 strokes

YANG-1, center

中央　*jung-1 yang-1*, center, central

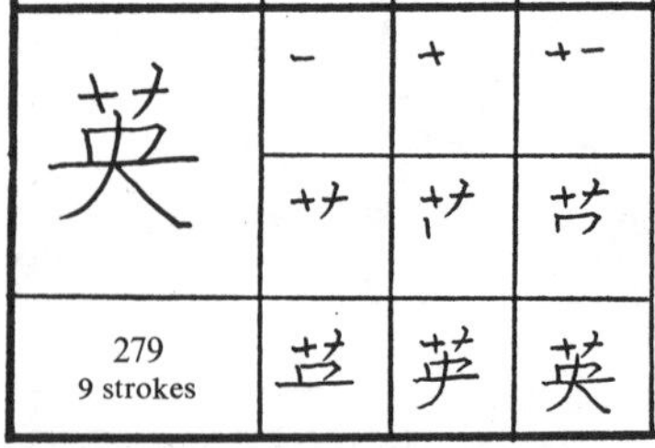

279
9 strokes

YING-1, be bold

The original meaning was "flower, to flower"; "grass" gave the meaning, and *yang-1* (278, above) suggested the sound. "Bold" is by sound-loan.

英國　*ying-1 gwo-2*, England

英里　*ying-1 li-3*, English mile

黑	丶	冂	冋	HEI-1, black. BLACK rad. (203)
	冋	四	四	*Hei-1* is said to be the picture of a man painted up with war paint and decorated with tattooing.
280 12 strokes	甲	里	黑	

占	丨	卜	卜	JAN-1, to divine
	占	占		*Jan-1* is a meaning-meaning compound: the "divine" rad. (118, above) + "mouth" = "to explain (orally) the divination cracks."
281 5 strokes				

點	丶	冂	冋	DYAN-3, dot
	四	甲	里	五點鐘 *wu-3 dyan-3 jung-1*, 5:00
	黑	黙	點	三點六 *san-1 dyan-3 lyou-4*, 3.6 點心 *dyan-3 syin-1*, snack, pastry
282 17 strokes				点

雨	一	一	一	YU-3, rain. RAIN rad. (173)
	币	雨	雨	The "rain" rad. is a picture of raindrops falling from clouds.
	雨	雨		雨點 *yu-2 dyan-3*, raindrop 雨衣 *yu-3 yi-1*, raincoat
283 8 strokes				

令	丿	人	今	LING-4, to command; command; LING-3, ream
	令	令		Usually printed 令.
				令兄 *ling-4 syung-1*, your older brother 一令紙 *yi-4 ling-3 jr-3*, ream of paper
284 5 strokes				

81

零	一	宀	二	**LING-2, zero; tiny bit**
	帀	雨	雨	The original meaning of this character was "drop," and it was a compound of "rain" for meaning and *ling-4* (284, above) for sound. The meaning "zero" may be an extension: "drop" > "tiny bit" > "virtually nothing" > "nothing"; or it may be a case of sound-loan. Usually printed 零.
285 13 strokes	零	零	零	

半	丶	丷	丷	**BAN-4, half**
	半	半		The vertical stroke bisects the "eight" rad. and the two "one" rads. to suggest "half."
286 5 strokes				一大半 *yi-2 da-4 ban-4*, majority 三點半 *san-1 dyan-3 ban-4*, 3:30 半天 *ban-4 tyan-1*, long time

多	丿	勺	夕	**DWO-1, be numerous**
	多	多	多	多半 *dwo-1 ban-4*, for the most part; probably 好多了 *hau-3 dwo-1 le*, Much better! 多謝 *dwo-1 sye-4*, Many thanks!
287 6 strokes				

少	丨	小	小	**SHAU-3, be few**
	少			多少 *dwo-1 shau-3*, How much? How many? 少了三個 *shau-3 le san-1 ge*, be three short 少你 *shau-3 ni-3*, lacking you
288 4 strokes				

句	丿	勺	勹	**JYU-4, sentence; verse line**
	句	句		句子 *jyu-4 dz-3*, sentence
289 5 strokes				

夠	ノ	ク	夕
	多	多	豹
290 11 strokes	夠	夠	夠

GOU-4, be enough

Dwo-1 "be numerous" suggests the meaning; *jyu-4* (289, above) once suggested the sound.

鬼	ノ	イ	白
	白	鱼	免
291 10 strokes	鬼	鬼	鬼

GWEI-3, ghost. GHOST rad. (194)

This character is said to be a picture of a ghost. That is a statement difficult to deny.

塊	一	十	土
	扌	圹	埔
292 13 strokes	坤	塊	塊

KWAI-4, clod, lump; a measure for dollars

The "earth" rad. gives the meaning; *gwei-3* (291, above) suggests the sound.

七塊錢　*chi-1 kwai-4 chyan-2*, seven dollars

块

毛	ノ	二	三
	毛		
293 4 strokes			

MAU-2, fur; a measure for dimes. FUR rad. (82)

Mau-2 is a picture of an animal's pelt.

毛筆　*mau-2 bi-3*, writing brush

毛衣　*mau-2 yi-1*, (wool) sweater

相	一	十	才
	木	机	机
294 9 strokes	朾	相	相

SYANG-1, mutual; SYANG-4, face, appearance; to examine

The original meaning was "to examine." The character is supposed to show someone studying a tree or piece of wood with his eye: a carpenter checking material.

相對　*syang-1 dwei-4*, be relative (not absolute)

首相　*shou-3 syang-4*, prime minister

想	一	十	才	SYANG-3, to think
	木	机	相	This character may stand for a word cognate with 294, above. The "heart" rad. means "mind" (as it often does), and the character can be explained as "to examine in the mind, to think." This character is then a reclarified compound.
295 13 strokes	相	想	想	想要 *syang-3 yau-4*, to feel like, to want to

得	丿	彳	彳	DEI-3, must; DE-2, to get; DE; a grammatical particle
	彳	彳	彳	得了 *de-2 le*, That does it! Enough!
				貴得多 *gwei-3 de dwo-1*, be much more expensive
296 11 strokes	得	得	得	看得見 *kan-4 de jyan-4*, be able to see

共	一	十	艹	GUNG-4, all together, collectively, joint
				Older forms have "clasp" (141, above) twice.
	艹	共	共	一共 *yi-2 gung-4*, all together
297 6 strokes				中共 *jung-1 gung-4*, "Chicoms"; Chinese communists

尤	一	ナ	尢	YOU-2, still more
	尤			
298 4 strokes				

京	丶	亠	亠	JING-1, capital
	古	古	宁	The character is a picture of a tall building (cp. 75, above), and this was its original meaning. It soon came to mean "tall buildings: capital."
				京都 *jing-1 du-1*, capital; Kyoto
299 8 strokes	宁	京		東京 *dung-1 jing-1*, Tokyo

| 就 | 丶 | 亠 | 古 | JYOU-4, then; only; to go to; to go with |
| 300 12 strokes | 亨 京 尤 | 京 就 | 京 就 | 就是 *jyou-4 shr-4*, be precisely . . .; namely . . .; That's right! 就有三個 *jyou-4 you-3 san-1 ge*, to have only three |

| 直 | 一 十 直 | 十 冇 | 广 直 | JR-2, be straight; to keep on; be a certain length Usually printed 直. 一直 *yi-4 jr-2*, so far; straight on 直三寸 *jr-2 san-1 tswun-4*, be three inches long |
| 301 8 strokes | | | | |

| 真 | 一 方 直 | 十 有 真 | 广 肖 真 | JEN-1, be real, be true; truly Often printed 眞. 眞相 *jen-1 syang-4*, true picture 眞是的 *jen-1 shr-4 de*, That's really too bad! 眞好 *jen-1 hau-3*, Great! |
| 302 10 strokes | | | | |

| 現 | 一 王 珇 | 二 玑 玥 | 干 玥 現 | SYAN-4, present, now 現錢 *syan-4 chyan-2*, ready money 兌現 *dwei-4 syan-4*, to cash a check; to fulfill a promise |
| 303 11 strokes | | | | 現 |

| 在 | 一 在 | 十 在 | 广 在 | DZAI-4, be at, be in, be on 現在 *syan-4 dzai-4*, now 在我看 *dzai-4 wo-3 kan-4*, as I see it 不在了 *bu-2 dzai-4 le*, no longer exists; be dead |
| 304 6 strokes | | | | |

	丶	⻁	⺕	**LYANG-2, be good**
良	⺕	自	良	The student should distinguish *lyang-2* from the "stubborn" rad. 艮 (31, above). 良心 *lyang-2 syin-1*, conscience
305 **7 strokes**	良			

	丿	人	仌	**SHR-2, food, to eat. FOOD rad. (184)**
食	今	仒	仓	The "food" rad. is a picture of a jar commonly used to hold food. 零食 *ling-4 shr-2*, snack
306 **9 strokes**	食	食	食	

	一	一	冂	**LYANG-3, two; a tael (ancient monetary unit)**
兩	帀	兩	兩	兩塊錢 *lyang-3 kwai-4 chyan-2*, two dollars 一兩金子 *yi-4 lyang-3 jin-1 dz-3*, a tael of gold
307 **8 strokes**	兩			兩口子 *lyang-3 kou-3 dz-3*, husband and wife 兩

	ノ	厂	万	**FAN-3, to turn back; to rebel**
反	反			相反 *syang-1 fan-3*, be the opposite of 反共 *fan-3 gung-4*, anti-Communist 反對 *fan-3 dwei-4*, to oppose
308 **4 strokes**				

	丿	人	仌	**SHR-2, food, to eat. FOOD rad. (184)**
食	今	仒	仓	Compare this with the form of the "food" rad. above (306). The form 食 is the form the "food" rad. usually takes when it is part of a character; 306, above, is the independent form.
309 **8 strokes** **(9 strokes)**	食	食		

FAN-4, cooked rice, food

Fan-4 is a sound-meaning compound. The "food" rad. gives the meaning; *fan-3* (308, above) suggests the sound.

310
12 strokes

TANG-2; the name of the T'ang Dynasty

311
10 strokes

TANG-2, sugar, candy

The "rice" rad. helps with the meaning; it often appears in characters for words that mean a powdery substance, grain, or granular foodstuffs. *Tang-2*, of course, is a phonetic.

白糖　*bai-2 tang-2*, white sugar

312
16 strokes

SHE-2, tongue. TONGUE rad. (135)

She-2 is a picture of a tongue sticking out of a mouth.

313
6 strokes

HWA-4, speech, language

Hwa-4 combines meanings: "words" + "tongue" = "speech, language."

說話　*shwo-1 hwa-4*, to speak
中國話　*jung-1 gwo-2 hwa-4*, the Chinese language

314
13 strokes

87

舍	丿	𠆢	𠆢	**SHE-4, home** Note the form of "man" at the top. *She-4* now = "man" + "tongue," which doesn't help much with the meaning "home." The character was originally a meaning-meaning compound, but its form has been corrupted. Memorize it.
	合	舎	舎	
315 8 strokes	舍	舍		舍弟 *she-4 di-4*, my younger brother

事	一	𠃌	彐	**SHR-4, affair, event** This character shows a hand holding a writing instrument. Originally, it meant "to hold office, to serve" and was supposed to suggest the scribes who were early rulers' most important servants.
	彐	事	事	
316 8 strokes	事			董事 *dung-3 shr-4*, member (of a board of directors)

情	丿	丄	忄	**CHING-2, emotion; circumstances** 事情 *shr-4 ching*, "affair, business" 情人 *ching-2 ren-2*, sweetheart 說情 *shwo-1 ching-2*, to ask a favor
	忄⁻	忄=	忄丰	
317 11 strokes	忄丰	情	情	

歌	丁	丁	可	**GE-1, song** The "yawn" rad. (to suggest the open mouth) combines with *ge-1* in this sound-meaning compound.
	哥	哥	哥	
318 14 strokes	歌	歌	歌	國歌 *gwo-2 ge-1*, national anthem

夂	丿	勹	夂	**JR-3, to follow. FOLLOW rad. (34)** The student should compare this with the "slow" rad. (337, below). The two rads. are identical in form. When the form occurs in characters above other elements, it is "follow" (as in 320, below); when the form occurs below other elements, it is "slow" (as in 340, below).
319 3 strokes				

各	ノ	ク	夂
	冬	各	各
320 6 strokes			

GE-4, each; various

各個 *ge-4 ge-4*, every one

各國 *ge-4 gwo-2*, various nations

客	丶	宀	宀
	宁	宏	客
321 9 strokes	客	客	客

KE-4, guest

客人 *ke-4 ren-2*, guest

請客 *ching-3 ke-4*, to give a party

气	ノ	一	气
322 3 strokes			

CHI-3, to beg

This character once was identical to the "breath" rad. (324, below). It was probably by sound-loan that it came to mean "to beg."

吃	丨	口	口
	口'	吃	吃
323 6 strokes			

CHR-1, to eat

吃飯　　　*chr-1 fan-4*, to eat

吃的東西　*chr-1 de dung-1 syi-1*, food, things to eat

吃力　　　*chr-1 li-4*, to require strength, be arduous

气	ノ	一	气
	气		
324 4 strokes			

CHI-4, breath. BREATH rad. (84)

The character is a picture of breath passing off in waves.

89

氣	ノ	⁻	乞	**CHI-4**, breath, animus, energy, soul
	气	气	气	客氣 *ke-4 chi-4*, be polite; to stand on ceremony
325 10 strokes	氣	氣	氣	生氣 *sheng-1 chi-4*, to get angry 別氣我 *bye-2 chi-4 wo-3*, Don't make me get mad! 气

月	)	刀	月	**ROU-4**, meat. MEAT rad. (130)
	月			Note that when the "meat" rad. occurs as a part of characters, it is identical in form to the "moon" rad. (178). The "meat" rad. as an independent character, however, has a different form (928, below).
326 4 strokes (6 strokes)				

能	㇄	厶	厶 丨	**NENG-2**, be able to
	自	自	育	*Neng-2* is listed in dictionaries under the "meat" rad. (326, above); that is the only way we know that this form is "meat."
327 10 strokes	能	能	能	能力 *neng-2 li-4*, ability 能够 *neng-2 gou-4*, be able to

曾	丶	丷	ㅛ	**TSENG-2**, already; **DZENG-1**, great grandparents or children through the male line
	甴	甶	甶	
328 12 strokes	曲	曲	曾	(日 160)

尸	フ	ㄱ	尸	**SHR-1**, corpse. CORPSE rad. (44)
				The character originally was a picture of a man lying down. The student should learn to distinguish the "corpse" rad. from the "door" rad. 戶 (391, below).
329 3 strokes				

會	ノ	入	仐	HWEI-4, to know how to, be able to; to meet; HWEI-3, a while; KWAI-4, to calculate
	仒	命	侖	會客 hwei-4 ke-4, to receive a guest
				學會 sywe-2 hwei-4, to learn, to master; academic society
330 13 strokes	侖	會	會	會子 hwei-2 dz-3, moment 会

以	ヽ	㇗	㇗	YI-3, using; taking; because of
				可以 ke-2 yi-3, may, be permitted to
	㇗	以		以東 yi-3 dung-1, to the east
				以外 yi-3 wai-4, beyond, outside of
331 4 strokes (5 strokes)				

原	一	厂	厂	YWAN-2, origin; a plain
				The character originally was "slope" + "white" + "water" and meant "spring." "Water" was corrupted into "small."
	厂	盾	盾	原子 ywan-2 dz-3, atom
				原先 ywan-2 syan-1, at first; previously
332 10 strokes	厡	原	原	

頁	一	丆	丆	YE-4, head. HEAD rad. (181)
				The character is a picture of a man's head. The student should learn to distinguish "head" from the "chief" rad. 首 (266, above) and from the "face" rad. 面 (610, below).
	丆	百	百	
333 9 strokes	頁	頁		頁

願	一	厂	厂	YWAN-4, be willing
				心願 syin-1 ywan-4, heart's desire
	盾	原	原	情願 ching-2 ywan-4, voluntarily
				有願 you-3 ywan-4, to have a vow
334 19 strokes	原	願	願	愿

91

音	`	亠	宀	YIN-1, tone. TONE rad. (180) The old form of the "tone" rad. was a mouth blowing on a flute—a pretty good way to suggest "tone." The modern form has been corrupted into "stand" over "say."
	立	立	产	
335 9 strokes	音	音	音	
意	`	宀	立	YI-4, idea, opinion, motive This character is often explained as "the tone in the heart" = "idea, motive, etc." 願意　ywan-4 yi-4, be willing 意見　yi-4 jyan-4, opinion 意外　yi-4 wai-4, unforeseeable
	音	音	音	
336 13 strokes	意	意	意	
夊	ノ	ク	夊	SWEI-1, slow. SLOW rad. (35) The student will remember that "slow" is identical in form to the "follow" rad. (319, above). When the form occurs below other elements in a character, it is the "slow" rad.; when it occurs above other elements in a character, it is the "follow" rad. The rarely seen independent form is printed 夂.
337 3 strokes				
爫	ノ	⺊	爫	JAU-3, claws. CLAWS rad. (87) This is the form of the "claws" rad. that is used as a part of characters. (For the independent form, see p. 267.) It is a picture. Often printed ⺤.
	爫			
338 4 strokes				
受	ノ	⺊	爫	SHOU-4, to receive The "crown" rad. is supposed to be an object being received from the "claws" (fingernails, hand) by the right hand. 受累　shou-4 lei-4, be troubled, be bothered 受看　shou-4 kan-4, be easy on the eyes
	爫	爫	爫	
339 8 strokes	受	受		

愛	ノ	ゟ	心
	心	心	心
340 13 strokes	恶	悉	愛

AI-4, to love

愛情　*ai-4 ching-2*, love (between a man and woman)

愛人　*ai-4 ren-2*, lover, husband, wife

愛國　*ai-4 gwo-2*, be patriotic

爱

仁	ノ	イ	仁
	仁		
341 4 strokes			

REN-2, humaneness, kindness

It is supposed that this word *ren-2* and the word *ren-2* 人 "man; be human" are cognates. The "two" rad., then, is a reclarification. The "two" is often explained philosophically: "two" = "another, other," and kindness is the most important virtue toward others.

乍	ノ	一	仁
	乍	乍	
342 5 strokes			

JA-4, suddenly

乍看　　*ja-4 kan-4*, at first sight

乍有乍沒　*ja-4 you-3 ja-4 mei-2*, Now it's here, now it's not.

作	ノ	イ	亻
	亻	仁	作
343 7 strokes	作		

DZWO-4, to do, to make

作飯　　*dzwo-4 fan-4*, to cook

作對　　*dzwo-4 dwei-4*, to oppose

作生日　*dzwo-4 sheng-1 r-4*, to have a birthday party

昌	丶	冂	曰
	日	日	昌
344 8 strokes	昌	昌	

CHANG-1, sunlight; splendor

This is a meaning-meaning compound: "sun" + "sun."

93

唱	丶	丨?	口	CHANG-4, to sing The "mouth" gives the meaning; chang-1 (344, above) suggests the sound. 唱歌 *chang-4 ge-1*, to sing
	口丨	口丨?	口丨?	
345 11 strokes	口曰	口曰?	唱	

上	丨	卜	上	SHANG-4, up, upon, above; to come or go up 上月 *shang-4 ywe-4*, last month 上千 *shang-4 chyan-1*, be close to a thousand 上學 *shang-4 sywe-2*, to go to school
346 3 strokes				

寫	丶	宀	宀	SYE-3, to write 寫字 *sye-3 dz-4*, to write 寫作 *sye-3 dzwo-4*, to write (e.g., a novel, a poem) 寫生 *sye-3 sheng-1*, to draw living things
	宁	宀	宁	
347 15 strokes	宜	寫	寫	(宀 232, 灬 34) 写

思	丨	冂	曰	SZ-1, to think, thought The character was originally "head" + "heart"; "head" was corrupted to "field." 思想 *sz-1 syang-3*, thought 意思 *yi-4 sz-1*, idea
	用	田	田丨	
348 9 strokes	思	思	思	

皀	丿	亻	勹	SYANG-1, be fragrant; the sweet smell of grain The character originally was a pan over a spoon and was perhaps supposed to suggest the smell of cooking grain. "Pan" has been corrupted into "white." *Syang-1* is not used in modern Chinese, but it is seen as a sound-component in modern characters.
	白	白	皀	
349 7 strokes	皀			

94

	ㄥ	ㄠ	乡	SYANG-1, country (opposite of city) 思鄉 *sz-1 syang-1*, to think of home
鄉	糹	纟	纟	
350 13 strokes	纟	纟	鄉	乡

	一	丁	下	SYA-4, be below 下月 *sya-4 ywe-4*, next month 鄉下 *syang-1 sya-4*, in the country; rural 以下 *yi-3 sya-4*, from now on; just after
下				
351 3 strokes				

	丨	冂	巾	JIN-1, cloth. CLOTH rad. (50) The character is a picture of a small piece of cloth—a kerchief, napkin, or towel—hanging down.
巾				
352 3 strokes				

	丨	冂	冂	MAU-4, to cover the eyes; to risk; to fake 冒名 *mau-4 ming-2*, to use someone else's name
冒	冃	冒	冒	
353 9 strokes	冒	冒	冒	

	丨	冂	巾	MAU-4, hat The "cloth" rad. gives the meaning; *mau-4* (353, above) gives the sound. 帽子 *mau-4 dz-3*, hat, cap
帽	巾'	帽	帽	
354 12 strokes	帽	帽	帽	

新	、	宀	立	SYIN-1, be new 新聞 *syin-1 wen-2*, news
	辛	亲	新	
355 13 strokes	新	新	新	(亲 213)

舊	一	艹	艹	JYOU-4, be old (things, not people) The original meaning of this character was "owl." The "grass" rad. represented the bird's "horns," the "dove" rad. helped further fix the meaning, and *jyou-4* (229, above) gave the sound. The meaning "old" is by sound-loan.
	花	芢	萑	
356 18 strokes	萑	雈	舊	(臼 229) 旧

異	丨	冂	田	YI-4, be strange
	田	甲	男	
357 11 strokes	畏	異	異	(田 23)

戈	一	十	士	TSAI-2, to wound The "lance" rad. gives the meaning; the other part of this character once gave the sound.
	弐	弐	戈	
358 6 strokes				

戴	十	士	吉	DAI-4, to wear (hats, glasses, gloves, etc.); honor 戴帽子 *dai-4 mau-4 dz-3*, to wear a hat 愛戴 *ai-4 dai-4*, love and honor
	吉	壴	異	
359 17 strokes	戴	戴	戴	

96

	丶	一	亠
文	文		

360
4 strokes

WEN-2, pattern; language, literature, culture; civil (as opposed to military). PATTERN rad. (67)

The character was a picture of a man with patterns worked onto his shirt.

中文 *jung-1 wen-2*, the Chinese language

	一	十	丷丿
茶	艹	茨	苳
	苳	茅	茶

361
10 strokes

CHA-2, tea

吃茶 *chr-1 cha-2*, to drink tea

茶點 *cha-2 dyan-3*, refreshments

茶會 *cha-2 hwei-4*, tea, reception

	丨	才	水
水	水		

362
4 strokes

SHWEI-3, water. WATER rad. (85)

The character is a picture of a stream of running water. This is the independent form of the rad.; you have already learned the other form of "three-dots-water."

水土 *shwei-3 tu-3*, climatic conditions

	一	一	一
西	丙	丙	西
	酉		

363
7 strokes

YOU-3, wine; the tenth "earthly branch." WINE rad. (164)

The "wine" rad. is a picture of a wine-jug; the horizontal stroke inside represents the liquid in it. The student should distinguish the "wine" rad. from "west" 西 (130, above).

	丶	冫	氵
酒	氵	沔	沔
	洒	酒	酒

364
10 strokes

JYOU-3, wine, alcoholic beverage

Jyou-3 combines meanings: "water" + "wine" = "wine, alcoholic beverage."

酒鬼 *jyou-2 gwei-3*, lush, alcoholic

				CHYU-3, to grab, to take hold of
取	一	丁	丌	The form, of course, is "right hand" + "ear"; the hand is supposed to be grabbing the ear, whence the meaning "to grab."
	丏	耳	耳	取得 *chyu-3 de-2*, to get, to obtain
365 8 strokes	耵	取		取笑 *chyu-3 syau-4*, to make fun of, to tease

				DZWEI-4, most
最	丶	冂	日	
	旦	무	昂	
366 12 strokes	骨	最	最	

				SHANG-4, still
尚	丨	丷	丷	尙且 *shang-4 chye-3*, even, still, yet
	凸	尚	尚	
367 8 strokes	尚	尚		

				CHANG-2, often, as a rule
常	丨	丷	丷	常常 *chang-2 chang-2*, often
	凸	尚	凿	常見 *chang-2 jyan-4*, be common
368 11 strokes	常	常	常	常會 *chang-2 hwei-4*, regular meeting

				GE-2, hide (as in "cowhide"). HIDE rad. (177)
革	一	十	廿	The character is a picture of a hide split and spread out to dry.
	廿	苫	苦	新革 *syin-1 ge-2*, to change (for the better)
369 9 strokes	苫	苩	革	

98

莫	一	十	艹	**JYAN-1**, be difficult, be in difficulty In the old form, some scholars see the picture of a man with his hands tied behind his back, whence "to be in difficulty."
	芢	芇	苫	
370 11 strokes	茦	茟	莫	

艱	艹	艹	苫	**JYAN-1**, be difficult This is the same word as 370, above; the character is reclarified with the "stubborn" rad.
	茦	莫	莫ヨ	
371 17 strokes	艱	艱	艱	艰

難	艹	苫	茦	**NAN-2**, be difficult 難吃 *nan-2 chr-1*, to taste bad 難道 *nan-2 dau-4*, It couldn't be that . . . ? You don't mean . . . ? 艱難 *jyan-1 nan-2*, be difficult, be in difficulty
	茦	茦	茦	
372 19 strokes	難	難	難	难

谷	丿	八	分	**GU-3**, valley. VALLEY rad. (150) The character is a picture. 山谷 *shan-1 gu-3*, ravine
	父	谷	谷	
373 7 strokes	谷			

容	丶	宀	宀	**RUNG-2**, to allow; face 容人 *rung-2 ren-2*, to tolerate people 笑容 *syau-4 rung-2*, smiling face 容或 *rung-2 hwo-4*, perhaps
	宀	穴	宓	
374 10 strokes	突	宏	容	

勿	ノ	勹	勹	**WU-4, must not, Don't!** This is said to be a picture of an old warning flag—"Stop!"—from which the meaning "must not" derives.
	勿			
375 **4 strokes**				

易	l	冂	日	**YI-4, to change; be easy** *Yi-4* originally meant "chameleon" and was a picture of the chameleon. The meaning "to change" is an easy extension of "chameleon." The meaning "be easy" is probably by sound-loan.
	日	尸	男	
376 **8 strokes**	易	易		容易 *rung-2 yi-4*, be easy

囱	ノ	亻	白	**TSUNG-1, smoke-hole, chimney, flue; CHWANG-1, window** The character is a picture.
	向	囱	囱	
377 **7 strokes**	囱			

囱心	ノ	亻	白	**TSUNG-1, excited, hurried** *Tsung-1* (377, above) gives the sound; the "heart" rad. gives the meaning.
	囱	囱	囱	
378 **11 strokes**	悤	悤	悤	

聰	一	丁	刀	**TSUNG-1, be intelligent** *Tsung-1* originally meant "be quick of hearing, be quick of apprehension," from which it easily came to mean "be quick to understand, be intelligent." The character is a sound-meaning compound. *Tsung-1* (378, above) gives the sound; the "ear" rad. gives the meaning.
	耳	耳	耴	
379 **17 strokes**	耴	聰	聰	聰

100

明	l	冂	月	**MING-2, be bright** "Sun" + "moon" = "light, bright." 聰明 *tsung-1 ming-2*, be intelligent 明白 *ming-2 bai-2*, to understand 明天 *ming-2 tyan-1*, tomorrow
	日	明	明	
380 **8 strokes**	明	明		

聽	一	刂	耳	**TING-1, to listen** Note the "ear" rad. in *ting-1*. 聽見 *ting-1 jyan-4*, to hear 聽說 *ting-1 shwo-1*, to hear it said that
	耳	耳	耳	
381 **22 strokes**	聽	聽	聽	(罒 132, 心 70) 听

今	丿	入	仐	**JIN-1, present, contemporary** 今天 *jin-1 tyan-1*, today 古今 *gu-3 jin-1*, past and present
	今			
382 **4 strokes**				

念	入	仐	今	**NYAN-4, to study** This character is supposed to be a meaning-meaning compound: "present"+the "heart" rad. (for "mind") = "to have present in the mind, to study." 念書 *nyan-4 shu-1*, to study
	念	念	念	
383 **8 strokes**	念			

攵	𠃊	勹	攵	**PU-3, knock. KNOCK rad. (66)** "Knock" is a picture of a hand knocking with a stick. This form is the form usually seen as a part of characters. (For the independent form, see p. 270.) Distinguish "knock" from "club" 殳 (183, above), "branch" 支 (271), and "pattern" 文 (360).
384 **4 strokes**				

孝	一	十	土	**SYAU-4, filial piety** The character combines meanings: the "old" rad. (138, above) + the "child" rad. = "filial piety." Note that the "old" rad. is abbreviated.
	耂	耂	耂	
385 7 strokes	孝			
教	土	耂	耂	**JYAU-1, to teach; JYAU-4, to tell; religion** This character is often written 教. 教書 *jyau-1 shu-1*, to teach 教學 *jyau-4 sywe-2*, teaching and learning 教會 *jyau-4 hwei-4*, the Church
	孝	孝	孝	
386 11 strokes	教	教	教	
曷	丨	冂	曰	**HE-2, what? why?** The form at the top is the "say" rad., not the "sun" rad.
	曰	曶	曷	
387 9 strokes	曷	曷	曷	
喝	丨	冂	口	**HE-1, to drink; HE-4, to shout** *He-2* (387, above) gives the sound; the "mouth" rad. gives the meaning. 喝茶 *he-1 cha-2*, to drink tea
	叩	呾	呬	
388 12 strokes	喝	喝	喝	
豕	一	丆	丂	**SHR-3, pig. PIG rad. (152)** The character is a picture of a pig.
	丂	豕	豕	
389 7 strokes	豕			

家	丶	丷	宀	JYA-1, home, house, family; specialist
	宀	宁	穷	*Jya-1* combines meanings: "pig" under "roof" = "home." Some commentators say the pig is really outside the house.
390 10 strokes	家	家	家	家鄉 *jya-1 syang-1*, home town, ancestral home 家母 *jya-1 mu-3*, my mother

戶	丿	勹	刍	HU-4, door. DOOR rad. (63)
	戶			The character is a picture. The student should distinguish it from "corpse" 尸 (329, above). Usually printed 户.
391 4 strokes				戶口 *hu-4 kou-3*, population; household 三戶家 *san-1 hu-4 jya-1*, three households

方	丶	二	亠	FANG-1, square. SQUARE rad. (70)
	方			方便 *fang-1 byan-4*, be convenient 東方 *dung-1 fang-1*, the East, the Orient 方言 *fang-1 yan-2*, dialect
392 4 strokes				

房	丿	勹	刍	FANG-2, house, building
	戶	戶	启	"Door" gives the meaning; *fang-1* (392, above) gives the sound.
393 8 strokes	房	房		房東 *fang-2 dung-1*, landlord

婁	丶	冂	曰	LOU-2; the name of a constellation; a surname
	曰	昌	串	There is no helpful explanation of this character. The student will want to note that it is a common "phonetic"—that is, it indicates the sound in a large number of common characters. 娄
394 11 strokes	婁	婁		

樓	一	十	才	**LOU-2**, building of two or more stories
	扗	桓	桓	樓房　*lou-2 fang-2*, building of two or more stories
395 15 strokes	樓	樓	樓	下樓　*sya-4 lou-2*, to go downstairs 樓下　*lou-2 sya-4*, downstairs　　楼

至	一	乙	云	**JR-4**, to reach. REACH rad. (133) The character is a picture of a bird alighting, from which came the idea "to reach."
	互	至	至	至今　*jr-4 jin-1*, up to the present time
396 6 strokes				至少　*jr-4 shau-3*, at the least

屋	ㄱ	コ	尸	**WU-1**, a room The "corpse" rad. here is supposed to mean "to lie or sit," and the character is explained: "where you come (reach) to lie or sit down—your room."
	尸	屋	屋	屋子　*wu-1 dz-3*, a room
397 9 strokes	居	屋	屋	房屋　*fang-2 wu-1*, houses, buildings

地	一	十	土	**DI-4**, place 地方　*di-4 fang-1*, place
	圤	地	地	土地　*tu-3 di-4*, land 地位　*di-4 wei-4*, job, status
398 6 strokes				

成	一	厂	厂	**CHENG-2**, to perfect; to become 成就　*cheng-2 jyou-4*, accomplishment
	厅	成	成	成立　*cheng-2 li-4*, to set up 兌成美金　*dwei-4 cheng-2 mei-3 jin-1*, to change into American money
399 7 strokes	成			

104

城	一	十	圤
	圫	圫	坊
400 9 strokes (10 strokes)	城	城	城

CHENG-2, city wall; city

The "earth" rad. gives the meaning, and *cheng-2* (399, above) gives the sound in this character.

交	丶	亠	宀
	六	交	交
401 6 strokes			

JYAU-1, to hand over, to exchange

The original meaning of this character was "to cross"; it was a picture of a man with crossed legs. The student should distinguish it from "pattern" 文 (360, above).

交易 *jyau-1 yi-4*, to trade

交情 *jyau-1 ching-2*, friendship

校	一	十	扌
	扌	朮	朾
402 10 strokes	朾	校	校

JYAU-4, to check; to collate; SYAU-4, school

校對 *jyau-4 dwei-4*, to proofread

學校 *sywe-2 syau-4*, school

校長 *syau-4 jang-3*, principal, college president

用	丿	冂	月
	月	用	
403 5 strokes			

YUNG-4, to use. USE rad. (101)

The vertical stroke in the center was thought by early scholars to be an arrow shot through the center of a target. From this they deduced a sequence of meanings: "apt—fit to the purpose—usable—to use."

甫	一	厂	冂
	同	甫	甫
404 7 strokes	甫		

FU-3, to begin

鋪	ノ	人	仐
	仐	全	金
405 15 strokes	金	鋪	鋪

PU-4, store; PU-1, to spread

The character is a sound-meaning compound. The "gold" rad. gives the meaning, and *fu-3* (404, above) suggests the sound.

鋪子 *pu-4 dz-3*, store, shop

铺

㠯	丨	厂	尸
	厒	㠯	
406 5 strokes			

YI-3, using, taking; because of

This is another way to write 以 (331, above). The student should distinguish this character from "bureaucrat" 臣 (491, below) and from "chief, large, great" 巨 (496, below).

官	、	宀	宀
	宀	宁	宁
407 8 strokes	官	官	

GWAN-1, mandarin; organ (of the body)

官事 *gwan-1 shr-4*, governmental affairs

官家 *gwan-1 jya-1*, government; the emperor

官話 *gwan-1 hwa-4*, "Mandarin" language

館	ノ	人	仐
	今	仒	食
408 16 strokes	食	飵	館

GWAN-3, big building; eatery

In the "eatery" sense, the "food" rad. gives the meaning; *gwan-1* (407, above) gives the sound.

飯館子 *fan-4 gwan-2 dz-3*, restaurant

馆

尼	コ	ヨ	尸
	尼	尼	
409 5 strokes			

NI-2, nun

106

呢	丨	冂	口	NE; a grammatical particle; NI-2, wool-stuff
	口⁊	口⁊	叨	*Ni-2* (409, above) gives the sound; the mouth here warns that the character may be a particle. The meaning "wool-stuff" comes by sound-loan.
410 8 strokes	呢	呢		呢大衣 *ni-2 da-4 yi-1*, woolen coat

所	丿	㇆	𠂆	SWO-3, place; which? what?
	户	户′	所	"Door" and "axe" here are supposed to combine to give the meaning "to build a living place," whence "place." The meanings "which? what?" are by sound-loan.
411 8 strokes	所	所		所以 *swo-2 yi-3*, therefore
交易所 *jyau-1 yi-4 swo-3*, stock exchange

車	一	亍	冃	CHE-1, car. CAR rad. (159) The character is a picture of a car or chariot.
	丏	直	亘	車房 *che-1 fang-2*, garage
車夫 *che-1 fu-1*, chauffeur
412 7 strokes	車			车

汽	丶	冫	氵	CHI-4, gas, steam The character combines meanings: "water" + "breath" (vapor) = "steam."
	氵	汢	汽	汽車 *chi-4 che-1*, automobile
汽水 *chi-4 shwei-3*, carbonated drink, soda water
413 7 strokes	汽			

火	丶	丷	少	HWO-3, fire. FIRE rad. (86) The character is a picture of flames rising. This is the independent form of "fire dots" (34, above).
	火			火車 *hwo-3 che-1*, train
火山 *hwo-3 shan-1*, volcano
414 4 strokes				

舟	ノ	イ	介	JOU-1, boat. BOAT rad. (137) The "boat" rad. is a picture of a boat.
	舟	舟	舟	
415 6 strokes				

船	ノ	イ	介	CHWAN-2, boat 下船 *sya-4 chwan-2*, to disembark 汽船 *chi-4 chwan-2*, steamship
	舟	舟	舟	
416 11 strokes	舟几	舟几	船	

飛	㇈	飞	飞	FEI-1, to fly. FLY rad. (183) *Fei-1* is the picture of a flying bird.
	飞	飞	飛	
417 9 strokes	飛	飛	飛	飞

幺幺	㇜	幺	幺	YOU-1, be small Note that this character is the "coil" rad. 幺 (25, above) doubled.
	幺㇜	幺幺	幺幺	
418 6 strokes				

幾	幺	幺幺	絲	JI-3, several
	丝	丝	幾	
419 12 strokes	幾	幾		几

108

機	一 十 才		**JI-1**, machine, mechanism; opportunity; be secret 飛機 *fei-1 ji-1*, airplane 機子 *ji-1 dz-3*, machine, mechanism 機會 *ji-1 hwei-4*, opportunity
420 16 strokes	機 機 機		机
行	ノ ㇒ 彳		**SYING-2**, to go; **HANG-2**, business firm. GO rad. (144) The left half of "go" is "step" (30, above). Originally the right half was identical (the similarity is still clear), and the character was easily explained: "step" + "step" = "to go."
421 6 strokes			
圭	一 十 土		**GWEI-1**, jade tablets or jade batons used in the old days as symbols of authority Note that *gwei-1* "earth" is used twice. These jade symbols were the tokens used in conferring fiefs (land).
422 6 strokes			
街	ノ ㇒ 彳		**JYE-1**, street *Jye-1* is a sound-meaning compound. The "go" rad. gives the meaning; *gwei-1* (422, above) at one time gave the sound.
423 12 strokes			
定	丶 ㇒ 宀		**DING-4**, to settle (a matter) 一定 *yi-2 ding-4*, certainly 定船 *ding-4 chwan-2*, to book passage 定錢 *ding-4 chyan-2*, money on deposit
424 8 strokes			

109

怎	ノ	′⊢	′ケ
	ケ	乍	乍
425 9 strokes	怎	怎	怎

DZEN-3, how? why?

The character is supposed to be a meaning-meaning compound: "suddenly" (342, above) + "heart" (mind) = "bewilderment" = the questions "how? why?"

怎麼　*dzem-3 ma*, how? why?

不怎麼　*bu-4 dzem-3 ma*, not very

人人	ノ	人	人ノ
	从		
426 4 strokes			

TSUNG-2, to follow; from

The character is a picture of one man following another. Compare 427, below.

從	ノ	′	彳
	彳	彳火	彳少
427 11 strokes	彳从	從	從

TSUNG-2, to follow; from

This is the same word as 426, above. The character has been "reclarified" with various additions.

從三點鐘　*tsung-2 san-1 dyan-3 jung-1*, since 3:00

從新　*tsung-2 syin-1*, again　　　从

回	l	冂	冋
	冋	回	回
428 6 strokes			

HWEI-2, to return; time, occurrence

The character is supposed to symbolize going around something until you return to the starting point.

回家　*hwei-2 jya-1*, to go home

下回　*sya-4 hwei-2*, next time

到	一	厶	云
	云	至	至
429 8 strokes	至	到	

DAU-4, to arrive at

The "reach" rad. gives the meaning; *dau-1* (205, above) gives the sound.

到了　*dau-4 le*, It's arrived.

到三點　*dau-4 san-1 dyan-3*, at 3:00

坐	丿	人	人人	DZWO-4, to sit down; to travel by
	쑤	坐	坐	*Dzwo-4* is a picture of two men sitting on the earth.
430 7 strokes				坐下　*dzwo-4 sya-4*, to sit down 坐船　*dzwo-4 chwan-2*, to travel by boat 坐飛機　*dzwo-4 fei-1 ji-1*, to travel by plane

來	一	厂	厃	LAI-2, to come
	夾	來	來	This character originally meant "wheat" and was a picture of growing wheat. The meaning "to come" is by sound-loan.
431 8 strokes	來	來		下來　*sya-4 lai-2*, to come down 從來　*tsung-2 lai-2*, customarily (in the past)　　　　来

去	一	十	土	CHYU-4, to go
	去	去		下去　　　*sya-4 chyu-4*, to go down 說來說去　*shwo-1 lai-2 shwo-1 chyu-4*, to say over and over
432 5 strokes				

站	丶	亠	亠	JAN-4, (taxi, bus) stand, to stand
	立	立	立丨	The "stand" rad. gives the meaning; *jan-1* (281, above) gives the sound.
433 10 strokes	站	站	站	火車站　*hwo-3 che-1 jan-4*, railroad station 汽車站　*chi-4 che-1 jan-4*, bus station

走	一	十	土	DZOU-3, to walk. WALK rad. (156)
	丰	丰	走	The character originally was a meaning-meaning compound: "man" + "foot." The modern character is somewhat corrupted.
434 7 strokes	走			他走了　*ta-1 dzou-3 le*, He's left. 走吧　　*dzou-3 ba*, Let's go!

起	土	‡	‡	CHI-3, to rise, to raise
	‡	走	走	*Ji-3* (273, above) suggests the sound in this character; the "walk" rad. is supposed to help with the meaning.
435 10 strokes	起	起		站起來 *jan-4 chi-3 lai-2*, to stand up 起飛 *chi-3 fei-1*, to take off (airplane)

昨	l	冂	日	DZWO-2, yesterday
	日	日′	日⌐	The "sun" rad. suggests the meaning; *ja-4* (342, above) once gave the sound. 昨天 *dzwo-2 tyan-1*, yesterday
436 9 strokes	昨	昨	昨	

旦	l	冂	日	DAN-4, dawn
	日	旦		The character is a picture of the sun just above the horizon to suggest "dawn."
437 5 strokes				

早	l	冂	日	DZAU-3, be early; long ago; Good morning!
	日	旦	早	早點 *dzau-2 dyan-3*, breakfast 早飯 *dzau-3 fan-4*, breakfast 早就 *dzau-3 jyou*, long ago
438 6 strokes				

兔	′	⼑	⼑	MYAN-3, to escape
	囪	肏	岛	*Myan-3* is supposed to be a picture of a running hare, whence "to escape." 免稅 *myan-3 shwei-4*, be exempt from taxes
439 7 strokes	免	兔		免得 *myan-3 de-2*, to save (from inconvenience); to avoid

晚	l	Π	日
	日ˊ	日ㄅ	日ㄅ
440 12 strokes	日ㄅㅁ	日ㄅㄗ	晚

WAN-3, be late; evening

Myan-3 (439, above) used to give the sound of this character; "sun" gives the meaning.

晚飯 *wan-3 fan-4*, supper

昨晚 *dzwo-2 wan-3*, yesterday evening

故	一	十	亠
	古	古	古ㄴ
441 9 strokes	故ㄅ	故	

GU-4, ancient; to die; cause; intentionally

故事 *gu-4 shr-4*, story

故意 *gu-4 yi-4*, on purpose

故去 *gu-4 chyu-4*, to pass away, to die

巛	〈	巜	巛
442 3 strokes			

CHWAN-1, river. RIVER rad. (47)

This character is a picture of flowing water. The form given here is not seen independently but only as a part of other characters. (The independent form is given on p. 239.) Compare 560, below, for another form of "river" which may appear as a part of characters.

工	一	丁	工
443 3 strokes			

GUNG-1, work. WORK rad. (48)

Gung-1 is the picture of a carpenter's square.

工作 *gung-1 dzwo-4*, work, job

木工 *mu-4 gung-1*, carpenter

工夫 *gung-1 fu-1*, free time

巠	一	乛	巠
	巛	巠	巠
444 7 strokes	巠		

JING-1, warp (of fabric)

The character is a picture of threads run across a loom.

113

經	乚	幺	幺	**JING-1,** warp (of fabric); to pass through; literary classics In the sense of "warp," this is 444, above, reclarified with "silk." The other meanings are derived from "warp." 已經 *yi-3 jing-1*, already
	幺	糸	糸	
445 13 strokes	経	経	經	経
网	丨	冂	冈	**WANG-3,** net. NET rad. (122) The character is a picture of a net.
	冈	网	网	
446 6 strokes				
睘	丶	冂	四	**HWAN-2,** to return; still, as before Note that the "gown" rad. (109, above) appears in this character without its top dot. The explanation of *hwan-2* is very complicated and unsatisfactory. It occurs often as a part of characters to give the sound.
	罒	晉	睘	
447 13 strokes	睘	睘	睘	(口 33)
還	罒	罒	晉	**HWAN-2,** to return; **HAI-2,** still 還鄉 *hwan-2 syang-1*, to return to one's native place 還是 *hai-2 shr*, still 還有 *hai-2 you-3*, furthermore
	睘	睘	睘	
448 16 strokes	睘	還	還	还
裏	丶	亠	亠	**LI-3,** lining; inside The character combines the meaning of "gown" and the sound of *li-3* (106, above). 裏子 *li-2 dz-3*, lining 城裏 *cheng-2 li-3*, in the city
	啇	宣	审	
449 13 strokes	裏	裏	裏	里

| 刖 450 6 strokes | ノ | 刀 | 月 |
| | 月 | 刖 | 刖 |

YWE-4, to cut off the foot (or feet) as punishment

This was one of the punishments prescribed for certain crimes by ancient Chinese law. It is, of course, no longer the practice. The character is a sound-meaning compound; "knife" is for meaning, *ywe-4* (178, above) for sound.

前 451 9 strokes	`	ヽ	丷
	亠	广	前
	肖	前	前

CHYAN-2, front, in front of

從前 *tsung-2 chyan-2*, in the past

前兩天 *chyan-2 lyang-3 tyan-1*, the past two days

前門 *chyan-2 men-2*, (at) the front door

後 452 9 strokes	ノ	ク	彳
	彳	径	径
	移	後	後	后

HOU-4, back, in back of

前後 *chyan-2 hou-4*, in front and back; from beginning to end

後來 *hou-4 lai-2*, and then, after that

後天 *hou-4 tyan-1*, (on) the day after tomorrow

豆 453 7 strokes	一	丁	一
	一	戸	戸
	豆		

DOU-4, flask; bean, pea. FLASK rad. (151)

The character is a picture of a flask. The meaning "bean, pea" occurs by sound-loan.

豆子 *dou-4 dz-3*, bean, pea

土豆 *tu-3 dou-4*, potato

頭 454 16 strokes	一	豆	豆
	豆	頭	頭
	頭	頭	头

TOU-2, the head; a suffix used to form nouns and noun-phrases

Dou-4 (453, above) suggests the sound; the "head" rad. gives the meaning.

一頭牛 *yi-4 tou-2 nyou-2*, cow

木頭 *mu-4 tou-2*, wood

後頭 *hou-4 tou-2*, in back

115

	一	十	土
寺	土	寺	寺
455 6 strokes			

SZ-4, (Buddhist) monastery

The character = "earth" over "thumb." There is no satisfactory explanation. *Sz-4* occurs as a part of many common characters to give the sound, and in these characters it usually indicates the sound *shr*.

	丨	冂	日
時	日	日⁻	日⁺
456 10 strokes	日土	時	時

SHR-2, time

The "sun" rad. gives the meaning; *sz-4* (455, above) gives the sound.

時事　*shr-2 shr-4*, current events

不時　*bu-4 shr-2*, from time to time

時常　*shr-2 chang-2*, often

时

	丿	亻	亻
候	亻'	亻⁻	亻⁻
457 10 strokes	亻⁻	候	候

HOU-4, to wait; to pay the bill; climate; a period of time

時候　*shr-2 hou*, time

問候　*wen-4 hou-4*, to ask after someone

火候　*hwo-3 hou-4*, time required to cook something

	一	丆	丆
百	丆	百	百
458 6 strokes			

BAI-3, one hundred

Bai-2 (231, above) gives the sound; the "one" rad. suggests that the meaning is numerical.

	丿	彡	彡
爲	彡	彡	彡
459 12 strokes	彡	爲	爲

WEI-4, for; WEI-2, to be, to act, to do

The character is supposed to be the picture of some animal, variously given as "monkey," "elephant," etc. The present meanings are all sound-loan. Common variant 为.

爲甚麼　*wei-4 shem-2 ma*, why?

爲人　*wei-2 ren-2*, character; to act properly

为

116

主	`、`	`一`	`二`	**JU-3**, lord, host; principal; to indicate
	`主`	`主`		*Ju-3* (61, above) gives the sound; the character "king" gives the meaning.
460 5 strokes				主人 *ju-3 ren-2*, host, landlord 主張 *ju-3 jang-1*, to advocate, to propose 主意 *ju-3 yi-4*, idea, plan

住	`丿`	`亻`	`亻`	**JU-4**, to live; to stay; to stop
	`仁`	`住`	`住`	住戶 *ju-4 hu-4*, group of people living under one roof; family
461 7 strokes	`住`			站住 *jan-4 ju-4*, to stop, to halt 問住 *wen-4 ju-4*, to stump with a question

第	`丿`	`ﾉ`	`ʅ`	**DI-4**; a prefix to numbers (forms ordinals)
	`竹`	`竺`	`竺`	第一 *di-4 yi-1*, first, the first 第四天 *di-4 sz-4 tyan-1*, the fourth day
462 11 strokes	`笃`	`第`	`第`	

年	`丿`	`ﾉ`	`ﾉ二`	**NYAN-2**, year
	`厂`	`乍`	`年`	The rad. of *nyan-2* is "shield" 干 (87, above).
463 6 strokes				去年 *chyu-4 nyan-2*, last year 今年 *jin-1 nyan-2*, this year 明年 *ming-2 nyan-2*, next year

凵	`凵`	`凵`		**KAN-3**, bowl. BOWL rad. (17)
				Kan-3 is a picture of a bowl.
464 2 strokes				

117

屮	ㄴ	ㄩ	屮	CHE-4, sprout. SPROUT rad. (45) The "sprout" rad. is a picture of a sprout.
465 **3 strokes**				

出	ㄴ	ㄩ	屮	CHU-1, to come out, to go out; to produce The character is supposed to be a sprout pushing out of a bowl.
	出	出		出來　*chu-1 lai-2*, to come out 出門　*chu-1 men-2*, to go out (of the house)
466 **5 strokes**				出國　*chu-1 gwo-2*, to go abroad

等	ノ	ト	ㄻ	DENG-3, to wait; to equal; rank; "etc." 等候　　　*deng-3 hou-4*, to wait for
	ㄻㄻ	竺	竻	馬牛羊等　*ma-3 nyou-2 yang-2 deng-3*, horses, cows, sheep, etc.
467 **12 strokes**	笁	等	等	

把	一	丁	扌	BA-3, to grasp; a measure for things with handles; handful; to guard; a particle used to bring direct objects in front of the verb; BA-4, handle
	扣	扣	把	一把米　*yi-4 ba-3 mi-3*, handful of rice 把門　　*ba-3 men-2*, to guard the door
468 **7 strokes**	把			把兄弟　*ba-3 syung-1 di-4*, sworn brothers

夬	ㄱ	ㄢ	尹	JYWE-1, archer's thimble; GWAI-4, to divide The character may be a picture of a man drawing his bow or fitting the thimble before he draws. It occurs as a part of characters to give sometimes the sound *jywe*, sometimes the sound *gwai* (or *kwai*).
	夬			
469 **4 strokes**				

118

快	⼂	⼃	⼁⼃	KWAI-4, be fast; soon; be happy; be sharp
	忄⼂	忄⼂	忄夬	快車 *kwai-4 che-1*, express train
470 7 strokes	快			快刀 *kwai-4 dau-1*, sharp knife

曼	⼂	冂	日	MAN-4, be long, to stretch out
	日	昌	罒日	
471 11 strokes	冒	旻	曼	

慢	⼂	⼃	⼁⼃	MAN-4, be slow
	忄冂	忄日	忄罒日	慢車 *man-4 che-1*, local train
	慢	慢	慢	快慢 *kwai-4 man-4*, speed
472 14 strokes				慢走 *man-4 dzou-3*, Watch your step! "Take care of yourself!" (said to a departing guest)

冉	⼁	冂	内	RAN-3, be tender, be flexible; whiskers
	内	冉		The character originally was a picture of whiskers.
473 5 strokes				

再	一	冂	冉	DZAI-4, again; another, more
	再			再見 *dzai-4 jyan-4*, Goodbye!
				再給三個 *dzai-4 gei-3 san-1 ge*, to give three more
474 6 strokes				再說 *dzai-4 shwo-1*, and furthermore

119

羊	﹑	⸴⸴	⸞⸞	YANG-2, sheep. SHEEP rad. (123)
	⸞⸞	羊	羊	The student already has learned one form of the "sheep" rad. (see 115, above). The form here is used as a part of characters and does not occur as an independent character.
475 6 strokes				

着	﹑	⸴⸴	⸞⸞	JE; a verb-suffix: "continuing . . . "; JAU-2, to ignite, to touch; verb ending: "to succeed in . . . "; JAU-1, to suffer from; That's right!
	⸞⸞	羊	羊	Distinguish this character from "look at" 看 (121, above).
476 11 strokes (12 strokes)	羊	着	着	

件	ノ	イ	亻	JYAN-4; a measure for events, official documents, articles of clothing, pieces of furniture
	仁	仁	件	零件 *ling-2 jyan-4*, component; spare part, accessory
477 6 strokes				

曲	⎸	冂	冃	CHYU-1, to twist; CHYU-3, song
	冉	曲	曲	The character once was a picture of an earthworm and had the meanings "earthworm; to twist." The rad. is now the "say" rad. (82, above).
478 6 strokes				唱曲 *chang-4 chyu-3*, to sing a song 作曲 *dzwo-4 chyu-3*, to compose (music)

豐	⎸	冂	冃	LI-3, ritual dish
	冉	曹	曹	*Li-3* was a picture of a vessel (the "flask" rad.) holding flowers. The flowers have been corrupted to "twist."
479 13 strokes	豐	豐	豐	(口 33)

120

示	、	㇋	礻	**SHR-4, sign. SIGN rad. (113)** *Shr-4* means "sign" in various senses, including "signs from heaven" and omens as well as the sense of "to exhibit, to show, to proclaim." It is supposed to be a picture of a wooden sign—perhaps of an ancestral tablet. This form of "sign" should be distinguished from the 衤 form of "gown" (910, below). Often printed 示.
480 4 strokes (5 strokes)	礻			

禮	礻	礻刀	礻刀	**LI-3, ritual; manners** This character is 479, above, reclarified with the "sign" rad. Here, as often, the "sign" rad. occurs in a character related to religion or religious matters. 禮帽　*li-3 mau-4*, top hat
481 17 strokes	礻曲	礻曲	礻豊	礼
	禮	禮	禮	

拜	一	二	三	**BAI-4, to worship** The rad. in this character is the "hand" rad. (41, above). Note that its form here is slightly distorted (cp. 121, above). *Bai-4* originally had two "hands" + "to lower." "Lower the hands" = "to worship." 禮拜　*li-3 bai-4*, to worship; week
	手	拜	拜	
482 9 strokes	拜			

拿	丿	人	스	**NA-2, to pick up** The character combines meanings: "to join" + "hand" = "to pick up." 拿起來　*na-2 chi-3 lai-2*, to pick up 拿走　　*na-2 dzou-3*, to take away 拿住　　*na-2 ju-4*, to hold onto firmly
	合	合	合	
483 10 strokes	合	拿		

進	丿	亻	个	**JIN-4, to enter** 進去　*jin-4 chyu-4*, to enter 進口　*jin-4 kou-3*, to import 進行　*jin-4 sying-2*, to make progress with; to pull strings
	佳	佳	佳	
484 11 strokes	隹	進	進	进

121

送	`丶`	`丷`	`丷`
	`丷`	`关`	`关`
485 9 strokes	`䒑`	`送`	`送`

SUNG-4, to send; to see off; to see home

送行　*sung-4 sying-2*, to see off

送禮　*sung-4 li-3*, to send a present

不送　*bu-2 sung-4*, (by guest) Don't bother seeing me off; (by host) Excuse me for not seeing you off.

因	`丨`	`冂`	`冂`
	`因`	`因`	`因`
486 6 strokes			

YIN-1, cause, because

Karlgren says the basic meaning is "cause" in a legal sense and explains the character as "a man (the "big" rad.) in prison."

因爲　*yin-1 wei-4*, because

因此　*yin-1 tsz-3*, because of this

信	`丿`	`亻`	`亻`
	`亻`	`信`	`信`
	`信`	`信`	`信`
487 9 strokes			

SYIN-4, sincerity; to believe; letter

The character shows "a man standing by his word," whence "sincere; to believe."

相信　*syang-1 syin-4*, to believe

信用　*syin-4 yung-4*, trustworthiness

信件　*syin-4 jyan-4*, mail, letters

禸	`丿`	`冂`	`巾`
	`禸`	`禸`	
488 5 strokes			

ROU-3, to track (as in "track bear"). TRACK rad. (114)

The character, especially in its old forms, looks like the view of an animal walking away from the viewer; you can see its hind-legs, its tail, and the arch of its back.

禺	`丿`	`冂`	`日`
	`日`	`禺`	`禺`
	`禺`	`禺`	`禺`
489 9 strokes			

YU-2, monkey

The character is a picture of a monkey.

萬	一	十	十十	**WAN-4**, ten thousand This character was a picture of a scorpion, and the original meaning was "scorpion." It is used to mean "ten thousand" by sound-loan. 千萬 *chyan-1 wan-4*, ten million; by all means 万
490 13 strokes	芍	苩	苩	
	萬	萬	萬	

臣	一	厂	厂	**CHEN-2**, bureaucrat. BUREAUCRAT rad. (131) Learn to distinguish the "bureaucrat" rad. from "using, taking" 臣 (406, above) and from *jyu-4* "chief, large, great" 巨 (496, below).
491 7 strokes (6 strokes)	臣	臣	臣	
	臣			

緊	臣	臣丿	臤	**JIN-3**, be tense, be urgent, be tight 太緊 *tai-4 jin-3*, be too tight (as shoes can be) 緊張 *jin-3 jang-1*, be excited; be tense; exciting 要緊 *yau-4 jin-3*, be important 緊
	臤	堅	堅	
492 14 strokes	緊	緊	緊	

正	一	丁	下	**JENG-4**, true, truly; be in the midst of 正吃飯 *jeng-4 chr-1 fan-4*, be in the midst of eating 正在 *jeng-4 dzai-4*, be in the midst of 正好 *jeng-4 hau-3*, Perfect!
	正	正		
493 5 strokes				

必	丿	心	心	**BI-4**, must 必得 *bi-4 dei-3*, must 必要 *bi-4 yau-4*, be necessary, be essential 必定 *bi-4 ding-4*, certainly
	必	必		
494 5 strokes				

123

	、	亠	宀
夜	宀	疒	彷
495 8 strokes	夜	夜	

YE-4, night

The character is classified in dictionaries under the "dusk" rad. 夕 (117, above). Note that the form of the rad. is corrupted a little in ye-4. The "lid" and "man" used to help give the sound.

半夜　ban-4 ye-4, midnight

	一	厂	尸
巨	尸	巨	
496 5 strokes			

JYU-4, chief, large, great

Jyu-4 is classified in dictionaries under the "work" rad. 工 (443, above). Note that "work" is distorted some in *jyu-4*. The original meaning of *jyu-4* is supposed to have been "a large carpenter's square, with handle," and the character was a picture.

	一	厂	戊
戊	戊	戊	
497 5 strokes			

WU-4, the fifth "heavenly stem"

The character used to mean "lance, halberd" and was a picture. Learn to tell it from *syu-1* (498, below).

	一	厂	戌
戌	戌	戌	戌
498 6 strokes			

SYU-1, the eleventh "earthly branch"

The original meaning of *syu-1* was "to destroy, to kill." The "one" rad. is supposed to show a wound made by the lance or halberd (497, above).

	卜	止	止
歲	产	芦	岁
499 13 strokes	岁	岁	歲

SWEI-4, harvest; year; be . . . years old

他幾歲了　ta-1 ji-3 swei-4 le, How old is he? (assuming less than ten)

歲入　swei-4 ru-4, annual income

(止　195)

山
夕

	、	亠	亡
忘	亡	忘	忘
500 7 strokes	忘		

WANG-4, to forget

The "heart" gives the meaning; *wang-2* (68, above) gives the sound. Compare 69, above, and note that *wang-2* + "heart" at the side means "be busy," while *wang-2* + "heart" below means "to forget."

忘八   *wang-2 ba-1*, tortoise; cuckold (note the change to *wang-2*)

	、	⋎	亇
差	⺍	羊	羊
501 9 strokes (10 strokes)	羊	差	差

CHA-4, to differ, to fall short, to owe; CHA-1, differ; difference (arithmetical); mistake; CHAI-1, to send; to commission; official

差不多   *cha-4 bu-4 dwo-1*, be almost the same

差事   *chai-1 shr-4*, work, job, official assignment

差別   *cha-1 bye-2*, difference

	一	二	于
开	开		
502 4 strokes			

JYAN-1, to raise in both hands

	丨	冂	冃
開	冃丨	門	門
503 12 strokes	門	開	開	开

KAI-1, to open

開門   *kai-1 men-2*, to open the door

開車   *kai-1 che-1*, to drive a car

水開了   *shwei-3 kai-1 le*, The water's boiling.

	L	丩	丩
丱	丱	丱	
504 5 strokes			

GWAN-4, the two tufts of hair on a child's head (a traditional way to dress children's hair in China)

The character is a picture of the two tufts of hair sticking up.

125

絲絲	ㄥ	幺	幺	GWAN-1, (in weaving) to run the threads through a web
	幺幺	幺幺	幺幺	The "coil" rad. (repeated) represents the silk or other thread in this process, and *gwan-4* (504, above) gives the sound.
505 **11 strokes**	絲	絲	絲	

關	丨	冂	甲	GWAN-1, to shut; barrier
	門	門	門	關門 *gwan-1 men-2*, to shut the door 關心 *gwan-1 syin-1*, be concerned about 關稅 *gwan-1 shwei-4*, customs duty
506 **19 strokes**	關	關	關	关

刻	、	亠	亡	KE-4, quarter of an hour; to engrave or carve; be stingy; be sarcastic
	歺	亥	亥	The original meaning was "carve.""Knife" gave the meaning; *hai-4* (250, above) gave the sound.
507 **8 strokes**	刻	刻		三點一刻 *san-1 dyan-3 yi-2 ke-4*, 3:15

找	一	扌	扌	JAU-3, to look for; to visit; to give change
	扌	扐	找	The student should distinguish *jau-3* from *wo-3* 我 (44, above).
508 **7 strokes**	找			找不着 *jau-3 bu-4 jau-2*, can't find 找到 *jau-3 dau-4*, to find

包	ノ	勹	勹	BAU-1, to wrap
	勹	包		包起來 *bau-1 chi-3 lai-2*, to wrap up 包工 *bau-1 gung-1*, to do contract work 包飯 *bau-1 fan-4*, to board at a place
509 **5 strokes**				

	`	冂	口	**PAU-3, to run** The "foot" rad. gives the meaning; *bau-1* (509, above) suggests the sound. 跑道 *pau-3 dau-4*, racetrack; runway (for airplanes)
跑	卩	𧾷	𧾷	
510 12 strokes	𧾷	趵	跑	

	`	冂	冖	**GU-3, bone.** BONE rad. (188) The top part is supposed to show the bone inside the flesh. Note the "meat" rad. (flesh) at the bottom. 骨頭 *gu-3 tou-2*, bone 頭骨 *tou-2 gu-3*, skull
骨	冎	冎	咼	
511 10 strokes	骨	骨	骨	

	`	冂	冂	**GWA-3, skeleton; bone with the meat stripped off** This character is the "bone" rad. minus its lower part, the "meat" rad.
冎	冎	冎	咼	
512 6 strokes				

	`	冂	冂	**KWAI-1, puckered mouth** The "mouth" rad. gives the meaning in this character; *gwa-3* (512, above) gives the sound. This character occurs in a number of characters to give the sounds *gwo* or *hwo*.
咼	冎	冎	咼	
513 9 strokes	咼	咼	咼	

	冂	冂	冂	**GWO-4, to go over** 過來 *gwo-4 lai-2*, come over 過去 *gwo-4 chyu-4*, to go over; to die; in the past 過重 *gwo-4 jung-4*, be overweight
過	咼	咼	過	
514 12 strokes	過	過	过	

127

| 自 515 6 strokes | ノ | イ | 冇 | DZ-4, nose; self; from. SMALL NOSE rad. (132) |
| | 白 | 自 | 自 | The character is supposed to be a picture of a nose. It is called "small nose" to distinguish it from the "big nose" rad. 鼻 (p. 289) that also means "nose." Distinguish "small nose" from "eye" 目 (120, above). |

釆 516 7 strokes	ノ	⺀	⺁	BYAN-4, to sift. SIFT rad. (165)
	丷	平	釆	Note that "sift" = "left" + "rice." If it helps, the student can think of the "left" rad. as the sifter with the rice falling through below it. Distinguish from *tsai-3* "cull" (517, below) and from "grain" 禾 and "tree" 木 (65 and 64, above).
	釆			

采 517 8 strokes	ノ	⺀	⺍	TSAI-3, to cull; bright colors
	丷	丷	平	Though this character seems to be composed of "claws" over "tree," it is found in dictionaries under the "sift" rad. 釆 (516, above). The "claws" are supposed to represent a hand picking fruit from a tree, whence "to cull." The meaning "bright colors" is by sound-loan.
	采	采		

菜 518 12 strokes	一	十	艹	TSAI-4, vegetables; course or dish in a Chinese meal
	艹	艹	芯	作菜 *dzwo-4 tsai-4*, to cook 要菜 *yau-4 tsai-4*, to order (in a restaurant)
	芓	芽	菜	

| 丁 519 2 strokes | 一 | 丁 | | DING-1, person; nail; be strong; single; the fourth "heavenly stem" The character is a picture of a nail. |

打	一	十	扌	DA-3, to beat; from; DA-2, dozen 打開 *da-3 kai-1*, to open 打入 *da-3 ru-4*, to branch out (in business); to force a way into 打聽 *da-3 ting-1*, to inquire
	扌	打		
520 5 strokes				
算	丿	卜	广	SWAN-4, to add up; to add in; to consider as 打算 *da-3 swan-4*, to plan to 算了 *swan-4 le*, That's enough! Forget it!
	竹竹	竹	筲	
521 14 strokes	筲	算	算	
刃	刁	刀	刃	REN-4, knife edge, blade The character is "knife" with an additional stroke to call attention to the blade.
522 3 strokes				
忍	刁	刀	刃	REN-3, to bear, to endure The "heart" rad. gives the meaning; *ren-4* (522, above) gives the sound. 忍受 *ren-3 shou-4*, to endure, to "stand"
	刃	忍	忍	
523 7 strokes	忍			
認	丶	亠	言	REN-4, to recognize; to admit 認得 *ren-4 de-2*, to recognize 認爲 *ren-4 wei-2*, to think, to feel 認眞 *ren-4 jen-1*, be conscientious
	言	訂	訒	
524 14 strokes	認	認	認	认

129

	`丶`	`亠`	`亠`	JR-1, to command; weapon; to stick to Karlgren explains the character by analyzing the "tone" rad. as "speak, give commands" and says, "the man with a lance who gives commands." This character gives the sound in a number of common modern characters.
戠	`立`	`立`	`音`	
525 12 strokes	`戠`	`戠`	`戠`	**(日 82)**

	`亠`	`言`	`言`	SHR-2, to know, knowledge; SHR-4, knowledge
識	`言`	`訐`	`諳`	認識 *ren-4 shr-2*, to recognize, to know 識字 *shr-2 dz-4*, be literate 常識 *chang-2 shr-4*, general knowledge
526 19 strokes	`識`	`識`	`識`	识

	`丶`	`亠`	`宀`	FANG-4, to lay down, to put; to tend; to lend; to fire (a weapon)
放	`方`	`方`	`方`	放手 *fang-4 shou-3*, to let go of 放心 *fang-4 syin-1*, be at ease about 放學 *fang-4 sywe-2*, to get out of class, to get out of school
527 8 strokes	`放`	`放`		

	`丿`	`亻`	`仁`	DI-3, foundation; bottom; to go down
氐	`氏`	`氐`		The little horizontal stroke at the bottom gives the meaning; the rest of the character, *shr-4* (224, above), once gave the sound.
528 5 strokes				

	`丶`	`亠`	`广`	DI-3, foundation; bottom
底	`广`	`庐`	`庐`	The word is the same as 528, above; the character is reclarified with "lean-to." 底子 *di-2 dz-3*, background, origin, foundation; original copy
529 8 strokes	`底`	`底`		底下 *di-3 sya-4*, underneath, below 年底 *nyan-2 di-3*, year's end

路	⺆	口	⻊	**LU-4, road; kind, sort** The "foot" rad. gives the meaning; the rest of the character once gave the sound. 路過 *lu-4 gwo-4*, to go past 走路 *dzou-3 lu-4*, to walk 路子 *lu-4 dz-3*, method, way
	⻊	趵	足	
530 13 strokes	趵	趵	路	
疒	⺀	⺀	广	**NI-4, be sick. SICK rad (104)** The character represents a man stretched out on his bed, whence "be sick." Compare the "bed" rad. (849, below).
	广	疒		
531 5 strokes				
内	丨	冂	内	**NEI-4, inside** *Nei-4* is a picture of a man entering a space marked off by the "borders" rad. (The rad. is "enter," not "man.") 内地 *nei-4 di-4*, interior (of a country) 三天内 *san-1 tyan-1 nei-4*, within three days
	内			
532 4 strokes				
丙	一	厂	丙	**BING-3, fish tail; the third "heavenly stem"** *Bing-3* looks like a picture of a fish tail.
	丙	丙		
533 5 strokes				
病	⺀	⺀	广	**BING-4, sickness, be sick** The character combines the "sick" rad. for meaning with *bing-3* (533, above) for sound. 看病 *kan-4 bing-4*, to see a doctor; to examine a patient
	疒	疒	疒	
534 10 strokes	病	病	病	

131

	一	十	土	FENG-1, to seal up; a measure for letters
封	圡	𡗗	圭	一封信 yi-4 feng-1 syin-4, letter 信封 syin-4 feng-1, envelope
535 9 strokes	封	封	封	

	ノ	⺈	白	BAI-2, silk; riches; a surname
帛	白	白	白	The character has "cloth" for meaning, bai-2 (231, above) for sound.
536 8 strokes	帛	帛		

	一	十	土	BANG-1, to help; clique, group
幫	圭	封	封	幫忙 bang-1 mang-2, to help 幫手 bang-1 shou-3, helper
537 17 strokes	封	幫	幫	幫

	ノ	二	千	CHWEI-2, to droop
垂	牛	乑	乑	Chwei-2 originally was a picture of a tree with drooping leaves. The character is now classified under the "earth" rad. 土 in Chinese dictionaries.
538 8 strokes	垂	垂		

	丨	冂	月	SHWEI-4, to sleep; to lie down
睡	月	目'	盰	In this character, chwei-2 (538, above) is probably there to give the sound. Shwei-4 can also be explained as a meaning-meaning compound: "eye" + "droop" = "to sleep."
539 13 strokes	睡	睡	睡	

帶	一	ナ	世	DAI-4, belt; to wear around the waist; to bring along
				帶錢　　dai-4 chyan-2, to bring money
	世	世	世	帶孩子　dai-4 hai-2 dz-3, to bring children along
540 11 strokes	帶	帶	帶	帶

犬	一	ナ	大	CHYWAN-3, dog. DOG rad. (94)
	犬			The student will note that the "dog" rad. = "big" + "dot." Care should be taken to distinguish "dog" from "big" 大 (50, above) and from tai-4 "extremely" 太 (74, above).
541 4 strokes				

哭	丶	丷	口	KU-1, to cry, to howl
	口口	丷口	哭	Ku-1 combines meanings: "dog" + "mouth" + "mouth" = "to howl, to cry."
542 10 strokes	哭	哭		

平	一	一	刁	PING-2, to weigh; be even, be calm, be level, be flat
	平	平		Ping-2 is a picture of scales in balance.
				平常　ping-2 chang-2, be ordinary
				平等　ping-2 deng-3, be equal
543 5 strokes				平原　ping-2 ywan-2, plain

應	丶	二	广	YING-1, to promise; ought; YING-4, to respond; to turn out to be true
	广	府	府	應用　　ying-1 yung-4, to put into practice
				應得的　ying-1 de-2 de, ought to get
544 17 strokes	雁	應	應	(彳　4)　　　　応

133

當	丨	⺌	少	DANG-1, to serve as; in the presence of; the very same . . . ; DANG-3, to think (mistakenly) that . . . ; DANG-4, to think (mistakenly) that; to pawn
	屵	尚	尚	應當 *ying-1 dang-1*, ought to
545 13 strokes	當	當	當	當時 *dang-1 shr-2*, (at) that time 当

法	丶	冫	氵	FA-3, method, way, law; FA-2, method; FA-4, doctrine
	氵一	汁	汢	法官 *fa-3 gwan-1*, judge 說法 *shwo-1 fa-4*, to expound Buddha's doctrine
546 8 strokes	法	法		法國 *fa-4 gwo-2*, France

怕	丿	忄	忄	PA-4, to fear
	忄	忄	怕	"Heart"+"white"="to fear." *Bai-2* "white" (231, above) is probably there to give the sound.
547 8 strokes	怕	怕		怕太太 *pa-4 tai-4 tai-4*, be henpecked

完	丶	宀	宀	WAN-2, to finish
	宀	宀	宇	完不了 *wan-2 bu-4 lyau-3*, can't be finished 完成 *wan-2 cheng-2*, to complete 用完 *yung-4 wan-2*, to use up
548 7 strokes	完			

辛	丶	亠	亠	SYIN-1, bitter, toilsome; the eighth "heavenly stem." BITTER rad. (160)
	亇	立	立	There is no helpful explanation of this rad. The student should be careful to distinguish it from *sying-4* "be lucky" 幸 (89, above).
549 7 strokes	辛			辛艱 *syin-1 jyan-1*, be difficult

辡	丶	亠	亣	**BYAN-4, to wrangle** *Byan-4* is supposed to combine meanings. The "bitter" rad. repeated = "bitter against bitter": "to recriminate, to wrangle, to dispute."
	亣	立	立	
550 14 strokes	辛	辛立	辡	

辦	丶	亠	亣	**BAN-4, to manage; to punish** *Byan-4* (550, above) suggests the sound; the "strength" rad. helps with the meaning. 辦法 *ban-4 fa-3*, method, way
	亣	立	辛	
551 16 strokes	辦	辦	辦	办

覺	亻	乍	钌	**JYWE-2, to feel; JYAU-4, to sleep** 覺得 *jywe-2 de-2*, to feel 睡覺 *shwei-4 jyau-4*, to sleep 覺着 *jywe-2 je*, to feel (physically)
	钌	臼	鸤	
552 20 strokes	覺	覺	覺	(見 214)　　覚

昔	一	十	丗	**SYI-2, ancient** The original meaning of this character was "meat dried in the sun; to age," and the top part of the old character was a picture of meat. The sun can still be found in the modern character. The meaning "ancient" derives from the earlier meaning "to age."
	丗	芈	芌	
553 8 strokes	昔	昔		

錯	丿	人	亼	**TSWO-4, to make a mistake** 不錯 *bu-2 tswo-4*, be pretty good 錯過 *tswo-4 gwo-4*, to miss a chance
	仐	全	金	
554 16 strokes	金	釷	錯	错

135

襄	丶	亠	宀	**HWAI-2**, to hug, to hide Note that the outer parts (top and bottom) of this character form the "gown" rad. (109, above). The rest of the character is supposed to represent something hidden in the clothes or something hugged against the bosom.
	襾	帝	帘	
555 16 strokes	寏	襄	襄	(Ⅲ 132)

壞	一	十	土	**HWAI-4**, be bad, be rotten, be sly 壞人 *hwai-4 ren-2*, evil person 車壞了 *che-1 hwai-4 le*, The car broke down. 不壞 *bu-2 hwai-4*, be pretty good
	扩	坛	垆	
556 19 strokes	壿	壞	壞	坏

河	丶	冫	氵	**HE-2**, river *Ke-3* (77, above) gives the sound; the "water" rad., of course, gives the meaning. 河道 *he-2 dau-4*, river course, riverbed 河口 *he-2 kou-3*, mouth of a river
	氵	汀	汀	
557 8 strokes	河	河		

魚	丿	刀	𠂊	**YU-2**, fish. FISH rad. (195) *Yu-2* is a picture of a fish.
	甬	甬	角	
558 11 strokes	魚	魚	魚	鱼

永	一	丁	丬	**YUNG-3**, be eternal The character is supposed to be a picture of water currents and thus suggests "go on and on" like flowing water: "be eternal." 永不 *yung-3 bu*, never . . .
	永	永		
559 5 strokes				

《《	〈	巛		**CHWAN-1**, river. RIVER rad. (47) This character is a picture of flowing water. Compare 442, above, which is another form of this rad. (The independent form is on p. 239.) This form occurs only as a part of characters.
560 2 strokes (3 strokes)				

羕	⸍⸌	丷	半	**YANG-4**, be long *Yang-4* combines *yang-2* (475, above) for sound with "be eternal" for meaning.
	羊	美	羊	
561 11 strokes	羕	羕	羕	

樣	一	十	才	**YANG-4**, kind, sort 一樣　　*yi-2 yang-4*, be alike 樣子　　*yang-4 dz-3*, style 怎麼樣　*dzem-3 ma yang-4*, How about . . . ? "How's everything?"
	木	朴	栏	
562 15 strokes	样	样	樣	样

條	丿	亻	伋	**TYAU-2**, section; a measure for roads, rivers, fishes, some animals; note (short message) 一條魚　*yi-4 tyau-2 yu-2*, fish 便條　　*byan-4 tyau-2*, brief note 條件　　*tyau-2 jyan-4*, terms, conditions
	伬	伩	條	
563 10 strokes	俢	條	條	条

冫	丶	冫		**BING-1**, ice. ICE rad. (15) Note the similarity between the "ice" rad. and the "three-dots-water" form of the "water" rad. The "ice" rad. has two dots instead of three. Often printed ⸜.
564 2 strokes				

137

次	丶	ン	冫	**TSZ-4**, a time; a measure for times or occasions; next (in order); order; be inferior to 下次　*sya-4 tsz-4*, next time 次要　*tsz-4 yau-4*, second most important 眞次　*jen-1 tsz-4*, It's really inferior.
	汐	泘	次	
565 6 strokes				

短	丿	丄	乍	**DWAN-3**, be short (opposite of long); lack 長短　*chang-2 dwan-3*, length
	夕	矢	矢	
566 12 strokes	矢口	短	短	

比	一	七	七	**BI-3**, to set side by side, to compare. COMPARE rad. (81) The modern character looks like "ladle" + "ladle" (137, above). The old forms have two men standing side by side. In any case, there are two similar objects side by side, as if for comparison.
	比			
567 4 strokes				

亟	一	了	丩	**JI-2**, to hurry
	弔	丮	永	
568 9 strokes	亟	亟		

極	一	十	才	**JI-2**, to reach an extreme; extremely; pole (extreme point) 極了　*ji-2 le*, extremely 極點　*ji-2 dyan-3*, extreme point 極力　*ji-2 li-4*, with all one's strength
	木	打	柯	
569 12 strokes	柯	極	極	极

138

南	一	ナ	广	NAN-2, south 南方　*nan-2 fang-1*, the South 西南　*syi-1 nan-2*, southwest 南極　*nan-2 ji-2*, South Pole
	方	肏	南	
570 9 strokes	南	南	南	

北	丿	ㅓ	土	BEI-3, north 城北　*cheng-2 bei-3*, north of the city 東北　*dung-1 bei-3*, northeast 北京　*bei-3 jing-1*, Peking 北平　*bei-3 ping-2*, Peking
	北	北		
571 5 strokes				

左	一	ナ	左	DZWO-3, left (opposite of right) 左不是　*dzwo-3 bu-2 shr-4*, nothing but 想左了　*syang-3 dzwo-3 le*, to think incorrectly 左手　*dzwo-2 shou-3*, left hand
	左	左		
572 5 strokes				

右	一	ナ	右	YOU-4, right (opposite of left) 左右　*dzwo-3 you-4*, approximately 右耳　*you-4 er-3*, right ear 左也 . . . 右也　*dzwo-3 ye-3 . . . you-4 ye-3*, 　　"either way . . ."
	右	右		
573 5 strokes				

穴	丶	丷	宀	SYWE-4, cave. CAVE rad. (116) This rad. is a picture.
	宀	穴		
574 5 strokes				

邊	白	自	鼻	**BYAN-1, side, region** 北邊 *bei-3 byan-1*, north side, northern region 左邊 *dzwo-3 byan-1*, left side 裏邊 *li-3 byan-1*, inside
	鼻	息	鼻	
575 **19 strokes**	邊	邊		(自 515, 方 392) 边
牙	一	二	千	**YA-2, tooth. TOOTH rad. (92)** The "tooth" rad. is a picture. 牙行 *ya-2 hang-2*, licensed broker 牙子 *ya-2 dz-3*, decorative edge; broker 門牙 *men-2 ya-2*, incisor
	牙			
576 **4 strokes**				
穿	、	'	宀	**CHWAN-1, to don, to wear; to thread; to pierce** 看穿 *kan-4 chwan-1*, to see right through
	宀	穴	空	
577 **9 strokes**	空	穿	穿	
袁	一	十	土	**YWAN-2, robe** Note that in this character the top part of the "gown" rad. 衣 (109, above) has been corrupted into "earth." *Ywan-2* is still classified in dictionaries under the "gown" rad., and the relation of its meaning to "gown" is clear enough.
	吉	吉	声	
578 **10 strokes**	声	袁	袁	
遠	土	吉	声	**YWAN-3, be far away** 永遠 *yung-2 ywan-3*, forever, always 遠東 *ywan-3 dung-1*, Far East 遠心力 *ywan-3 syin-1 li-4*, centrifugal force
	袁	袁	袁	
579 **13 strokes**	遠	遠	遠	远

近	ノ	イ	仁	**JIN-4, be near** The sound of *jin-4* is indicated by *jin-1* (262, above); "halt" is there for meaning. 近年 *jin-4 nyan-2*, (in) recent years 近來 *jin-4 lai-2*, recently
	斤	斤	近	
580 7 strokes	近			
凶	ノ	メ	凶	**SYUNG-1, be cruel, be unlucky, be calamitous** The "bowl" rad. in this character used to be a pit, and the X shape was a man falling, legs up, into the pit: "calamity."
	凶			
581 4 strokes				
离	`	亠	宀	**LI-2, hobgoblin** This character is a picture of a hobgoblin. Note that, with the "track" rad. as its lower part, the hobgoblin has hind legs and a tail. The top parts, "lid" + "cruel," have been corrupted from the original picture.
	文	卤	卤	
582 11 strokes	离	离	离	
离隹	亠	文	卤	**LI-2, to depart from; from** 離開 *li-2 kai-1*, to leave 離間 *li-2 jyan-1*, to cause a rift between 離奇 *li-2 chi-2*, be strange, be weird
	离	离	离	
583 19 strokes	離	離	離	离
僉	ノ	人	스	**CHYAN-1, all, together** Note that the top part of *chyan-1—ji-2* "get together" (175, above)—gives the meaning. The lower part, "mouth" + "mouth" and "man" + "man," seems simply to reinforce the idea of getting together or collecting.
	合	合	合	
584 13 strokes	僉	僉	僉	僉

臉	丿	刀	月	**LYAN-3, face**
	肑	脸	脸	The "meat" rad. gives the meaning in this character; the *chyan-1* (584, above) part suggests the sound.
585 17 strokes	脸	臉	臉	臉子 *lyan-2 dz-3*, appearance, looks 門臉 *men-2 lyan-3*, façade 臉

數	丶	口	日	**SHU-4, number; SHU-3, to enumerate**
	昌	婁	婁	歲數 *swei-4 shu-4*, (person's) age 數目 *shu-4 mu*, number, amount
586 15 strokes	婁	數	數	數學 *shu-4 sywe-2*, mathematics 数

洗	丶	冫	氵	**SYI-3, to wash; to massacre, to wipe out**
	汁	汢	汫	
587 9 strokes	洪	洗	洗	

往	丿	彳	彳	**WANG-3 (also WANG-4), toward; former**
	彳	彳	彳	往東 *wang-3 dung-1*, eastward 往後 *wang-3 hou-4*, from now on
588 8 strokes	彳	往		往往 *wang-2 wang-3*, sometimes

每	丿	丿	仁	**MEI-3, each**
	勾	匂	每	每一個 *mei-3 yi-2 ge*, each 每天 *mei-3 tyan-1*, every day
589 7 strokes	每			每次 *mei-3 tsz-4*, each time

142

但	ノ	イ	亻
	伵	佢	但
590 7 strokes	但		

DAN-4, but; only

但是 *dan-4 shr-4*, but

不但 *bu-2 dan-4*, not only . . .

圣	フ	ヌ	圣
	圣	圣	
591 5 strokes			

KU-1, to work in the fields

The character appears to combine meanings: "right hand" + "earth" = "to work in the fields." In modern Chinese, it is commonly seen only as a part of characters.

怪	ノ	忄	忄
	忄フ	忄ヌ	怪
592 8 strokes	怪	怪	

GWAI-4, to blame; to consider weird, be weird

寄怪 *chi-2 gwai-4*, be peculiar, weird

别怪他 *bye-2 gwai-4 ta-1*, Don't blame him.

然	ノ	ク	夕
	夕	夕-	夘
593 12 strokes	夕犬	然	然

RAN-2, so, like this

The character originally meant "to roast," and it combined meanings: "meat" (slightly deformed) + "dog" + "fire." "So, like this" comes by sound-loan.

然後 *ran-2 hou-4*, afterward

必然 *bi-4 ran-2*, certainly

午	ノ	⺈	仁
	午		
594 4 strokes			

WU-3, noon; the seventh "earthly branch"

The character once meant "to knock against" and was a picture of a battering-ram. Compare the "shield" rad. (87, above). All other meanings are by sound-loan.

下午 *sya-4 wu-3*, afternoon

正午 *jeng-4 wu-3*, high noon

許	、	丶	言	SYU-3, to permit; to promise; perhaps
	言	訂	訐	許可　*syu-2 ke-3*, to permit, permission
595 11 strokes	訐	許		許多　*syu-3 dwo-1*, very many; many things　　　　　　　許

才	一	十	才	TSAI-2, substance; natural capacity, talent, genius; then (and not till then); only
				Distinguish *tsai-2* from "thumb" 寸 (186, above) and from "hand" 扌 (14, above).
596 3 strokes				

果	丨	冂	日	GWO-3, fruit; result; really
	日	旦	甲	*Gwo-3* is a picture of fruit on a tree. 水果　*shwei-2 gwo-3*, fruit 果仁　*gwo-3 ren-2*, nut
597 8 strokes	畀	果		果然　*gwo-3 ran-2*, indeed, certainly

課	、	丶	言	KE-4, lesson, course; class; section
	訂	訊	誯	下課　*sya-4 ke-4*, Class dismissed. 課本　*ke-4 ben-3*, textbook
598 15 strokes	諤	誤	課	人事課　*ren-2 shr-4 ke-4*, personnel section　　课

世	一	十	廿	SHR-4, world; generation
	廿	世		This character is actually three "ten" rads. 十 (the vertical stroke on the left one is bent for the sake of design) written together to suggest "thirty years": "a generation."
599 5 strokes				今世　*jin-1 shr-4*, this age; contemporary

144

介	ノ	人	介
	介		
600 4 strokes			

JYE-4, be between; to regard as important

介意　jye-4 yi-4, to notice; to take offense at

界	丨	冂	日
	田	田	甲
601 9 strokes	界	界	界

JYE-4, boundary; world; scope

世界　shr-4 jye-4, world

邊界　byan-1 jye-4, border

海	丶	∶	氵
	氵	汐	汇
602 10 strokes	海	海	海

HAI-3, sea

海關　hai-3 gwan-1, customshouse; Customs

地中海　di-4 jung-1 hai-3, Mediterranean

上海　shang-4 hai-3, Shanghai

部	丶	二	亠
	立	立	音
603 11 strokes	音	部	部

BU-4, set; portion, part; department; a measure for vehicles

部分　bu-4 fen, portion, part

部門　bu-4 men-2, section, department

部長　bu-4 jang-3, department head

黄	一	十	廿
	芇	苧	苩
604 11 strokes	黄	黄	黄

HWANG-2, be yellow. YELLOW rad. (201)

黄豆　hwang-2 dou-4, soybean

黄河　hwang-2 he-2, the Yellow River

(田　23)

145

總	ㄥ	ㄠ	ㄠ	DZUNG-3, to add together; always; probably, surely 總是 *dzung-3 shr-4*, always 總共 *dzung-3 gung-4*, altogether 總數 *dzung-3 shu-4*, total, total amount
	幺	糸勹	絇	
605 17 strokes	絢	總	總	总
連	一	冂	白	LYAN-2, to connect; continuously; including; company (military); even 連着 *lyan-2 je*, continuous, continuously 連長 *lyan-2 jang-3*, company commander 連一個 *lyan-2 yi-2 ge*, even one
	亘	車	車	
606 10 strokes	連	連		连
只	丶	冂	口	JR-3, just, only 只得 *jr-3 de-2*, can do nothing but . . . 只好 *jr-2 hau-3*, can do nothing but . . . 只有 *jr-2 you-3*, can do nothing but . . . 只是 *jr-3 shr-4*, but; only
	尸	只		
607 5 strokes				
特	丿	𠂉	牛	TE-4, be special 特別 *te-4 bye-2*, be special; especially 特點 *te-4 dyan-3*, special feature 特爲 *te-4 wei-4*, especially for; purposely
	牜	牡	牪	
608 10 strokes	特	特		
而	一	丆	丆	ER-2, beard; and, and yet, but. BEARD rad. (126) *Er-2* is a picture of a beard. Distinguish it from "face" 面 (610, below). 而且 *er-2 chye-3*, and moreover . . . 而已 *er-2 yi-3*, That's all.
	丙	而	而	
609 6 strokes				

面 610 9 strokes	一	丆	丆	MYAN-4, face. FACE rad. (176)
	丏	而	而	This character is a picture.
	而	面	面	右面 *you-4 myan*, on the right; right side

面子 *myan-4 dz-3*, face, social standing; width (of textiles)

面目 *myan-4 mu-4*, facial appearance; behavior

洋 611 9 strokes	丶	冫	氵	YANG-2, ocean; foreign
	氵	氵	氵	大西洋 *da-4 syi-1 yang-2*, the Atlantic
	氵	洋	洋	太平洋 *tai-4 ping-2 yang-2*, the Pacific

洋鬼子 *yang-2 gwei-2 dz-3*, "foreign devil" (derogatory)

| 于 612 3 strokes | 一 | 二 | 于 | YU-2, on, to, at |

余 613 7 strokes	丿	入	人	YU-2, I, me
	仐	仐	仐	
	余			

除 614 10 strokes	乛	乛	阝	CHU-2, except; to divide (arithmetic); to remove
	阝	阼	阼	除去 *chu-2 chyu*, in addition to; to remove
	阼	除	除	除了 . . . 以外 *chu-2 le . . . yi-3 wai-4*, in addition to

除夕 *chu-2 syi-4*, (on) New Year's Eve

147

江	`	⠄	氵	**JYANG**-1, river
	氵	汀	江	長江 *chang-2 jyang-1*, the Yangtze River
615 6 strokes				江西 *jyang-1 syi-1*, Kiangsi 江北人 *jyang-1 bei-3 ren-2*, person from north of the Yangtze

全	ノ	入	仝	**CHYWAN**-2, be complete, completely; all, the whole
	仐	全	全	The student should distinguish this from the "gold" rad. 金 (94, above). 完全 *wan-2 chywan-2*, be complete; completely, perfectly
616 6 strokes				全部 *chywan-2 bu-4*, whole thing; completely

乾	一	十	古	**GAN**-1, be dry; unadorned; to use up; in name only
	古	直	車	乾洗 *gan-1 syi-3*, to dry-clean 乾唱 *gan-1 chang-4*, to sing unaccompanied
617 11 strokes	車	軋	乾	用乾 *yung-4 gan-1*, to use up　　　　　干

爭	ノ	⺊	⺈	**JENG**-1, to argue, to fight
	爫	爫	鱼	The character shows two hands struggling over an object. 爭取 *jeng-1 chyu-3*, to work hard for
618 8 strokes	爭	爭		爭氣 *jeng-1 chi-4*, be determined; to prove one's ability

淨	`	⠄	氵	**JING**-4, to clean, be clean; net (as opposed to gross); everywhere
	氵	氵	浐	乾淨 *gan-1 jing-4*, be clean 淨得 *jing-4 de-2*, net profit
619 11 strokes	淨	淨	淨	淨拿 *jing-4 na-2*, to net, to clear (so much money)

148

胡	一	十	十	HU-2, Tartars; Mongols; foolish
				胡說 *hu-2 shwo-1*, to talk nonsense; "Nonsense!"
	古	刮	胡	胡來 *hu-2 lai-2*, to not know what you are doing, "to mess around"
620 9 strokes	胡	胡		

湖	丶	冫	氵	HU-2, lake
				湖北 *hu-2 bei-3*, Hupeh
	汁	沽	沽	湖南 *hu-2 nan-2*, Hunan
621 12 strokes	湖	湖	湖	

商	丶	亠	亠	SHANG-1, quotient; commerce; merchant
				商人 *shang-1 ren-2*, businessman
	产	产	产	商船 *shang-1 chwan-2*, merchant ship
				進口商 *jin-4 kou-3 shang-1*, importer
622 11 strokes	商	商	商	

業	丨	丬	⺌	YE-4, business; profession; property
				商業 *shang-1 ye-4*, business
	业	业	业	業主 *ye-4 ju-3*, property owner
623 13 strokes	業	業	業	业

民	一	二	尸	MIN-2, folk, people
				人民 *ren-2 min-2*, people
	尸	民		民法 *min-2 fa-3*, civil law
				民主 *min-2 ju-3*, democracy, be democratic
624 5 strokes				

	丨	少	屵	DANG-3, association; political party
黨	屵	嵩	嵩	國民黨 *gwo-2 min-2 dang-3*, Kuomintang, Chinese Nationalist Party 民主黨 *min-2 ju-2 dang-3*, Democratic Party
625 20 strokes	當	黨	黨	党

	丶	亠	产	CHAN-3, to produce, product; property
産	文	产	产	出産 *chu-1 chan-3*, to produce, production output 共産黨 *gung-4 chan-2 dang-3*, Communist Party
626 11 strokes	产	产	産	産業 *chan-3 ye-4*, property (real estate) 产

	一	冂	冃	JAN-3, to behead; to cut asunder
斬	曰	亘	車	The character is explained as "a chariot with axes in it."
627 11 strokes	斬	斬	斬	斬

	一	冂	曰	JAN-4, temporarily
暫	車	斬	斬	暫時 *jan-4 shr-2*, temporarily 暫且 *jan-4 chye-3*, for a short time 暫辦法 *jan-4 ban-4 fa-3*, temporary measure
628 15 strokes	斬	斬	暫	暫

	丶	冫	氵	HWAI-2; the name of the Hwai River
淮	氵	泸	汴	淮河 *hwai-2 he-2*, the Hwai River 淮南 *hwai-2 nan-2*, Hwainan (Anhwei Province)
629 11 strokes	淮	淮	淮	

150

準	丶	氵	汀	JWUN-3, water-level; standard; to regulate; be accurate 準時 *jwun-3 shr-2*, be on time
	汀	泄	淮	
630 13 strokes	淮	準		准

久	丿	勺	久	JYOU-3, to last for a long time The student should distinguish this character from "slow" and "follow" (337 and 319, above). 永久 *yung-2 jyou-3*, eternally, permanently 長久 *chang-2 jyou-3*, be long (in time)
631 3 strokes				

癶	㇆	㇆	㇆′	BWO-4, back. BACK rad. (105) The character shows two things faced away from each other, that is, back to back. Hence the idea "back."
	㇆″	癶		
632 5 strokes				

發	㇆	㇆″	癶	FA-1, to send out, to bring out, to shoot 發行 *fa-1 sying-2*, to issue (bonds, banknotes); to publish 發行 *fa-1 hang-2*, to sell wholesale 發現 *fa-1 syan-4*, to discover
	癹	癹	發	
633 12 strokes	發	發	發	发

冓	一	二	⟊	GOU-4, webwork, interlacery The character is supposed to originally have been the picture of a webwork fishtrap. It now means "inner rooms," perhaps by sound-loan.
	井	丼	丼	
634 10 strokes	冓	冓	冓	

Character	Stroke order			Definition
講 635 17 strokes				**JYANG-3**, to speak; be conscientious about 講話 *jyang-3 hwa-4*, talk, to make a speech 講數學 *jyang-3 shu-4 sywe-2*, to lecture on mathematics 讲
種 636 14 strokes				**JUNG-3**, kind, sort, species; **JUNG-4**, to plant, to sow, to grow 種子 *jung-2 dz-3*, seed 黃種人 *hwang-2 jung-3 ren-2*, Orientals (people of the Yellow Race) 種地 *jung-4 di-4*, to farm 种
罒 637 5 strokes (6 strokes)				**WANG-3**, net. NET rad. (122) This form of "net" occurs only as a part of characters. (The independent form is 446, above.) Note that this form of the "net" rad. is identical to a form of the "eye" rad. (132, above). Sometimes only trial and error with the dictionary can determine which is the rad.
傅 638 12 strokes				**FU-4**, to teach, teacher; a surname The student should distinguish this character from *chwan-2* "transmit" 傳 (640, below). 傅粉 *fu-4 fen-3*, to make up, to put on face powder
專 639 11 strokes				**JWAN-1**, solely 專家 *jwan-1 jya-1*, specialist 專門 *jwan-1 men-2*, specialized, speciality 專車 *jwan-1 che-1*, special car 专

152

傳	ノ	亻	仁
640 13 strokes	伩	俥	俥
	俥	僡	傳

CHWAN-2, to transmit; JWAN-4, record, biography

傳說　*chwan-2 shwo-1*, to spread a rumor; rumor; legend

傳敎　*chwan-2 jyau-4*, to proselytize

自傳　*dz-4 jwan-4*, autobiography

传

| 虫 | 丶 | 口 | 口 |
| 641
6 strokes | 中 | 虫 | 虫 |

CHUNG-2, bug; HWEI-3, reptile. BUG rad. (142)

This character is a picture of a bug.

雖	丶	口	口
642 17 strokes	吕	吊	虽
	蜀	雖	雖

SWEI-1, SWEI-2, although

雖然　*swei-1 ran-2*, although

虽

象	ノ	⺈	乌
643 12 strokes	刍	豸	豸
	象	象	象

SYANG-4, elephant; image

The character is a picture of an elephant.

現象　*syan-4 syang-4*, phenomenon

像	ノ	亻	亻
644 14 strokes	亻	俗	偁
	傄	像	像

SYANG-4, to look like; picture, portrait, statue; such as . . .

象

153

几	ノ	几	
645 2 strokes			

JI-1, table. TABLE rad. (16)

Ji-1 is a picture of a table. The student will want to distinguish it from "legs" 儿 and from "man with amputated foot" 兀 (57 and 58, above). Reading pronunciation *ji-3*.

茶几 *cha-2 ji-1*, tea table

歺	丶	⺊	⺊
	歺	歺	
646 5 strokes (4 strokes)			

DAI-3, chip. CHIP rad. (78)

The character is supposed to be a picture of bone chips. The student should distinguish it from the "dusk" rad. 夕 (117, above). This form of "chip" occurs only as a part of characters. (Its independent form is 727, below.)

亮	丶	亠	亠
	亠	吉	亭
647 9 strokes	高	亭	亮

LYANG-4, be bright; to show

亮刀 *lyang-4 dau-1*, to draw a knife

佔	ノ	亻	亻
	仆	价	佔
648 7 strokes	佔		

JAN-4, to occupy, to constitute

佔多數 *jan-4 dwo-1 shu-4*, to constitute the majority

軍	丶	冖	冖
	冖	冒	宣
649 9 strokes	宣	軍	

JYUN-1, military, army; army corps

軍官 *jyun-1 gwan-1*, military officer

軍長 *jyun-1 jang-3*, corps commander

軍事 *jyun-1 shr-4*, military affairs

軍

運	丶	⼍	⼎	**YUN-4**, to transport; fate, luck 運河 *yun-4 he-2*, canal 運用 *yun-4 yung-4*, to utilize 運氣 *yun-4 chi*, luck
	冒	宣	軍	
650 12 strokes	軍	渾	運	运
越	土	丰	走	**YWE-4**, to pass over, to exceed; (if repeated) the more . . . the more . . . 越界 *ywe-4 jye-4*, to encroach 越發 *ywe-4 fa-1*, more than before 越來越 *ywe-4 lai-2 ywe-4*, to get more and more . . .
	走	走	走	
651 12 strokes	起	趆	越	
敢	⼶	⼷	子	**GAN-3**, dare 敢情 *gan-3 ching*, of course; after all 不敢當 *bu-4 gan-3 dang-1*, You flatter me.
	亓	育	身	
652 12 strokes	身	敢	敢	
並	丶	⼀	丷	**BING-4**, side by side; and; actually; moreover 並不 *bing-4 bu*, actually not; certainly not 並且 *bing-4 chye-3*, moreover
	丷	計	並	
653 8 strokes	並	並		
非	丨	⼅	⼅	**FEI-1**, be wrong, be false; not. WRONG rad. (175) 是非 *shr-4 fei-1*, right and wrong 並非 *bing-4 fei-1*, It's not that . . . 非常 *fei-1 chang-2*, exceptionally
	非	非	非	
654 8 strokes	非	非		

155

造	ノ	广	屮	**DZAU-4**, to manufacture, to build; party to a lawsuit 原造　　*ywan-2 dzau-4*, plaintiff 造汽車　*dzau-4 chi-4 che-1*, to make cars 造反　　*dzau-4 fan-3*, to rebel, to revolt
	屮	生	告	
655 10 strokes	告	浩	造	

於	、	二	宀	**YU-2**, to; with reference to; than 於是　*yu-2 shr-4*, thereupon 於我　*yu-2 wo-3*, for me, with reference to me 多於　*dwo-1 yu-2*, be more than
	方	方'	於	
656 8 strokes	於	於		

束	一	冂	戸	**SHU-4**, bundle; to bind *Shu-4* is a picture of a bundle. 束手　*shu-4 shou-3*, be helpless 束身　*shu-4 shen-1*, to control oneself
	束	束	束	
657 7 strokes	束			

敕	束	束	束	**CHR-4**, to correct; imperial orders
	束	敕	敕	
658 11 strokes	敕			

整	一	冂	束	**JENG-3**, to tinker with; to give trouble; whole; exactly 整兩點　*jeng-3 lyang-2 dyan-3*, 2:00 sharp 整天　　*jeng-3 tyan-1*, all day
	敕	敕	整	
659 16 strokes	整	整	整	

156

紀	ㄥ	ㄠ	ㄠ	JI-4, record; year; age; JI-3, to order 紀念 *ji-4 nyan-4*, to commemorate 年紀 *nyan-2 ji-4*, age 軍紀 *jyun-1 ji-3*, military discipline
	ㄠ	糸	糹	
660 9 strokes	糹	紀		紀

樹	才	木	木	SHU-4, tree 果樹 *gwo-3 shu-4*, fruit tree 樹枝 *shu-4 jr-1*, tree branch
	村	桔	桔	
661 16 strokes	桔	樹	樹	(木 64) 树

皮	丿	尸	巾	PI-2, bark, leather, skin, fur. SKIN rad. (107) The character is supposed to show a hand flaying off pieces of hide. Note the "right hand" rad. 又 in *pi-2*. 皮帶 *pi-2 dai-4*, leather belt 皮包 *pi-2 bau-1*, leather bag
	皮	皮		
662 5 strokes				

活	丶	冫	氵	HWO-2, be alive; be movable; work (usually, manual work) 活水 *hwo-2 shwei-3*, running water 活字 *hwo-2 dz-4*, movable type 作活 *dzwo-4 hwo-2*, to work; to do needle-work
	氵	汗	汗	
663 9 strokes	汗	活	活	

石	一	丆	石	SHR-2, rock; DAN-4, a picul (133⅓ pounds). ROCK rad. (112) The "mouth" is supposed to be a rock that has rolled to the foot of the cliff. 石頭 *shr-2 tou-2*, stone, rock 石像 *shr-2 syang-4*, stone statue
	石	石		
664 5 strokes				

SZ-1, silk; trace, a bit

This character is composed of two "silk" rads., side by side.

絲作的 *sz-1 dzwo-4 de*, be made of silk

665
12 strokes

TSAU-3, grass. GRASS rad. (140)

This form of the "grass" rad. is composed of two "sprout" rads. (465, above), side by side, to suggest "grass" sprouting up. The student has learned another form of "grass" (192, above). The form here is the independent form.

666
6 strokes

BYAN-4, change

變成 *byan-4 cheng-2*, to change into

(幺 25)

667
22 strokes

BU-4, step, pace; on foot

Bu-4 used to be a picture of two feet or of a foot in two positions to suggest motion. In the modern form, one of these feet is corrupted into "few."

步行 *bu-4 sying-2*, to go on foot

步子 *bu-4 dz-3*, pace, step

668
7 strokes

HU-1, tiger. TIGER rad. (141)

The character is a picture of a tiger.

669
6 strokes

虍	⺊	广	庐
	虍	虏	虏
670 13 strokes	虏	虏	虏

JYU-4, wild boar

Jyu-4 combines meanings: "tiger" + "pig" = "tiger-pig, a pig fierce as a tiger." Thus: "wild boar."

據	一	十	扌
	扩	捤	捤
671 16 strokes	捤	據	據

JYU-4, according to; to take in your hand; evidence, proof

Jyu-4 (670, above) gives the sound; "hand" gives the meaning "to take in the hand." Other meanings are derivative.

據說 *jyu-4 shwo-1*, People say . . .

佔據 *jan-4 jyu-4*, to occupy (by force) 据

炎	丶	丷	丷
	火	灶	灶
672 8 strokes	炎	炎	

YAN-2, to blaze

Yan-2 combines meanings: "fire" over "fire" = "to blaze." As a part of characters, this character usually indicates the sound *dan* or *tan*.

談	丶	亠	二
	言	言	訁
673 15 strokes	訁	談	談

TAN-2, to chat, to talk about

The "word" rad. gives the meaning; *yan-2* (672, above) here has the sound value *tan*.

談話 *tan-2 hwa-4*, to talk; statement 谈

淡	丶	冫	氵
	氵	氵	氵
674 11 strokes	淡	淡	

DAN-4, weak, thin, insipid, pale

看得很淡 *kan-4 de hen-3 dan-4*, be indifferent to

生意很淡 *sheng-1 yi-4 hen-3 dan-4*, Business is poor.

159

垚	一	十	土	**LU-4, clod, lump of earth** The "earth" rad. at the bottom gives the meaning; the sound is suggested by the rest of the character, which has been corrupted from *lyou-4* (149, above).
	丰	去	圥	
675 8 strokes	坴	垚		

陸	⁻	了	阝	**LU-4, land** This word is likely cognate with *lu-4* "clod" (675, above). The character is reclarified with the "mound" rad. 大陸　*da-4 lu-4*, continent, mainland 陸軍　*lu-4 jyun-1*, army　　陆
	阝⁻	阝⁺	阝±	
676 11 strokes	阝圭	陕	陸	

丸	丿	九	丸	**WAN-2, bullet, BB, pill, ball** The student should distinguish *wan-2* from *fan-2* "common" 凡 (682, below) and from *ren-4* "blade" 刃 (522, above). 丸子　*wan-2 dz-3*, pill, small ball 魚丸　*yu-2 wan-2*, fish-ball (food)
677 3 strokes				

熱	⁻	十	土	**RE-4, be hot, to heat** 熱心　　*re-4 syin-1*, be enthusiastic 熱情　　*re-4 ching-2*, be passionate 熱力學　*re-4 li-4 sywe-2*, thermodynamics
	丰	去	坴	
678 15 strokes	執	執	執	(灬 34)　　热

鬥	丨	丨⁻	丨²	**DOU-4, to fight. FIGHT rad. (191)** The old form of this character was a picture of two men struggling with each other. Some scholars explain the modern form as "two kings confined in a small place, whence 'to fight.'" Distinguish from *men-2* "gate" 門 (45, above).　　斗
	丨ᶠ	丨王	丨王⁼	
679 10 strokes	丨王干	丨王王	丨王刂	

160

市	丶	亠	亠	SHR-4, market, marketplace; municipality; standard system of weights and measures
	市	市		市長　*shr-4 jang-3*, mayor
680 5 strokes				市寸　*shr-4 tswun-4*, Chinese standard inch

鬧	｜	匚	王	NAU-4, to make a disturbance; be disturbed by; to get (perhaps with difficulty)
	王	王王	鬥王	*Nau-4* combines meanings: "to fight in the marketplace" = "to make a disturbance."
681 15 strokes	鬥	鬧	鬧	鬧鐘　*nau-4 jung-1*, alarm clock　　　鬧

凡	ｊ	凡	凡	FAN-2, common, all
				Fan-2 is said to combine meanings: an object (the dot) thrown under a table may be any old thing you would leave under the table.
682 3 strokes				凡是　*fan-2 shr-4*, all those who are 平凡　*ping-2 fan-2*, be ordinary

恐	一	丁	工	KUNG-3, to fear
	卫	巩	巩	恐怕　*kung-3 pa-4*, be afraid that; "probably"
683 10 strokes	恐	恐	恐	恐嚇　*kung-3 he-4*, to threaten 恐水病　*kung-3 shwei-3 bing-4*, hydrophobia

云	一	二	云	YUN-2, to say
	云			*Yun-2* originally was a picture and meant "cloud." It came to mean "to say" by sound-loan.
684 4 strokes				

161

陰	ㄱ	阝	阝	YIN-1, shady, dark; "yin" in "yin and yang"; be cloudy; be crafty; secret; lunar; negative; incised; to deceive
	阝	阝𠆢	阝𠆢	陰天　*yin-1 tyan-1*, be overcast
				樹陰　*shu-4 yin-1*, shade of a tree
685 11 strokes	阝今	陰	陰	陰戶　*yin-1 hu-4*, female organ　　阴

易	丨	冂	日	YANG-2, be bright, brilliance
				This character originally meant "south slope of a hill" or "north side of a riverbank," i.e., the side that gets the sun (cp. 687, below). The student should distinguish this character from *yi-4* "to change; be easy" 易 (376, above).
	旦	昮	昜	
686 9 strokes	易	昜		

陽	ㄱ	阝	阝	YANG-2, sun, solar; "yang" in "yin and yang"; open; positive; male organ; to cut in relief
	阝日	阝日	阝日	This character is 686, above, reclarified with "mound."
				太陽　*tai-4 yang-2*, sun
687 12 strokes	陽	陽	陽	阳

虎	丨	卜	上	HU-3, tiger
				老虎　*lau-2 hu-3*, tiger
	产	庐	虍	馬馬虎虎　*ma-2 ma-3 hu-2 hu-3*, be careless, sloppy
688 8 strokes	處	虎		虎口　*hu-3 kou-3*, dangerous situation

丂	一	丂		KAU-3, breath, sigh
689 2 strokes				

号	丶	冂	口	HAU-4, to call, to cry out
	므	号		The character combines meanings: *kau-3* "a breath, a sigh" + "mouth" is used to suggest the idea "to call, to cry out." Compare 691, below.
690 5 strokes				

號	口	므	号	HAU-2, to cry out; HAU-4; appellations, means of identification: name, size, number, sign, mark; order; bugle
	号⌐	号⌐	号⌐	號頭 *hau-4 tou-2*, number 問號 *wen-4 hau-4*, question mark
691 13 strokes	號	號	號	號令 *hau-4 ling-4*, order 号

予	ㄱ	ㄱ	孒	YU-2, to give; I
	予			The student should learn to tell *yu-2* apart from the "child" rad. 子 (18, above) and the "spear" rad. 矛 (840, below).
692 4 strokes				

預	ㄱ	ㄱ	予	YU-4, beforehand; to anticipate
	予⌐	矛	預	The "head" rad. here suggests the meaning "to anticipate"; *yu-2* (692, above) gives the sound.
	預	預	預	預算 *yu-4 swan-4*, to make advance plans 預先 *yu-4 syan-1*, beforehand 预
693 13 strokes				

備	ノ	亻	亻	BEI-4, to prepare, to get ready for
	什	㐅	㐅	預備 *yu-4 bei-4*, to get ready, to plan, preparation
	俌	備	備	準備 *jwun-3 bei-4*, to get ready; to intend to 備馬 *bei-4 ma-3*, to saddle a horse 备
694 12 strokes				

163

希	ノ	メ	ㄨ
	爻	爷	希
695 7 strokes	希		

SYI-1, be loose; be rare; to hope

The "crisscross" rad. is supposed to show the loose meshes of a cloth; the "cloth" rad. is there to help develop this meaning. The meaning "hope" (the most common modern use of this character) is evidently by sound-loan.

望	丶	亠	亡
	土	切	胡
696 11 strokes	朝	望	望

WANG-4, to look for; to expect; toward

希望 *syi-1 wang-4*, hope, to hope to
望東 *wang-4 dung-1*, eastward
名望 *ming-2 wang-4*, prestige

紅	ㄥ	幺	幺
	幺	糸	糸
697 9 strokes	糸一	紅丁	紅工

HUNG-2, be red

紅茶　　　 *hung-2 cha-2*, "black" tea
紅人　　　 *hung-2 ren-2*, Amerindian; favorite of an important person
紅十字會　 *hung-2 shr-2 dz-4 hwei-4*, Red Cross

紅工

切	一	七	切
	切		
698 4 strokes			

CHYE-1, to slice, to carve; be tangent (in geometry); CHYE-4, be sure to; be close to

親切 *chin-1 chye-4*, be closely related to

代	ノ	イ	仁
	代	代	
699 5 strokes			

DAI-4, to take the place of; an age

代表　　 *dai-4 byau-3*, to represent, representative
代數學　 *dai-4 shu-4 sywe-2*, algebra
古代　　 *gu-3 dai-4*, ancient times

袋	イ	代	代	**DAI-4, bag, pocket** The "gown" rad. gives the meaning in this character; *dai-4* (699, above) gives the sound. 口袋 *kou-3 dai-4*, bag, pocket
	代	伐	伐	
700 11 strokes	伐	伐	袋	

妾	丶	二	亠	**JYE-4, wife of inferior rank, concubine** *Jye-4* is explained: "to stand" + "woman" = a woman who stands when her husband or wives of superior status are present; therefore, "concubine." This explanation, historically not accurate, can help you remember the character in any case.
	亣	立	竒	
701 8 strokes	妾	妾		

接	一	十	扌	**JYE-1, to receive; to connect; to meet; to catch; to take over** 接着 *jye-1 je*, continuously; after that; serially 接着 *jye-1 jau-2*, to meet (cp. *jye-1 je*, above) 接頭 *jye-1 tou-2*, to contact (about arrangements); be familiar with
	扩	护	拉	
702 11 strokes	挼	接	接	

化	ノ	イ	化	**HWA-4, to change; to melt; to evaporate; -ize, -ify** If "man" + "ladle" suggests "alchemy" to you, you can use that as a mnemonic for *hwa-4*. "Alchemy" = "to transmute, to change." 化學 *hwa-4 sywe-2*, chemistry 工業化 *gung-1 ye-4 hwa-4*, to industrialize
	化			
703 4 strokes				

花	一	十	十一	**HWA-1, flower, blossom; flowery; design; cotton; to spend; fireworks** 花樣 *hwa-1 yang-4*, design, pattern 花子 *hwa-1 dz-3*, beggar 花生 *hwa-1 sheng-1*, peanut
	十ナ	ナ	艻	
704 8 strokes	花	花		

聲耳	士	声	声	SHENG-1, sound, tone; to declare; reputation
	声	声	殸	The "ear" gives part of the meaning. The top part is an old meaning-meaning compound itself: a musical instrument + "club" = to strike the musical instrument with a stick, "to make sounds." 声
705 17 strokes	殸	聲耳	聲	聲音 *sheng-1 yin*, sound

襄	丶	亠	亠口	SYANG-1, to take off, to disrobe
	亠口口	空	窊	Note that the "gown" rad. occurs as part of this character to give the meaning. The significance of the rest of *syang-1* is not known.
706 17 strokes	窒	襄	襄	

讓	亠	言	言口	RANG-4, to yield, to allow; to lower (in price); to offer; to step aside; to cause, to make; by
	言口	言谷	言谷	讓步 *rang-4 bu-4*, to concede, to compromise
707 24 strokes	讓	讓	讓	让

類頁	丷	半	米	LEI-4, class, species, kind
	类	类	类	人類 *ren-2 lei-4*, mankind 分類 *fen-1 lei-4*, to classify 相類 *syang-1 lei-4*, be similar
708 19 strokes	類	類頁	類頁	(米 101, 頁 333) 米大

休	丿	亻	仁	SYOU-1, to rest; to cease; to divorce
	什	仕	休	*Syou-1* combines meanings and is supposed to show a man resting under a tree, whence "to rest."
709 6 strokes				休學 *syou-1 sywe-2*, to drop out (of school) 休業 *syou-1 ve-4*, to close a business (for a holiday or vacation)

166

息	ノ	イ	介	SYI-2, to breathe; to rest; to stop, to cease; a surname
	自	自	自	*Syi-2* is supposed to combine "nose" + "heart" to suggest "to breathe." (The significance of "heart" is, perhaps, obscure.)
710 10 strokes	息	息	息	休息　*syou-1 syi-2*, to rest

式	一	二	下	SHR-4, form, fashion, model, style
	工	式	式	新式　*syin-1 shr-4*, new style 式子　*shr-4 dz-3*, formula
711 6 strokes				

登	ノ	ヲ	ヺ	DENG-1, to go up; to press down on with the foot; to publish
	ヺ″	癶	癶	The "flask" used to be a pedestal; the "back-to-back" showed two feet that had climbed onto it.
	登	登	登	登報　*deng-1 bau-4*, to publish (in a newspaper or magazine)
712 12 strokes				登第　*deng-1 di-4*, to pass an exam

燈	丶	丷	少	DENG-1, lantern, lamp
	火	炒	炒	The "fire" rad. gives the meaning here; *deng-1* (712, above) gives the sound.
	烞	熔	燈	點燈　*dyan-3 deng-1*, to light a lamp 花燈　*hwa-1 deng-1*, colored lantern
713 16 strokes				灯

普	丶	丷	丷	PU-3, general, universal; a surname
	半	並	並	*Pu-3* combines the meanings "side by side" (653, above) + "sun" to suggest "all the places the sun shines": "universal, general."
	並	並	普	普希金　*pu-3 syi-1 jin-1*, Pushkin (the Russian poet)
714 12 strokes				

167

甬	⁊	⁻⁷	⁻⁷	YUNG-3, bulk measure: ten "pecks"
	甬	甬	甬	*Yung-3* originally meant "a big bell," and the character was a picture of the bell, with a hook at the top center by which the bell could be hung. It came by sound-loan to mean "bulk measure: ten 'pecks.'"
715 7 strokes				

通	⁊	⁻⁷	⁻⁷	TUNG-1, to go through; thoroughgoing, universal
	甬	甬	甬	普通 *pu-3 tung-1*, be universal, be widespread or common
716 10 strokes	通	通	通	通過 *tung-1 gwo-4*, to go through; to pass in a parliamentary meeting 通知 *tung-1 jr-1*, to inform; notice

電	一	一	雨	DYAN-4, electricity; lightning
	雨	雨	雨	The character shows a streak of lightning falling under the rain. 電燈 *dyan-4 deng-1*, electric light
717 13 strokes	電	電	電	電話 *dyan-4 hwa-4*, telephone 電氣 *dyan-4 chi-4*, electricity 电

收	㇄	㇉	屮	SHOU-1, to put away; to receive; to collect 收起來 *shou-1 chi-3 lai-2*, to put away
	屮	收	收	收入 *shou-1 ru-4*, income; to earn 收成 *shou-1 cheng-2*, harvest
718 6 strokes				

春	一	二	三	CHWUN-1, spring (the season)
	丰	夫	表	The character is supposed to show vegetation burgeoning in the sun. 春天 *chwun-1 tyan-1*, springtime
719 9 strokes	春	春	春	春青 *chwun-1 ching-1*, time of youth 春意 *chwun-1 yi-4*, lewd thoughts

| 兆

720
6 strokes | 丶 | 冫 | 刁 |
| | 兆 | 兆 | 兆 |

JAU-4, omen

Jau-4 shows the cracks on the heated tortoise shell which the early Chinese used for divination. (Read the note in 118, above).

兆頭 *jau-4 tou-2*, omen

預兆 *yu-4 jau-4*, signs of the times

跳 721 13 strokes	丨	冂	口
	묘	足	足
	足	跔	跳

TYAU-4, to jump

The "foot" rad. gives the meaning; *jau-4* (720, above) is supposed to give the sound.

跳遠 *tyau-4 ywan-3*, broad jump

跳行 *tyau-4 hang-2*, to skip a line

殺 722 10 strokes	丿	乂	乄
	禾	矛	杀
	杀几	殺	殺

SHA-1, to kill; to tighten (a belt); to add up; to sting, to hurt; to reduce; to brake, to stop

自殺 *dz-4 sha-1*, to commit suicide

殺車 *sha-1 che-1*, to brake (a car)

杀

| 処

723
5 strokes | 丿 | 勹 | 夂 |
| | 処 | 処 | |

CHU-4, place; CHU-3, to dwell

The character is composed of the "slow" rad. + the "table" rad. Originally "slow" was a picture of a man, and "table" was supposed to be a small stool. "Man" + "stool" is a good way to suggest "dwell," because the Chinese are fond of sitting outside their houses on little stools.

處 724 11 strokes	丨	卜	上
	广	声	虍
	虍	虙	處

CHU-4, place; CHU-3, to dwell

This is the same word as 723, above. The character is reclarified with "tiger," but nobody is quite sure why.

處世 *chu-4 shr-4, chu-3 shr-4*, to get along in the world (especially with other people)

處女 *chu-4 nyu-3, chu-3 nyu-3*, virgin

処

169

風	ノ	几	凡
	几	凤	凨
725 9 strokes	風	風	風

FENG-1, wind; news; custom; rumor; desire. WIND rad. (182)

The dictionaries say that *fan-2* (682, above) gives the sound; the "bug" gives the meaning, "because when the wind stirs, the bugs breed."

風聞 *feng-1 wen-2*, The rumor is . . . 风

俗	ノ	イ	亻
	亻	伀	伀
726 9 strokes	俗	俗	俗

SU-2, vulgar, common

The "valley" rad. is supposed to suggest "ravines, mountain country"; with the addition of "man," we get "hillbilly," hence "uncultivated, vulgar."

風俗 *feng-1 su-2*, custom

俗氣 *su-2 chi*, be in poor taste

歹	一	丆	歹
	歹		
727 4 strokes			

DAI-3, chip. CHIP rad. (78)

This character is supposed to be a picture of bone chips. Compare 歹 to the form of this rad. you have already learned (646, above). The form here may occur as an independent character. The student should learn to tell "chip" from "dusk" 夕 (117, above).

死	一	丆	歹
	歹	夗	死
728 6 strokes			

SZ-3, to die, be dead; stubbornly

Sz-3 combines meanings. The "ladle" rad. is corrupted from an earlier "man" rad., and "man" + "bone chips" is supposed to suggest death.

死亡 *sz-3 wang-2*, to die, death

死尸 *sz-2 shr*, corpse

題	冂	旦	早
	톼	是	是
729 18 strokes	題	題	題

TI-2, theme, subject

問題 *wen-4 ti-2*, question, problem

題目 *ti-2 mu-4*, topic, title, heading; problem, exercise

(日 160, 頁 333) 題

170

秋	´	´	千	**CHYOU-1, autumn** In China, after the grain is threshed, it is common to stack and burn the unusable stalks. These "grain fires" are a part of the autumn scene; whence, perhaps, this character. 秋天 *chyou-1 tyan-1*, autumn
730 9 strokes	千	禾	禾	
	禾´	秋	秋	
涼	`	´´	´`	**LYANG-2, be cool, be cold** Alternate form 凉. 涼快 *lyang-2 kwai-4*, be cool 着涼 *jau-1 lyang-2*, to catch cold
731 11 strokes	氵	汀	泞	
	涼	涼	涼	
員	l	⼝	口	**YWAN-2, be round; person with certain duties, member** "Mouth" + "cowrie" is supposed to suggest roundness. The meaning "member, etc." is by sound-loan. 教員 *jyau-4 ywan-2*, teacher 會員 *hwei-4 ywan-2*, member
732 10 strokes	尸	月	肖	
	昌	員	員	員
圓	l	冂	冂	**YWAN-2, be round; to make excuses; currency; to interpret** This character is used now rather than 732, above, to mean "round"; the character is reclarified with "surround." 美圓 *mei-3 ywan-2*, American currency
733 13 strokes	冋	同	冒	
	圓	圓	圓	圆
改	⼸	⼹	己	**GAI-3, to change** 改變 *gai-3 byan-4*, to change, change 改革 *gai-3 ge-2*, to reform, to improve 改良 *gai-3 lyang-2*, to improve, improvement
	己´	弘	改	
734 7 strokes	改			

171

理	一	二	干
	王	玑	玑
735 11 strokes	玾	珅	理

LI-3, principle; to set in order; to speak to; to pay attention to

Li-3 originally meant "veins in jade" and was a sound-meaning compound.

道理   *dau-4 li-3*, reason, logical basis; doctrine

理想   *li-2 syang-3*, ideal, be ideal

清	丶	丷	氵
	氵	沣	沣
736 11 strokes	清	清	清

CHING-1, be clear; to clear

"Water" gives the meaning; *ching-1* (198, above) gives the sound.

清理   *ching-1 li-3*, to clean up (literally or figuratively)

說不清   *shwo-1 bu ching-1*, be unable to express clearly

清白   *ching-1 bai-2*, unsullied

楚	一	十	才
	木	林	梺
737 13 strokes	梺	梺	楚

CHU-3, be distinct

清楚   *ching-1 chu-3*, be clear

記	丶	亠	言
	言	訐	訂
738 10 strokes	記		

JI-4, to remember; to record; mark, sign

The "word" rad. gives the meaning; *ji-3* (273, above) gives the sound.

記得   *ji-4 de-2*, to remember

記住   *ji-4 ju-4*, to fix in the mind

記者   *ji-4 je-3*, reporter

记

留	ノ	亻	厶
	幻	幼	留
739 10 strokes	留	留	留

LYOU-2, to keep; to stay; to ask someone to stay; to leave behind

留聲機   *lyou-2 sheng-1 ji-1*, record player

傳留   *chwan-2 lyou-2*, to hand down

留心   *lyou-2 syin-1*, be careful

刀口	フ	刀	刀
	刀口	召	
740 5 strokes			

JAU-4, to summon; SHAU-4; a place name

The meaning "to summon" comes by combining "mouth" for meaning with *dau-1* (102, above) for sound.

紹	ㄑ	幺	幺
	幺	幺	紅
741 11 strokes	紅刀	紹刀	紹

SHAU-4, to join together

The "silk" rad. suggests the meaning; *jau-4, shau-4* (740, above) gives the sound.

介紹 *jye-4 shau-4*, to introduce

紹

管	ノ	ㅏ	斤
	斤	竹	竺
742 14 strokes	笢	筦	管

GWAN-3, reed, pipe; to manage; to guarantee

For the basic meaning "pipe," the "bamboo" rad. gives the meaning; *gwan-1* (407, above) gives the sound. Other meanings are by sound-loan.

管理 *gwan-2 li-3*, to manage

勸	一	艹	艼
	芇	萑	萑
743 20 strokes	雚	雚	勸

CHYWAN-4, to exhort

The "strength" rad. gives the meaning in this character; *gwan-4* (193, above) suggests the sound.

勸過來 *chywan-4 gwo lai*, to bring someone around to your way of thinking

(力 206)

劝

安	丶	丶	宀
	宀	安	安
744 6 strokes			

AN-1, be peaceful, be at ease, peace; to install

An-1 is a famous meaning-meaning character: "one woman under your roof means peace."

安全 *an-1 chywan-2*, be safe, safety

安定 *an-1 ding-4*, be secure, steady

173

案	丶	宀	宀	AN-4, table; case at law; bill (legislative); legal record
	安	安	安	*An-1* (744, above) gives the sound; the "tree" rad. suggests "table."
745 10 strokes	宰	宰	案	辦案子 *ban-4 an-4 dz-3*, to handle a legal case 畫案 *hwa-4 an-4*, drawing table

求	一	十	寸	CHYOU-2, to reach for; to beg
	寸	求	求	求乞 *chyou-2 chi-3*, to beg 求親 *chyou-2 chin-1*, to seek a marriage alliance; to propose
746 7 strokes	求			求心力 *chyou-2 syin-1 li-4*, centripetal force

救	一	十	寸	JYOU-4, to rescue
	求	求	求	求救 *chyou-2 jyou-4*, to ask for help 救生 *jyou-4 sheng-1*, to save a life
747 11 strokes	求	救	救	救火車 *jyou-4 hwo-3 che-1*, fire engine

光	丨	丩	少	GWANG-1, light, brightness; to make bare; be used up; only
	屮	少	光	吃光 *chr-1 gwang-1*, to eat up 陽光 *yang-2 gwang-1*, sunlight
748 6 strokes				光陰 *gwang-1 yin-1*, time

無	丿	亇	亇	WU-2, to lack, not to have; not . . .
	亇	冊	無	無非 *wu-2 fei-1*, only 無從 *wu-2 tsung-2*, not knowing where it is best to start
749 12 strokes	無	無	無	無用 *wu-2 yung-4*, be useless 无

174

侖	ノ	人	今	**LWUN-2, to arrange** This character combines meanings. The bottom part means "documents." The top part means "to get together." Combined, "to get together, to collect" and "documents" are supposed to suggest "to arrange."
	今	合	侖	
750 8 strokes	侖	侖		
論	、	亠	言	**LWUN-4, to discuss; theory; -ism; LWUN-2; first syllable in *Analects* (a Confucian book)** 論文 *lwun-2 wen-2*, dissertation; essay 無論 *wu-2 lwun-4*, no matter; regardless of 論理 *lwun-4 li-3*, logic
	言	訂	論	
751 15 strokes	論	論	論	论
亭	、	亠	宀	**TING-2, kiosk** The top part is a slightly abbreviated "tall" rad. (75, above), which, as the student will remember, is a picture of a tower. *Ding-1* (519, above) gives the sound.
	亩	高	亭	
752 9 strokes	亭	高	亭	
停	ノ	イ	个	**TING-2, to stop** 停止 *ting-2 jr-3*, to stop (doing something) 停車 *ting-2 che-1*, to park 停火 *ting-2 hwo-3*, cease-fire
	仁	佰	佰	
753 11 strokes	停	停	停	
隋	⁊	了	阝	**DWO-2, mincemeat; SWEI-2; the name of a dynasty** In the case of *dwo-2*, the "meat" rad. gives the meaning. The rest of the character once gave the sound.
	阝-	阝ナ	阝ナ	
754 12 strokes	隋	隋	隋	

隨	⁊	了	阝	SWEI-2, to follow; any, all 隨便 *swei-2 byan-4*, at your convenience, Do as you please. 隨時 *swei-2 shr-2*, any time 隨員 *swei-2 ywan-2*, attaché
	阝⁴	陸	隋	
755 15 strokes	隋	隋	隨	隨

量	丨	冂	日	LYANG-2, to consider carefully; to weigh, to measure; LYANG-4, quantity, volume, capacity; to weigh; to estimate The bottom part of this character used to be *jung-4* "be heavy" 重 (242, above). It has been corrupted into "village" in the modern form. The sun used to be merely an object being weighed.
	旦	旦	昌	
756 12 strokes	昌	量	量	

倍	丿	亻	亻	BEI-4, times, fold The student should distinguish *bei-4* from *bu-4* "a set, etc." 部 (603, above). 三倍 *san-1 bei-4*, three times as much 倍數 *bei-4 shu-4*, multiple
	亻	亻	亻	
757 10 strokes	位	倍	倍	

賤	丨	冂	目	JYAN-4, be cheap; be humble; be unresponsive The "cowrie" rad. gives the meaning; *jyan-1* (166, above) suggests the sound. 賤賣 *jyan-4 mai-4*, to sell at a low price
	貝	貝	賎	
758 15 strokes	賎	賤	賤	賤

剛	丨	冂	冈	GANG-1, just now; exactly; only; be firm, be hard 剛才 *gang-1 tsai-2*, just now 剛直 *gang-1 jr-2*, be firm in one's principles 剛好 *gang-1 hau-3*, Perfect!
	冈	岡	岡	
759 10 strokes	岡	剛	剛	剛

㔾

760
2 strokes

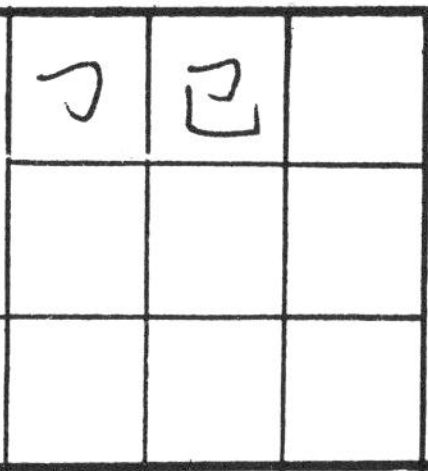

JYE-2, seal. SEAL rad. (26)

The student has learned the independent form of the "seal" rad. already: 卩 (84, above). The form here only occurs as a part of characters. Distinguish "seal" from "self" 己, "already" 已, and *sz-4* 巳 (273–275, above).

危

761
6 strokes

WEI-2, danger; be lofty

The character is explained as "a man at the top of a cliff or slope, looking down at something that has fallen off."

危樓 *wei-2 lou-2*, tall building

險

762
16 strokes

SYAN-3, be dangerous

危險 *wei-2 syan-3*, be dangerous, danger

險些 *syan-3 sye-1*, nearly, almost

险

厚

763
9 strokes

HOU-4, be thick; be generous

厚實 *hou-4 shr-2*, be thick

厚道 *hou-4 dau-4*, be generous

舛

764
6 strokes

CHWAN-3, to face away, to oppose, be discordant. DISCORD rad. (136)

The original form of this character was two men facing away from each other. From "face away," of course, come the other ideas of "oppose, be discordant." It is counted here as 6 strokes, but is often actually written, as here, in 7 strokes.

既	亻	勹	白	**JI-4**, be finished; since, now that; already; a surname. Usually written 既. 既然 *ji-4 ran-2*, this being the case . . . 既是 *ji-4 shr-4*, this being the case . . . 既而 *ji-4 er-2*, then; before long
765 11 strokes	自	皀	卽	
	皀	卽	既	

辰	一	厂	厇	**CHEN-2**, early; the fifth "earthly branch." EARLY rad. (161) The character can mean "early" in the sense "early in the day" or "early in the year." One modern scholar (Kuo Mo-jo) thinks it is a picture of a stone tool used in ancient times to break the soil for cultivation.
766 7 strokes	厇	辰	辰	
	辰			

石研	一	丆	石	**YAN-2**, to grind fine; to do research, to investigate thoroughly The "stone" rad. suggests the meaning "to grind." *Jyan-1* (502, above) is supposed to help with the sound. 研求 *yan-2 chyou-2*, to research
767 11 strokes	石	石	石二	
	研	砼	研	

究	丶	宀	宀	**JYOU-4, JYOU-1**, to look into 研究 *yan-2 jyou-1*, research, to research; knowledge 究辦 *jyou-4 ban-4*, to prosecute and settle a case 究問 *jyou-4 wen-4*, to investigate in detail; to try a case
768 7 strokes	宀	宂	究	
	究			

貫	乚	毌	毌	**GWAN-4**, to string together; to pierce *Gwan-4* is a picture of two cowries strung together on a string, the way cash (Chinese coins) was later. The form of the top cowrie is slightly corrupted.
769 11 strokes	毌	毌	貫	貫
	貫	貫	貫	

178

實

770
14 strokes

SHR-2, fruit; be solid; true, real

實在 *shr-2 dzai-4*, truly

實現 *shr-2 syan-4*, to come true

實得 *shr-2 de-2*, net income

实

簡

771
18 strokes

JYAN-3, to abridge; be simple; letter

Variant 簡.

簡直 *jyan-3 jr-2*, simply; frankly

簡字 *jyan-3 dz-4*, simplified Chinese character

(竹 54, 日 160)

简

單

772
12 strokes

DAN-1, be odd (numbered); be single, be simple; list

簡單 *jyan-3 dan-1*, be simple

開單子 *kai-1 dan-1 dz-3*, to make a list

單位 *dan-1 wei-4*, unit

単

背

773
9 strokes

BEI-4, back; to turn one's back on; be bad; to memorize; to recite; BEI-1, to carry on the back

背着 *bei-4 je*, behind someone's back; contrary to . . .

背後 *bei-4 hou-4*, in back of; behind someone's back

背包 *bei-4 bau-1*, knapsack

景

774
12 strokes

JING-3, scene, scenery; outlook

背景 *bei-4 jing-3*, background

景象 *jing-3 syang-4*, "the situation"; state of affairs

風景 *feng-1 jing-3*, scenery, landscape

同	丨	冂	冂	TUNG-2, be the same; with, together
	冋	同	同	同意 *tung-2 yi-4*, to agree
				同學 *tung-2 sywe-2*, classmate
775 6 strokes				同樣 *tung-2 yang-4*, all the same, nevertheless

巽	フ	ㄋ	巳	SYUN-4, to yield, be yielding
	巳フ	巴	㠯	
776 12 strokes	㠲	巽	巽	

選	フ	ㄋ	巳	SYWAN-3, to choose; brief
	巴	巽	巽	選民 *sywan-3 min-2*, the enfranchised; those who can vote
				文選 *wen-2 sywan-3*, anthology
777 15 strokes	巽	選	選	選間 *sywan-3 jyan-1*, brief space; little while 选

結	ㄥ	ㄠ	幺	JYE-2, to tie together; JYE-2, JYE-3, knot; JYE-1, to bear fruit
	幺	幺	糸	結果 *jye-2 gwo-3*, result; The outcome was . . .
				結論 *jye-2 lwun-4*, conclusion, deduction
778 12 strokes	結	結	結	結實 *jye-1 shr-2*, to bear fruit 结

昏	丿	𠂆	仁	HWUN-1, dusk, darkness
	氏	氏	昏	The top of this character used to be *di-3* "foundation; bottom; to go down" (528, above), and the character was a meaning-meaning compound: "go down" + "sun" = "darkness, dusk." The dot has dropped
779 8 strokes	昏	昏		out of *di-3* in the modern form.

180

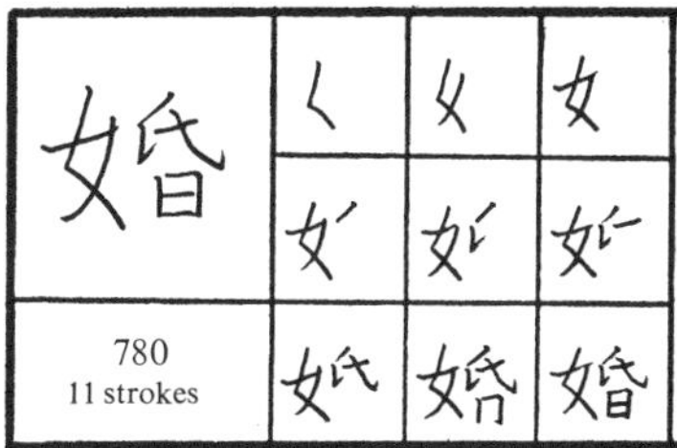

780
11 strokes

HWUN-1, marriage

結婚 *jye-2 hwun-1*, to marry, marriage

離婚 *li-2 hwun-1*, to divorce

婚禮 *hwun-1 li-3*, wedding, marriage ceremony

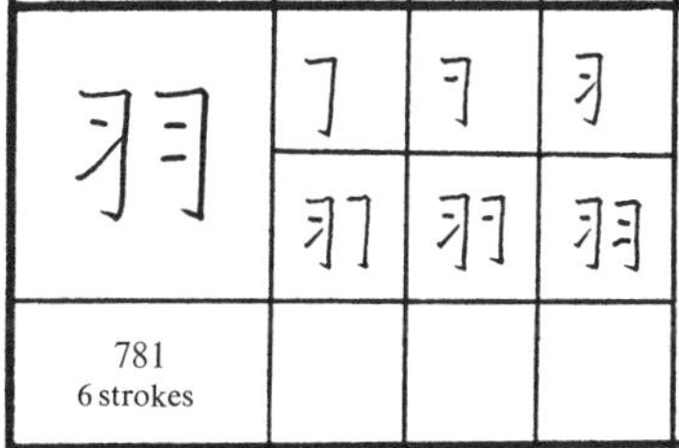

781
6 strokes

YU-3, wings. WINGS rad. (124)

The character is a picture. Printed 羽.

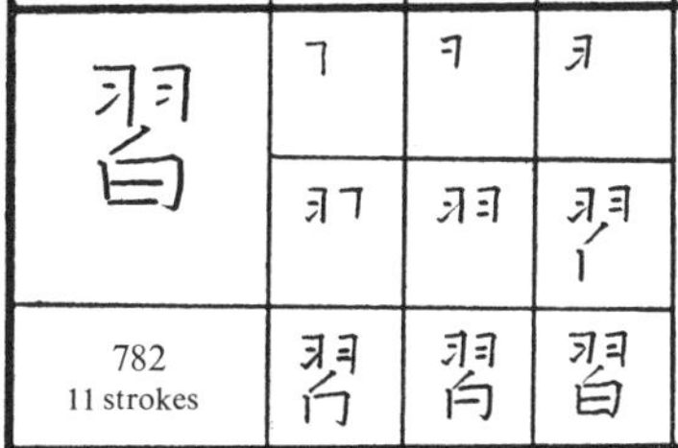

782
11 strokes

SYI-2, to practice; practice, habit

學習 *sywe-2 syi-2*, to study

習氣 *syi-2 chi-4*, habits (good or bad)

習題 *syi-2 ti-2*, school exercise, academic problem

习

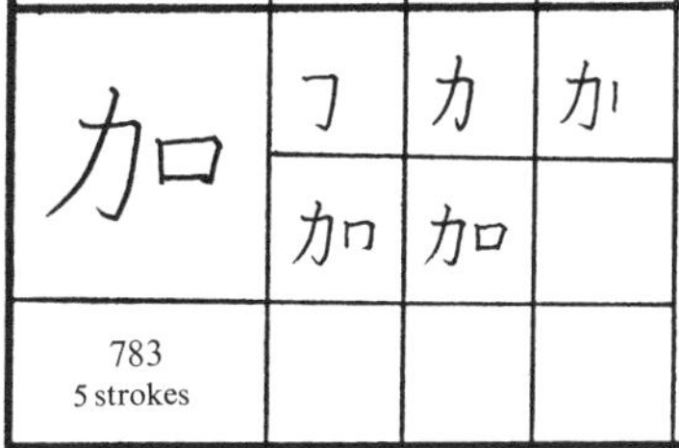

783
5 strokes

JYA-1, to add, to increase, plus . . .

加一倍 *jya-1 yi-2 bei-4*, double

加入 *jya-1 ru-4*, to join an organization

加快 *jya-1 kwai-4*, to speed up

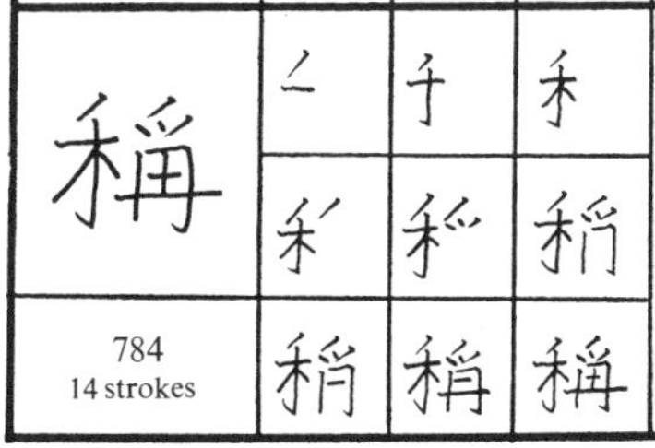

784
14 strokes

CHENG-1, to weigh; name; CHEN-4, to own; to suit; CHENG-4, steelyard

名稱 *ming-2 cheng-1*, name

稱道 *cheng-1 dau-4*, to praise

稱心 *chen-4 syin-1*, accord with one's wishes

称

	、	宀	宀	PANG-2, other; side, beside
旁	宀	宀	声	旁邊　*pang-2 byan-1*, beside; the area near
				旁人　*pang-2 ren-2*, other people
785 10 strokes	声	㢏	旁	旁聽　*pang-2 ting-1*, to audit (a course)

	一	十	扌	AN-4, to press with the finger or thumb; according to
按	扌	扩	护	按着　*an-4 je*, according to
				按月　*an-4 ywe-4*, by the month
786 9 strokes	按	按	按	按理　*an-4 li-3*, Logically . . .

	𡿨	女	女	RU-2, be like; be as good as; according to; if
如口	如	如	如	如意　*ru-2 yi-4*, be satisfied
				如今　*ru-2 jin-1*, nowadays
787 6 strokes				如果　*ru-2 gwo-3*, if

	、	` `	氵	JYWE-2, to decide; decidedly; to execute (a person); to burst
決	氵	氵	決	決定　*jywe-2 ding-4*, to decide, decision
				決不　*jywe-2 bu*, be determined not to (do something)
788 7 strokes	決			決心　*jywe-2 syin-1*, determination

	一	十	艹	HWA-2, flowers; glory; Chinese
華	艹	芏	芋	中華民國　*jung-1 hwa-2 min-2 gwo-2*, The Republic of China
				華美　*hwa-2 mei-3*, Sino-American; be splendid and beautiful
789 10 strokes (12 strokes)	茾	莑	華	華北　*hwa-2 bei-3*, North China　华

SYING-4, nature, temperament

記性 *ji-4 sying-4*, memory

人性 *ren-2 sying-4*, human nature

性情 *sying-4 ching*, temperament, disposition

790
8 strokes

AI-2, DAI-1, be stupid, be idiotic

791
7 strokes

BAU-3, to protect; guarantee, surety

保險 *bau-2 syan-3*, to insure, insurance

保管 *bau-2 gwan-3*, to hold in trust, to take care of (legally)

保全 *bau-3 chywan-2*, to keep intact, to pre-serve

792
9 strokes

SYANG-4, toward, to face; habitually in the past

向來 *syang-4 lai-2*, always; up till now

向着 *syang-4 je*, toward, facing

一向 *yi-2 syang-4*, up to now

793
6 strokes

JYE-4, to lend; to borrow

借給 *jye-4 gei-3*, to lend

借據 *jye-4 jyu-4*, notes (receipts for loans)

借光 *jye-4 gwang-1*, Excuse me.

794
10 strokes

183

規	一	二	夫	GWEI-1, (drawing) compasses; rule, regulation; to correct (a fault); fee
	夫	刔	刔	日規 *r-4 gwei-1*, sundial
				規勸 *gwei-1 chywan-4*, reprimand
795 11 strokes	耒目	規	規	規定 *gwei-1 ding-4*, to make a regulation 規

觀	一	卄	廿	GWAN-1, to look at, view
				觀念 *gwan-1 nyan-4*, concept
	芇	萑	萑	觀點 *gwan-1 dyan-3*, viewpoint
				旁觀 *pang-2 gwan-1*, be a spectator
796 24 strokes (25 strokes)	雚	觀	觀	觀

社	丶	ラ	礻	SHE-4, society
				The character combines meanings: "sign" + "earth" = "altar to the spirits of the land" (original meaning), "tutelary deity, village, society."
	礻	礻	礻十	
797 7 strokes	礻十	社		社會 *she-4 hwei-4*, society

度	丶	亠	广	DU-4, to pass through; degree, rule, extent
	广	庐	庐	度過 *du-4 gwo-4*, to pass through (a period of time)
				度數 *du-4 shu-4*, degree
798 9 strokes	庐	庐	度	高度 *gau-1 du-4*, altitude

由	丨	冂	冂	YOU-2, to rest with, be up to (someone), from, by; cause
	由	由		自由 *dz-4 you-2*, be free, freedom
				由於 *you-2 yu-2*, due to
799 5 strokes				理由 *li-3 you-2*, reason

184

命 800 8 strokes	ノ 合 合	人 合 命	合 合	MING-4, destiny, fate; life; order 生命 *sheng-1 ming-4*, life 革命 *ge-2 ming-4*, to carry out a revolution; revolution 命令 *ming-4 ling-4*, order, command
注 801 8 strokes	丶 氵 汁	冫 汀 注	氵 汀	JU-4, to comment on; to concentrate on; note, commentary; to pour into; bet 注重 *ju-4 jung-4*, to emphasize 貫注 *gwan-4 ju-4*, to pay sharp attention to 下注 *sya-4 ju-4*, to get down a bet
展 802 10 strokes	⁊ 尸 展	⊐ 屏 展	尸 屈 展	JAN-3, to unroll; to postpone 發展 *fa-1 jan-3*, to develop, development 展開 *jan-3 kai-1*, to open out 展性 *jan-3 sying-4*, malleability
替 803 12 strokes	一 夫 替	二 夫夫 替	丰 夫夫 替	TI-4, for, in place of, to substitute 替工 *ti-4 gung-1*, substitute workman 代替 *dai-4 ti-4*, to represent; in place of 替壞 *ti-4 hwai-4*, to decay, to decline
祖 804 9 strokes	丶 礻 祖	冫 初 祖	礻 初 祖	DZU-3, ancestor 祖先 *dzu-3 syan-1*, ancestor(s) 祖父 *dzu-3 fu-4*, paternal grandfather 祖國 *dzu-3 gwo-2*, fatherland

185

丟	ノ	二	千
	壬	丢	丟
805 **6 strokes**			

DYOU-1, to lose

Note that this character is simply *chyu-4* "to go" with a "left" rad. over it.

丟臉 *dyou-1 lyan-3*, "to lose face"

丟人 *dyou-1 ren-2*, "to lose face"

走丟 *dzou-3 dyou-1*, to lose your way

體	口	冂	冎
	骨	骨	骨
806 **23 strokes**	骨曲	體	體

TI-3, body

身體 *shen-1 ti-3*, body

體重 *ti-3 jung-4*, weight (of humans)

體面 *ti-3 myan-2*, be pretty; be in good taste; honor

(骨 511, 曲 478)

体

示	一	二	亓
	亓	示	
807 **5 strokes**			

SHR-4, sign. SIGN rad. (113)

Compare this to the form of the "sign" rad. already learned: 礻 (480, above).

示意 *shr-4 yi-4*, to show what you mean or intend

宗	丶	丷	宀
	宀	宇	宇
808 **8 strokes**	宗	宗	

DZUNG-1, ancestor; law case; batch

Dzung-1 combines meanings. "Roof" over the "sign" rad. (for spiritual manifestations) suggests the altar to the ancestors which every Chinese family has in its house.

祖宗 *dzu-3 dzung-1*, ancestor

鹿	亠	广	户
	户	鹿	鹿
809 **11 strokes**	鹿	鹿	鹿

LU-4, deer. DEER rad. (198)

The character is a picture of a deer.

| 印 810 4 strokes | ㇒ | 亻 | 幻 |
| | 印 | | |

ANG-2, to lift up; to hold high office

The right half of this character, the "seal" rad., suggests the high office of which the seal was a symbol; the left half of the character is a "man" rad., slightly distorted. The two halves combine to give the meaning.

迎 811 7 strokes	㇒	亻	幻
	卬	卬	迎
	迎		

YING-2, to face, toward; to meet

歡迎　hwan-1 ying-2, to welcome

迎接　ying-2 jye-4, to receive or welcome someone

迎面　ying-2 myan-2, facing each other; the space opposite

| 申 812 5 strokes | 丨 | 冂 | 日 |
| | 日 | 申 | |

SHEN-1, to stretch; to state, to inform; Shanghai; the ninth "earthly branch"

The old character was two hands stretching an object (the "down" rad.). The modern form is "field" + "down."

申請　shen-1 ching-3, to apply for

申報　shen-1 bau-4, to report (to a superior)

神 813 9 strokes	丶	宀	衤
	礻	礻	初
	初	神	神

SHEN-2, spirit, god

神話　shen-2 hwa-4, myth

留神　lyou-2 shen-2, be careful

神經　shen-2 jing-1, nerves; be insane, insanity

政 814 9 strokes	一	丁	下
	下	正	正
	政	政	政

JENG-4, government; political; administration

政體　jeng-4 ti-3, system of government

政界　jeng-4 jye-4, government circles

政客　jeng-4 ke-4, politician (pejorative usage)

付	ノ	イ	仁	**FU-4**, to hand over; set The "thumb" (representing a hand) hands over something to the "man." 付清　　*fu-4 ching-1*, to clear, to pay off (an account, a debt) 付表決　*fu-4 byau-3 jywe-2*, to put to the vote of a parliamentary body
	付	付		
815 5 strokes				

府	丶	亠	广	**FU-3**, prefecture; palace 政府　　*jeng-4 fu-3*, government 府上　　*fu-3 shang-4*, (your) residence (polite expression)
	广	疒	庐	
816 8 strokes	府	府		

賈	一	丆	冖	**JYA-4**, price; **GU-3**, merchant; to sell The "cowrie" rad. gives the meaning here; *sya-4* "cover" (122, above) suggests the sound. 賈人　　*gu-3 ren-2*, merchant
	兩	兩	西	
817 13 strokes	胃	賈	賈	(貝　123)　　　　　　　　賈

價	ノ	イ	仁	**JYA-4**, price This is the same word as 817, above. The character is reclarified with "man." 價錢　　*jya-4 chyan-2*, price 原價　　*ywan-2 jya-4*, original price
	伒	価	価	
818 15 strokes	僧	價	價	价

彡	ノ	彡	彡	**SHAN-1**, streaks. STREAKS rad. (59) The character is a picture.
819 3 strokes				

188

影 820 15 strokes	丿 日 景	冂 旦 景	月 昌 影	YING-3, shadow, image, photograph 電影　*dyan-4 ying-3*, movie 陰影　*yin-1 ying-3*, shadow, shade 影射　*ying-3 she-4*, to counterfeit, to forge (京　299)
壬 821 4 strokes	丿 壬	二	千	REN-2, to carry on the shoulder; great; the ninth "heavenly stem" The character seems to show the "knight" rad. carrying some object (the "left" rad.) thrown over his shoulder. Originally the character was a picture of the standard carrying pole with an object fixed to each end for balance; at the center was the carrier.
任 822 6 strokes	丿 仁	亻 仟	亻 任	REN-4, to allow; term of office; responsibility; to employ; to endure 任用　*ren-4 yung-4*, to appoint 任免　*ren-4 myan-3*, hiring and firing 任命　*ren-4 ming-4*, appointment; nomination
何 823 7 strokes	丿 何 何	亻 何	亻 何	HE-2, what 任何　*ren-4 he-2*, any 何必　*he-2 bi-4*, Why must . . . ? 如何　*ru-4 he-2*, how? in what way? How about . . . ?
詳 824 13 strokes	丶 言 言	亠 言 詳	言 言 詳	SYANG-2, in detail; to know 詳談　*syang-2 tan-2*, to discuss in detail 詳情　*syang-2 ching-2*, detailed information 不詳　*bu-4 syang-2*, be unknown 详

189

細	㇂	幺	幺	**SYI-4, be fine, be thin** Note that the rads. in *syi-4* are the same as in *lei-4* 累 (29, above), but the position is different. Originally *syi-4* had "silk" + "head" = "hair"; therefore, "fine." "Head" was corrupted.
	幺	幺	糸	
825 11 strokes	約	細	細	詳細 *syang-2 syi-4*, be in detail 细

惜	㇒	㇚	小	**SYI-1, to pity** 可惜 *ke-3 syi-1*, unfortunately; Alas! 愛惜 *ai-4 syi-1*, to love and take care of
	忄一	忄艹	忄艹	
826 11 strokes	忄艹	惜	惜	

根	一	十	才	**GEN-1, root; square root; a measure for long, thin things** 根本 *gen-1 ben-3*, be basic, fundamental; from the beginning 根據 *gen-1 jyu-4*, to base something on; according to; basis 方根 *fang-1 gen-1*, square root
	木	杧	柙	
827 10 strokes	柤	根	根	

史	㇒	冂	口	**SHR-3, history; historian** In old forms, the bottom part of *shr-3* was a right hand (still discernible) holding "a case containing the bamboo slips on which history is written." The character now is classified in dictionaries under "mouth" (33, above).
	史	史		
828 5 strokes				

吏	一	一	亠	**LI-4, civil servant** *Li-4* originally was just a variant of *shr-3* (828, above). The student should learn to tell apart 828 and 829.
	亖	吏	吏	
829 6 strokes				

190

使	ノ	イ	イ	SHR-3, envoy; to use; to cause; with
	イ゠	イ゠	イ゠	使得 *shr-3 de-2*, to make; to cause; be able to use; be all right
830 8 strokes	使	使		大使 *da-4 shr-3*, ambassador 使命 *shr-3 ming-4*, mission, assignment

味	丶	口	口	WEI-4, flavor, odor; a measure for medicines and for courses (of a meal)
	口゠	口゠	口゠	味覺 *wei-4 jywe-2*, sense of taste 味官 *wei-4 gwan-1*, taste organs
831 8 strokes	味	味		氣味 *chi-4 wei-4*, smell, flavor

亂	ノ	乀	厶	LWAN-4, be disorderly, disorder
	厶	矞	矞	內亂 *nei-4 lwan-4*, civil war 亂首 *lwan-4 shou-3*, causes of a disorder; rebel leader
832 13 strokes	亂	亂	亂	亂眞 *lwan-4 jen-1*, be a good imitation (of a painting or sculpture) 乱

辰	ノ	厂	厂	PAI-4, branch off
	厎	厎	辰	The character is a picture of a stream dividing, from which comes the meaning "to branch off." The character 834, below, is now usually used in this sense.
833 6 strokes				

派	丶	丶	氵	PAI-4, to branch off; to appoint; school or sect; to levy; to distribute
	氵	氵	氵	派稅 *pai-4 shwei-4*, to levy taxes 黨派 *dang-3 pai-4*, political party
834 9 strokes	派	派	派	派出所 *pai-4 chu-1 swo-3*, precinct house

				JU-4, to help
助	㇑	冂	月	幫助　*bang-1 ju-4*, to help, help
	月	且	助	助手　*ju-4 shou-3*, assistant
835 7 strokes	助			助教　*ju-4 jyau-4*, teaching assistant

				SHE-4, to establish; if
設	、	亠	亖	設備　*she-4 bei*, equipment
	言	言	言	設立　*she-4 li-4*, to set up
836 11 strokes	訁	設	設	設法　*she-4 fa-3*, to figure out a way; to try to　　設

				YI-1, to heal
醫	一	三	医	醫生　*yi-1 sheng*, medical doctor
	医	医	殹	醫方　*yi-1 fang-1*, prescription (medical)
837 18 strokes	殹	醫	醫	醫學　*yi-1 sywe-2*, medical science (矢　63,　酉　363)　　　医

				YWAN-4, public building; courtyard; *yüan* (one of the five branches of the Chinese government)
院	㇇	了	阝	
	阝	阝	阝	電影院　*dyan-4 ying-3 ywan-4*, movie theater
				立法院　*li-4 fa-3 ywan-4*, the "Legislative Yüan"
838 10 strokes	阮	院	院	醫院　　*yi-1 ywan-4,* hospital

				FU-2, to serve; to swallow; be used to; clothes
服	㇒	几	月	衣服　*yi-1 fu-4*, clothes (note change from *fu-2* to *fu-4*)
	月	肌	服	說服　*shwo-1 fu-2*, to convince
839 8 strokes	服	服		服從　*fu-2 tsung-2*, to obey

	ㄱ	▽	ㄲ
矛	予	矛	

840
5 strokes

MAU-2, spear. SPEAR rad. (110)

This character is a picture of a spear. The student should learn to distinguish the "spear" rad. from yu-2 "to give; I" 予 (692, above).

	▽	予	矛
務	矛'	矛'	敄
	敄	敄	務

841
11 strokes

WU-4, affairs; must

务

務必　wu-4 bi-4, without fail

服務　fu-2 wu-4, to serve, service

外務　wai-4 wu-4, foreign affairs

	⺌	⺍	⺣
精	米	米=	料
	料	精	精

842
14 strokes

JING-1, essence, spirit, sperm; very; to be skillful; be essential, pure; be smart

精神　jing-1 shen-1, spirit, vitality

精明　jing-1 ming-2, be shrewd

精通　jing-1 tung-1, to know very well

	ㄑ	么	女
奴	奴	奴	

843
5 strokes

NU-2, handmaiden, slave

The character combines meanings.

奴才　nu-2 tsai-2, slave

奴性　nu-2 sying-4, be servile, servile disposition

	ㄑ	么	女
努	奴	奴	努
	努		

844
7 strokes

NU-3, to strive, to work hard at

努力　nu-3 li-4, "put your back into it," effort

努着　nu-3 jwo-2, to hurt oneself through overexertion

193

	ノ	亡	台	**DUNG-4, to move**
動				活動 *hwo-4 dung-4*, be active, activity
	台	自	重	動機 *dung-4 ji-1*, motive, intention
845				動員 *dung-4 ywan-2*, to mobilize (troops), mobilization
11 strokes	重	動	動	动

	宀	艹	生	**KAU-4, to lean on, to depend on**
靠				可靠 *ke-3 kau-4*, be reliable
	牛	告	告	靠近 *kau-4 jin-4*, be near to
				靠背 *kau-4 bei-4*, chair back
846	靠	靠	靠	
15 strokes				(非 654)

	彳	又		**YIN-3, to march. MARCH rad. (54)**
廴				*Yin-3* is a picture of a man marching out. The student should be careful to distinguish "march" from the form ⻍ of the "halt" rad. (171, above).
847				
3 strokes				

	⁊	ヨ	ヨ	**JYAN-4, to set up; Fukien**
建				建設 *jyan-4 she-4*, to build, to build up
	聿	圭	聿	建立 *jyan-4 li-4*, to establish
				建造 *jyan-4 dzau-4*, to build, to make
848	建	建		
9 strokes				

	⌐	丬	丬	**CHYANG-1, bed. BED rad. (90)**
爿				This rad. is a picture of a bed. The student should learn to distinguish it from the "slice" rad. 片 (927, below).
	爿			
849				
4 strokes				

牆	㇄	丬	爿	CHYANG-2, wall
	爿	爿	爿	*Chyang-1* (849, above) gives the sound. The right half of this character used to be "wheat" (cp. 431, above) over a picture of "a double wall for storing grain."
850 17 strokes	牆	牆	牆	牆面 *chyang-2 myan-4*, be uneducated 墙

蒦	一	十	艹	HWO-4, to catch in hunting; to measure
	艹	艹	萑	The character shows a hand catching a bird. The bird either has a crest or is hidden in the grass. The meaning "to measure" is by sound-loan.
851 13 strokes (14 strokes)	萑	蒦	蒦	(隹 39)

護	丶	二	言	HU-4, to protect
	言	訂	評	保護 *bau-3 hu-4*, to protect 護士 *hu-4 shr-4*, nurse 救護 *jyou-4 hu-4*, to rescue, to save
852 20 strokes	謹	護	護	(言 38) 护

莫	一	十	艹	MU-4, evening; MWO-4, don't; no one
	艹	莒	莒	The old form had "grass-sun-grass": the sun in the grass; therefore, "evening, late." The bottom "grass" has been corrupted into "big." The meanings "don't" and "no one" are by sound-loan.
853 10 strokes	莒	莫	莫	莫非 *mwo-4 fei-1*, Is it possible that . . .?

模	一	十	才	MWO-2, pattern (pronounced MU-2 in some compounds); be indistinct
	木	杧	村	模子 *mu-2 dz-3*, mold, die 模樣 *mu-2 yang*, facial appearance, face 模表 *mwo-2 byau-3*, model, example
854 14 strokes (15 strokes)	楷	模	模	

修	亻	亻	仁	**SYOU-1**, to repair, to build; be long; to study This character is also written 修, whence its official count of 10 strokes. 修理 *syou-1 li-3*, to fix 修改 *syou-1 gai-3*, to revise 自修 *dz-4 syou-1*, to educate oneself; study period (in school)
	仆	仪	攸	
855 9 strokes (10 strokes)	攸	修	修	

省	丶	丿	小	**SHENG-3**, province; to save 省錢 *sheng-3 chyan-2*, be economical 省得 *sheng-3 de-2*, lest 河北省 *he-2 bei-3 sheng-3*, Hopei Province
	少	少	省	
856 9 strokes	省	省	省	

尺	ㄱ	コ	尸	**CHR-3**, a Chinese "foot" (about 14 English inches; pronounced CHR-2 in some compounds); ruler 尺寸 *chr-2 tswun*, size (in feet and inches) 市尺 *shr-4 chr-3*, Chinese standard foot 一根尺 *yi-4 gen-1 chr-3*, ruler
	尺			
857 4 strokes				

萈	一	十	艹	**HWAN-2**, mountain sheep with horns *Hwan-2* undoubtedly was a picture of the animal to which it refers.
	艹	苎	莧	
858 11 strokes (12 strokes)	莧	萈	萈	(見 214)

寬	丶	丷	宀	**KWAN-1**, be broad The dot is sometimes omitted when this character is written by hand. 寬大 *kwan-1 da-4*, be spacious; to fit loosely; be lenient 寬厚 *kwan-1 hou-4*, be generous 寬容 *kwan-1 rung-2*, to tolerate 寬
	宀	宀	宵	
859 14 strokes (15 strokes)	窟	寬	寬	

系 860 7 strokes	ノ	ᡭ	幺
	幺	糸	糸
	系		

SYI-4, to tie; department (of a college); system

社會學系 *she-4 hwei-4 sywe-2 syi-4*, sociology department

太陽系 *tai-4 yang-2 syi-4*, solar system

系數 *syi-4 shu-4*, coefficient

縣 861 16 strokes	丨	门	目
	旦	早	県
	県	縣	縣

SYAN-4, a *hsien* (administrative district, similar to a U.S. county)

縣長 *syan-4 jang-3*, magistrate of a *hsien*

縣令 *syan-4 ling-4*, magistrate of a *hsien*

(目 120)

县

| 公 862 4 strokes | ノ | 八 | 公 |
| | 公 | | |

GUNG-1, public; male; equitable; metric; "Mr."; grandfather

公尺 *gung-1 chr-3*, meter

公社 *gung-1 she-4*, commune

公使 *gung-1 shr-3*, minister (diplomatic)

哉 863 9 strokes	一	十	土
	士	吉	吉
	哉	哉	哉

DZAI-1; a sentence-final particle, expressing doubt or regret; Alas!

鐵 864 21 strokes	ノ	入	仐
	仐	金	鉅
	鐥	鐘	鐵

TYE-3, iron; be strong

鐵路 *tye-3 lu-4*, railroad

鐵軍 *tye-3 jyun-1*, strong army

鐵定 *tye-3 ding-4*, to decide definitely

铁

台	ㄥ	ㄙ	ㄙ
	台	台	
865 5 strokes			

YI-2, I, me; TAI-2; the name of a group of stars in Ursa Major

There is no helpful explanation of this character. It occurs fairly often in other characters to suggest the sound. Sometimes it indicates a *yi* sound, sometimes a *tai* sound, and sometimes a *jr* or *shr* sound.

治	丶	冫	氵
	氵	治	治
866 8 strokes	治	治	

JR-4, to govern; to heal, to treat

政治　*jeng-4 jr-4*, politics

治理　*jr-4 li-3*, to govern

治病　*jr-4 bing-4*, to treat an illness

吾	一	丁	五
	五	吾	吾
867 7 strokes	吾		

WU-2, I, me; a surname

吾人　*wu-2 ren-2*, we, us

吾愛　*wu-2 ai-4*, address to someone held in affection (translation of English "my dear")

吾兄　*wu-2 syung-1*, "you" (polite: to a friend)

語	丶	亠	亖
	言	言	訂
868 14 strokes	語	語	語

YU-3, language, speech

語言　*yu-3 yan-2*, language

國語　*gwo-2 yu-3*, *Kuo-yǔ* (the Chinese national language)

語法　*yu-2 fa-3*, grammar

语

弗	ㄱ	コ	弓
	弗	弗	
869 5 strokes			

FU-2, not; not willing

This character originally meant "rope" and was a picture of a piece of rope (the "bow" rad.) tying two things—now "left" and "down"—together. The meaning "not; not willing" comes by sound-loan.

費	ㄱ	⊐	弓	FEI-4, to waste; expense, fee
				費錢 *fei-4 chyan-2*, be expensive
	弗	弗	費	學費 *sywe-2 fei-4*, tuition
				費用 *fei-4 yung-4*, expense
870 12 strokes	費	費	費	(貝 123) 費

其	一	十	卄	CHI-2, his, her, its, their
				其實 *chi-2 shr-2*, The fact is . . .
	卄	甘	其	尤其是 *you-2 chi-2 shr-4*, especially
				其次 *chi-2 tsz-4*, next in order; second
871 8 strokes	其	其		

餘	丿	人	亼	YU-2, surplus, remainder
				其餘 *chi-2 yu-2*, the rest of it
	今	仺	食	餘數 *yu-2 shu-4*, balance, remainder; complement of a number
				餘閒 *yu-2 syan-2*, leisure, spare time
872 15 strokes	飠	飠	餘	(余 613) 余

勢	土	坴	夫	SHR-4, power; momentum; tendency
				勢力 *shr-4 li-4*, influence
	坴	坴乚	執	時勢 *shr-2 shr-4*, current situation
				勢派 *shr-4 pai-4*, scale; aspect, conditions
873 13 strokes	執	執	勢	(坴 675) 势

範	丿	广	斤	FAN-4, pattern; rule
				模範 *mwo-2 fan-4*, model
	斤斤	竹	竹	範本 *fan-4 ben-3*, textbook of examples or models
874 15 strokes	軍	範	範	(車 412) 范

199

韋	ㄱ	カ	土	WEI-2, to walk off, to walk in opposite directions; soft leather. WALK OFF rad. (178)
	孛	吾	吾	This character used to have "foot" as its top part and its bottom part with a circle in between; it was supposed to suggest two feet walking off in opposite directions.
875 9 strokes	韋	韋	韋	韦

圍	丨	冂	冋	WEI-2, to go around; circumference
	冋	円	同	範圍　fan-4 wei-2, scope, sphere 圍牆　wei-2 chyang-2, enclosing wall 桌圍　jwo-2 wei-2, curtain hung before a table
876 12 strokes	圍	圍	圍	囲

彼	ノ	ク	彳	BI-3, the other; he, she
	彳	彷	彴	彼此　bi-2 tsz-3, each other, mutually 彼處　bi-3 chu-4, (in) that place 彼等　bi-2 deng-3, they
877 8 strokes	彼	彼		

允	ㄥ	ㄙ	允	YUN-3, to consent; true, sincere
	允			允許　yun-2 syu-3, to permit, permission 允從　yun-3 tsung-2, to assent 允當　yun-3 dang-4, be suitable, satisfactory
878 4 strokes				

充	丶	亠	亡	CHUNG-1, to fill up; to pretend to be
	云	产	充	The student should distinguish this character from kang-4 "be high" 亢 (952, below). 充分　chung-1 fen-4, be adequate 冒充　mau-4 chung-1, to act falsely as, to impersonate 充足　chung-1 dzu-2, be sufficient
879 6 strokes				

統 880 12 strokes				TUNG-3, to control; all; succession

統 880 12 strokes

TUNG-3, to control; all; succession

總統 *dzung-2 tung-3*, president (of a government)

傳統 *chwan-2 tung-3*, tradition

統一 *tung-3 yi-1*, to unify, unity

统

推 881 11 strokes

TWEI-1, to push; to elect; to make excuses; to cut, to clip; to deduce

推行 *twei-1 sying-2*, to carry into operation

推動 *twei-1 dung-4*, to put into action; to promote; to propel

推子 *twei-1 dz-3*, barber's clippers

答 882 12 strokes

DA-2, to answer; DA-1, answer

回答 *hwei-2 da-1*, answer, to answer

答應 *da-1 ying-4*, to answer; to agree to

答數 *da-2 shu-4*, answer (to a math problem)

貨 883 11 strokes

HWO-4, goods; currency

國貨 *gwo-2 hwo-4*, native products

洋貨 *yang-2 hwo-4*, imports

通貨 *tung-1 hwo-4*, currency

货

咸 884 9 strokes

SYAN-2, all; a surname

JYAN-3, decrease; "minus"

減少 *jyan-2 shau-3*, to decrease; to subtract

減價 *jyan-3 jya-4*, to cut prices; to hold a sale

五減三 *wu-3 jyan-3 san-1*, five minus three

885
12 strokes

(口 33)

SYING-2, form

形勢 *sying-2 shr-4*, appearance, condition of things; topographical

形容 *sying-2 rung-2*, to describe

情形 *ching-2 sying-2*, circumstances of a matter

886
7 strokes

SHENG-1, to ascend, to raise; Chinese dry quart (31.6 cubic inches); quart box

升子 *sheng-1 dz-3*, quart box

升學 *sheng-1 sywe-2*, be promoted to a higher school

一升米 *yi-4 sheng-1 mi-3*, quart of rice

887
4 strokes

DI-1, low, to lower

低頭 *di-1 tou-2*, to bow the head

低聲下氣 *di-1 sheng-1 sya-4 chi-4*, be meek

低地 *di-1 di-4*, lowlands

888
7 strokes

CHANG-2, be long. LONG rad. (168)

This form of the "long" rad. does not occur as an independent character; it occurs only as a part of characters. The student should be prepared, however, to recognize this form in characters as the "long" rad. The independent form has already been given: 長 (226, above).

889
7 strokes
(8 strokes)

降

890
10 strokes

JYANG-4, to descend; to lower; to demote; SYANG-2, to surrender; to control

降低 *jyang-4 di-1*, to drop

升降機 *sheng-1 jyang-4 ji-1*, elevator

下降 *sya-4 jyang-4*, to descend

昭

891
9 strokes

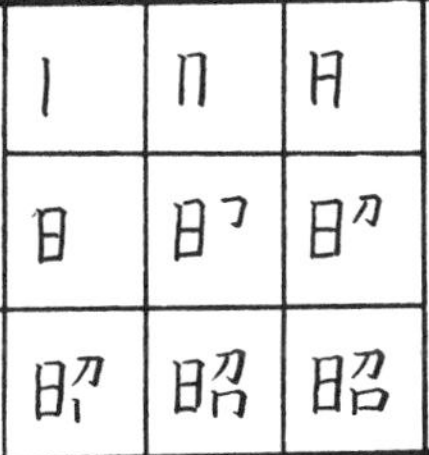

JAU-1, to shine

昭然 *jau-1 ran-2*, be clear, be evident

昭明 *jau-1 ming-2*, be bright

昭代 *jau-1 dai-4*, good times, a period of peace and prosperity

照

892
13 strokes

JAU-4, to reflect; to shine on; according to

按照 *an-4 jau-4*, according to . . .

照像 *jau-4 syang-4*, to take a photograph

護照 *hu-4 jau-4*, passport

忽

893
8 strokes

HU-1, suddenly; to neglect

忽然 *hu-1 ran-2*, all of a sudden

忽作忽止 *hu-1 dzwo-4 hu-1 jr-3*, starting and stopping, by fits and starts

忽忽 *hu-1 hu-1*, be confused, muddled

樂

894
15 strokes

YWE-4, music; LE-4, happiness

The character is a picture of musical paraphernalia—bells and so on—on a wooden stand (the "tree" rad.).

音樂 *yin-1 ywe-4*, music

快樂 *kwai-4 le-4*, be happy; happiness

乐

泉	ノ	⺅	白	**CHYWAN-2, a spring** The character is usually explained: "white" (for "pure") + "water" = "spring." 泉地 *chywan-2 di-4*, oasis 黄泉 *hwang-2 chywan-2*, "The Yellow Spring" (Hades)
	白	貞	身	
895 9 strokes	泉	泉		

線	く	幺	幺	**SYAN-4, thread, wire; clue** 八線 *ba-1 syan-4*, trigonometry 線人 *syan-4 ren-2*, stool pigeon 平行線 *ping-2 sying-2 syan-4*, parallel lines
	幺	幺	紗	
896 15 strokes	絁	綿	線	線

郵	ノ	二	千	**YOU-2, postal** 郵費 *you-2 fei-4*, postage 郵差 *you-2 chai-1*, mailman 郵件 *you-2 jyan-4*, mail
	壬	壬	垂	
897 11 strokes	垂	垂阝	郵	邮

局	⁊	⁊	尸	**JYU-2, office** 郵政局 *you-2 jeng-4 jyu-2*, post office 電報局 *dyan-4 bau-4 jyu-2*, telegraph office 電話局 *dyan-4 hwa-4 jyu-2*, telephone office
	尻	局	局	
898 7 strokes	局			

證	﹑	二	言	**JENG-4, proof, to prove; permit** 證據 *jeng-4 jyu-4*, proof 通行證 *tung-1 sying-2 jeng-4*, travel permit 證婚 *jeng-4 hwun-1*, to perform a wedding ceremony
	言	言	訂	
899 19 strokes	訟	諮	證	(登 712) 证

204

	、	⼋	宀
空	宀	宂	空
900 8 strokes	宆	空	

KUNG-1, be empty

The "cave" rad. gives the idea "be empty"; *gung-1* (443, above) suggests the sound.

空氣　*kung-1 chi-4*, air

太空員　*tai-4 kung-1 ywan-2*, astronaut

	⼃	⼓	勹
色	夕	多	色
901 6 strokes			

SE-4, color; looks; kind; desire; SHAI-3, color. COLOR rad. (139)

氣色　*chi-1 se-4*, complexion

足色　*dzu-2 se-4*, pure (of gold or silver)

好色　*hau-3 se-4*, be lustful

	⼁	冂	冏
困	用	困	困
902 7 strokes	困		

KWUN-4, difficulty, hardship; to trap; to maroon; to besiege; to sleep

The character is supposed to show a tree in a box, whence "difficulty."

困難　*kwun-4 nan-2*, be difficult, difficulty

困覺　*kwun-4 jyau-4*, to sleep

	氵	氵	汁
滿	汢	沽	滿
903 14 strokes	滿	滿	滿

MAN-3, be full

不滿　*bu-4 man-3*, be dissatisfied

滿足　*man-3 dzu-2*, to satisfy

滿意　*man-3 yi-4*, be satisfied

(氵 181)　　　満

	⼃	勹	勹
角	夕	角	角
904 7 strokes	角		

JYAU-3, horn; angle; corner; a measure for dimes; role; JYWE-2, role. HORN rad. (148)

The character is a picture of an animal's horn.

直角　*jr-2 jyau-3*, right angle

牛角　*nyou-2 jyau-3*, oxhorn

解

905
13 strokes

JYE-3, to loosen, to untie

解決　*jye-3 jywe-2*, to solve; to kill; solution

了解　*lyau-2 jye-3*, to understand

解放　*jye-3 fang-4*, to liberate

(刀　102)

組

906
11 strokes

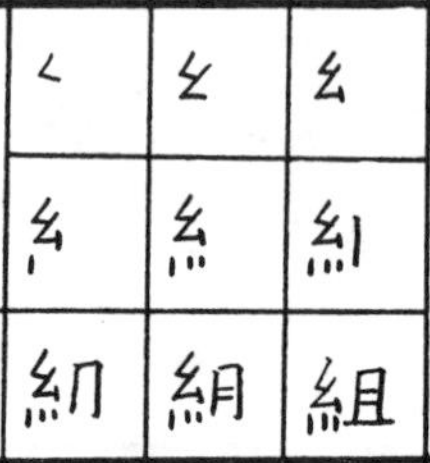

DZU-3, to organize; section, department

人事組　*ren-2 shr-4 dzu-3*, personnel department

組長　*dzu-2 jang-3*, section chief

組合　*dzu-3 he-2*, to consolidate; (mathematical) associations

组

織

907
18 strokes

JR-1, to weave

組織　*dzu-3 jr-1*, to organize, organization

(戠　525)

织

复

908
9 strokes

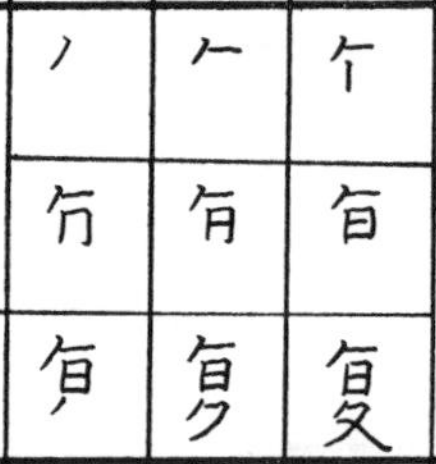

FU-2, to return

The "slow" rad. at the bottom is supposed to suggest the meaning of this character. The top part—now "left-one-sun"—once was a character that gave the sound. Compare 909, below.

復

909
12 strokes

FU-4, to return; to repeat; to reply

This is the same word as 908, above. The character is reclarified with the "step" rad.

復原　*fu-4 ywan-2*, to recover, to get better

復員　*fu-4 ywan-2*, to demobilize

复

衤	、	亠	礻	YI-4, gown. GOWN rad. (145)
	衤	衤		This form of the "gown" rad. occurs only as a part of characters. The student already has learned the independent form of "gown" (109, above). The student should distinguish this form of "gown" from the form of the "sign" rad. 礻 (480, above).
910 5 strokes (6 strokes)				

複	亠	礻	衤	FU-4, be complex; to repeat
	衤	衤	衤	重複 *chung-2 fu-4*, to duplicate 複寫紙 *fu-4 sye-3 jr-3*, carbon paper 複習 *fu-4 syi-2*, to review (e.g., school work)
911 14 strokes (15 strokes)	衤	複	複	复

雜	、	亠	亠	DZA-2, be mixed; be miscellaneous
	亣	杂	杂	複雜 *fu-4 dza-2*, be complex 雜貨 *dza-2 hwo-4*, sundries 雜亂 *dza-2 lwan-4*, be mixed up, be in disorder
912 18 strokes	新	雜	雜	(木 64, 隹 39) 杂

典	｜	冂	冃	DYAN-3, canon, canonic; to borrow or lend money on security of land or house
	由	曲	曲	字典 *dz-4 dyan-3*, dictionary of characters 典故 *dyan-3 gu-4*, classical allusion; historical background
913 8 strokes	典	典		

查	一	十	才	CHA-2, to investigate
	木	杢	杏	查病 *cha-2 bing-4*, be examined for disease 查字典 *cha-2 dz-4 dyan-3*, to look up in the dictionary 查點 *cha-2 dyan-3*, to check a list of goods
914 9 strokes	杳	查	查	

207

限

915
9 strokes

SYAN-4, limit

限定 *syan-4 ding-4*, to set a limit

限量 *syan-4 lyang-4*, limit; to estimate

有限 *you-3 syan-4*, be limited; "Ltd."

提

916
12 strokes

TI-2, to raise; to lift in the hand (pronounced DI-1 in some compounds)

提案 *ti-2 an-4*, to move (in a meeting); proposal

提出 *ti-2 chu-1*, bring up; to withdraw money

提前 *ti-2 chyan-2*, to move up (the date of an event)

肯

917
8 strokes

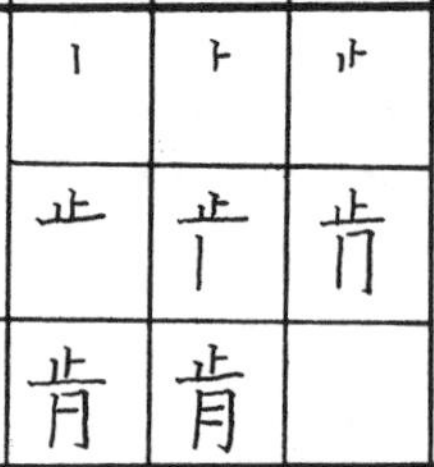

KEN-3, be willing (also read KENG-3)

肯定 *ken-3 ding-4*, to accept; to recognize (e.g., another nation)

冬

918
5 strokes

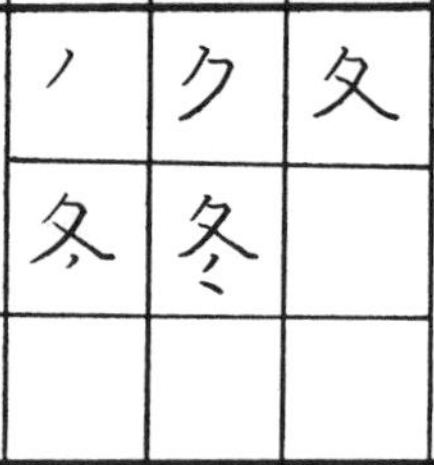

DUNG-1, winter

冬天 *dung-1 tyan-1*, winter; in winter

冬至 *dung-1 jr-4*, (at the time of) the winter solstice

冬令 *dung-1 ling-4*, winter

夏

919
10 strokes

SYA-4, summer

夏天 *sya-4 tyan-1*, (in) summer

夏至 *sya-4 jr-4*, summer solstice

夏令 *sya-4 ling-4*, summer

LENG-3, be cold

The "ice" rad. gives the meaning; *ling-4* (284, above) suggests the sound.

冷清 *leng-3 ching-1*, be lonely; be quiet and peaceful

冷貨 *leng-3 hwo-4*, unsalable goods

920
7 strokes

MIN-3, dish. DISH rad. (108)

The character is a picture. The student should be careful to distinguish "dish" from the "blood" rad. (922, below), from "net" 网 (637, above), and from "eye," 目 (132, above).

921
5 strokes

SYWE-3, blood. BLOOD rad. (143)

Sywe-3 is explained as a picture of a sacrificial dish with something in it. The "something in it" is represented in the modern character by the "left" rad. The student should note the warnings under 921, above, concerning rads. which are likely to be confused with this one.

922
6 strokes

CHYOU-2, prisoner

This character is a picture of a man in an enclosure, whence, "prisoner." The student should compare *chyou-2* to the bottom part of *he-2* "what?" 曷 (387, above) and note that they are not identical.

923
5 strokes

WEN-1, be kind

Wen-1 is "prisoner" over "dish," and the character is explained: "to feed a prisoner is to be kind." Usually written 昷.

924
10 strokes

209

溫	丶	冫	氵	**WEN-1, warm; review** Note that this character appears to be 924, above, reclarified with "water." 溫度 *wen-1 du-4*, temperature 溫習 *wen-1 syi-2*, review, study 溫泉 *wen-1 chywan-2*, hot spring
	氵	沪	泅	
925 13 strokes	浬	溫	溫	
該	丶	亠	言	**GAI-1, to owe; to be someone's turn; ought to; the said . . .** 應該 *ying-1 gai-1*, ought 該死 *gai-1 sz-3*, What a crime! Disgusting! 該我 *gai-1 wo-3*, It's my turn!
	言	訂	訂	
926 13 strokes	該	該	該	该
片	丿	丿	广	**PYAN-4, slice, to slice, piece; an expanse; PYAN-4, PYAN-1, card. SLICE rad. (91)** The student should distinguish the "slice" rad. from the "bed" rad. 爿 (849, above). 照片 *jau-4 pyan-4*, photograph
	片	片		
927 4 strokes				
肉	丨	冂	内	**ROU-4, meat; fruit pulp; be sluggish. MEAT rad. (130)** This is the form of the "meat" rad. that can occur as an independent character. The student has learned the form which may occur as a part of characters (326, above). This rad. is a picture of a piece of dried meat.
	内	肉	肉	
928 6 strokes				
星	丨	冂	日	**SYING-1, star, planet; a bit** 火星 *hwo-3 sying-1*, Mars 火星子 *hwo-3 sying-1 dz-3*, spark 星星 *sying-1 sying-1*, star
	日	昮	昇	
929 9 strokes	早	星	星	

210

期	一	十	甘	CHI-2, period; issue (of a magazine); to expect
	甘	且	其	星期 *sying-1 chi-2*, week
				期滿 *chi-2 man-3*, to expire
930 12 strokes	其	期	期	期望 *chi-2 wang-4*, to look forward to

叚	フ	コ	尸	JYA-3, to borrow; fake
	尸	尸	尸	Note that the right side of this character is not the "club" rad. (183, above). *Jya-3* is classified in dictionaries under the "right hand" rad. 又.
931 9 strokes	叚	叚	叚	

假	丿	亻	亻	JYA-3, to borrow; fake; JYA-4, vacation
	亻	亻	作	This is 931, above, reclarified with the "man" rad.
				假意 *jya-3 yi-4*, with false intent
				假如 *jya-3 ru-2*, if
932 11 strokes	作	假	假	放假 *fang-4 jya-4*, to have a vacation

與	ㄅ	ㄉ	ㄢ	YU-3, to hand over; with
	伤	伤	伤	與其 *yu-3 chi-2*, rather than
				與黨 *yu-2 dang-3*, allied political parties, collaborating parties
933 13 strokes	伤	伤	與	與國 *yu-3 gwo-2*, nations on friendly terms with each other 与

舉	ㄅ	ㄉ	ㄢ	JYU-3, to lift; to begin; behavior; all
	伤	伤	伤	選舉 *sywan-3 jyu-3*, to elect, election
				舉動 *jyu-3 dung-4*, behavior
934 16 strokes	與	舉	舉	舉行 *jyu-3 sying-2*, to hold (e.g., a meeting) 举

211

義	、	゛	丷
	羊	主	主
935 13 strokes	羊	義	義

YI-4, meaning; right conduct; public; free

義士 *yi-4 shr-4*, martyr

主義 *ju-3 yi-4*, doctrine, -ism

義務 *yi-4 wu-4*, duty; without pay; open to all

义

被	、	゛	ネ
	ネ	ネ	ネ
936 10 strokes	初	袖	被

BEI-4, quilt; by (sign of agent in passive construction); to be (sign of passive construction)

被子 *bei-4 dz-3*, quilt

被告 *bei-4 gau-4*, the accused; defendant

被死 *bei-4 sz-3*, to get killed

利	ノ	二	千
	千	禾	利
937 7 strokes	利		

LI-4, interest (on money); profit; be sharp

淨利 *jing-4 li-4*, net profit

複利 *fu-4 li-4*, compound interest

利用 *li-4 yung-4*, to make use of

存	一	ナ	オ
	存	存	存
938 6 strokes			

TSWUN-2, to keep, to store; deposit

存在 *tswun-2 dzai-4*, to exist, existence

存在主義 *tswun-2 dzai-4 ju-3 yi-4*, existentialism

保存 *bau-3 tswun-2*, to preserve

肖	丨	丷	少
	少	肖	肖
939 7 strokes	肖		

SYAU-4, to look like

Printed 肖.

肖像 *syau-4 syang-4*, photograph, portrait (painted or carved)

肖照 *syau-4 jau-4*, photograph

212

消	、	ニ	シ	**SYAU-1**, to consume, to abolish; be necessary
	シ	シ	シ	取消　*chyu-3 syau-1*, to abolish
940 10 strokes	シ	消	消	消化　*syau-1 hwa*, to digest, digestion 消息　*syau-1 syi*, news, information

制	ノ	⼂	仁	**JR-4**, to measure, to regulate; institution, system
	乍	乍	伟	限制　*syan-4 jr-4*, limit, to limit
941 8 strokes	伟	制		專制　*jwan-1 jr-4*, be despotic 制度　*jr-4 du-4*, system

考	一	十	土	**KAU-3**, to test, be tested; exam
				大考　*da-4 kau-3*, final exam
	耂	老	考	考查　*kau-3 cha-2*, to investigate
942 6 strokes				考古　*kau-2 gu-3*, to do archaeological research

試	、	二	言	**SHR-4**, to try
	言	言	言	考試　*kau-3 shr-4*, to take or give an exam; exam
943 13 strokes	試	試	試	口試　*kou-3 shr-4*, oral exam 筆試　*bi-3 shr-4*, written exam (口　33)　　試

彡	ノ	入	今	**JEN-3**, thick hair
	今	今		The character shows a "man" rad. over the "streaks" rad. It is supposed to be a picture of a man with thick, heavy hair.
944 5 strokes				

	ㄥ	ㄙ	ㄙ	TSAN-1, to take part in; to refer, to consult; SHEN-1, ginseng; sea slug
參	ㄙ	乡	矣	參加 *tsan-1 jya-1*, to take part in 參考 *tsan-1 kau-3*, to consult, to consider 參觀 *tsan-1 gwan-1*, to sightsee at
945 11 strokes	矣	參	參	參

	一	厂	厅	BYAU-1, long hair. HAIR rad. (190)
髟	手	長	長	The "streaks" rad. stands for hair; the "long" rad. gives the rest of the meaning.
946 10 strokes	髟	髟		

	ㄥ	ㄐ	ㄐ	JYANG-1, to take hold of; be about to, just; to nurture; JYANG-4, a general
將	爿	爿	爿	將就 *jyang-1 jyou*, to make do with; to compromise 將來 *jyang-1 lai-2*, in the future
947 11 strokes	將	將	將	少將 *shau-3 jyang-4*, rear admiral, major general　將

	丶	冖	罒	SHU-3, caterpillar
蜀	四	罒	罒	The oldest form of this character did not have the "bug" rad. in it and was a simple picture of a caterpillar. Some scribe re-clarified it with a "bug," and then, later on, another re-reclarified it with another bug. The common form now is 蠋.
948 13 strokes	蜀	蜀	蜀	(虫　641)

	乛	冖	尸	SHU-3, to belong to; genus, family; be subordinate
屬	屏	犀	属	屬於 *shu-3 yu-2*, to belong to; be tantamount to 屬國 *shu-3 gwo-2*, dependent territories; colonies
949 21 strokes	屬	屬	屬	屬性 *shu-3 sying-4*, qualities, attributes　屬

畢	丶	冂	曰	**BI-4, to finish**
				畢完 *bi-4 wan-2*, to finish
	旦	咠	咠	畢業 *bi-4 ye-4*, to graduate
				畢肖 *bi-4 syau-4*, be identical, exactly alike
950 11 strokes	昆	畢	畢	毕

拾	一	十	扌	**SHR-2, to pick up; to find; ten** This is a form of 十 used in accounting.
	扩	扒	扲	
951 9 strokes	拴	拾	拾	

亢	丶	亠	亠	**KANG-4, be high, to go high** The student should distinguish this character from *chung-1* "fill up" 充 (879 above).
	亢			
952 4 strokes				

航	丿	丆	丬	**HANG-2, to sail, to navigate**
				航空 *hang-2 kung-1*, air-, aeronautical, aeronautics
	舟	舟	舟	航行 *hang-2 sying-2*, to sail, to fly, to navigate
953 10 strokes	舟'	舟冖	航	航線 *hang-2 syan-4*, shipping route, flight route

旅	亠	亣	方	**LYU-3, to travel; troops, brigade**
				旅社 *lyu-3 she-4*, inn
	方'	方'	方冘	旅行 *lyu-3 sying-2*, to take a trip, to travel
954 10 strokes	斻	斻	旅	旅長 *lyu-2 jang-3*, brigade commander

急	ノ	ケ	刍	**JI-2**, be hurried; be upset; be urgent 急忙 *ji-2 mang-2*, be hassled, busy 急性 *ji-2 sying-4*, acute (said of a disease) 急難 *ji-2 nan-2*, desperate situation, emergency
	刍	刍	刍	
955 9 strokes	急	急	急	

寄	丶	丷	宀	**JI-4**, to mail, to send; to entrust; to dwell 寄存 *ji-4 tswun-2*, to deposit, deposits 寄生 *ji-4 sheng-1*, be parasitic 寄身 *ji-4 shen-1*, to stop at a place; to lodge
	宀	宀	宊	
956 11 strokes	宊	寄	寄	

票	一	一	一	**PYAU-4**, ticket, stamp, bank note, check, document; vote 支票 *jr-1 pyau-4*, check 郵票 *you-4 pyau-4*, postage stamp 傳票 *chwan-2 pyau-4*, summons (legal)
	西	西	西	
957 11 strokes	票	票	票	

布	一	ナ	右	**BU-4**, cotton cloth; to publish 一疋布 *yi-4 pi-3 bu-4*, piece of cloth 布西曼 *bu-4 syi-1 man-4*, Bushmen (a transliteration) 布景 *bu-4 jing-3*, stage scenery
	右	布		
958 5 strokes				

奐	ノ	勹	宀	**HWAN-4**, be loose
	台	奂	奂	
959 9 strokes	奂	奐	奐	

216

	`	冂	口
唤	口´	口⁷	吶

960
12 strokes

| 叨 | 唤 | 唤 |

HWAN-4, to call out

In this character, *hwan-4* (959, above) gives the sound; the "mouth" rad. gives the meaning.

唤起 *hwan-4 chi-3*, to incite, to stir up

	一	扌	才
换	扩	扩⁷	扨

961
12 strokes

| 扬 | 换 | 换 |

HWAN-4, to exchange

换錢 *hwan-4 chyan-2*, to change money

改换 *gai-3 hwan-4*, to change

對换 *dwei-4 hwan-4*, to exchange

	`	亠	六
啇	六	产	产

962
11 strokes

| 产 | 啇 | 啇 |

DI-1, stem, base

The student should distinguish this character from *shang-1* "merchant" 商 (622, above).

(口 33)

	亠	六	产
適	产	啇	啇

963
14 strokes

| 滴 | 滴 | 適 |

SHR-4, to reach; be suitable

適當 *shr-4 dang-4*, be proper, be suitable

合適 *he-2 shr-4*, be appropriate

適法 *shr-4 fa-3*, legal, according to the law

适

	一	卄	廿
鞋	苫	苣	革

964
15 strokes

| 革⁺ | 革± | 鞋 |

SYE-2, shoe

布鞋 *bu-4 sye-2*, cloth shoes

皮鞋 *pi-2 sye-2*, leather shoes

鞋底 *sye-2 di-3*, shoe sole

(口 33, 土 86)

217

德	ノ	ク	彳	**DE-2**, virtue; personal energy 德國　*de-2 gwo-2*, Germany 德政　*de-2 jeng-4*, good government that benefits the people 德行　*de-2 sying-4*, good conduct; good character
	彳十	彳古	彳声	
965 15 strokes	德	德	德	(▥　132)

彦	`	亠	文	**YAN-4**, decoration Note that *yan-4* is composed of the "pattern" rad., the "slope" rad., and the "streaks" rad. The relevance of "pattern" and "streaks" to "decoration" is clear enough; the "slope" rad. originally was part of the decoration and did not mean "slope."
	立	产	产	
966 9 strokes	彦	彦		

顏	文	产	彦	**YAN-2**, color; face The "head" rad. gives the meaning; *yan-4* (966, above) suggests the sound. 容顏　*rung-2 yan-2*, face; expression 顏色　*yan-2 se-4*, color 顏面　*yan-2 myan-4*, face
	彦丆	彦丙	彦百	
967 18 strokes	彦百	顏	顏	顔

係	ノ	亻	亻	**SYI-4**, to connect; be related; to be 關係　*gwan-1 syi-4*, relationship, relevance 係數　*syi-4 shu-4*, coefficient (mathematics)
	伙	俆	係	
968 9 strokes	係	係	係	系

烟	`	丷	少	**YAN-1**, smoke; tobacco, cigarette 烟袋　*yan-1 dai-4*, pipe (for tobacco) 烟子　*yan-1 dz-3*, soot 烟鬼　*yan-1 gwei-3*, opium addict
	火	灯	炉	
969 10 strokes	烟	烟	烟	

218

租	丶	乙	千	**DZU-1, rent, to rent** In China, rent traditionally was land rent and was paid in grain, hence the "grain" rad. in *dzu-1*. 租借　*dzu-1 jye-4*, to lease 租戶　*dzu-1 hu-4*, tenant
	矛	禾	利	
970 10 strokes	和	租	租	

需	宀	雨	雨	**SYU-1, to need** 需要　*syu-1 yau-4*, to need, need 必需　*bi-4 syu-1*, must 需求　*syu-1 chyou-2*, to require, to demand
	雨	雫	雫	
971 14 strokes	雫	需	需	(雨　283)

廣	亠	广	广	**GWANG-3, be broad** 廣東　*gwang-3 dung-1*, Canton 廣告　*gwang-3 gau-4*, advertisement 廣大　*gwang-3 da-4*, be big, massive
	庐	庐	庐	广
972 15 strokes	庐	廣	廣	(黃　604)

值	丿	亻	仁	**JR-2, be worth, to have a (certain) value** Usually printed 值. 值錢　*jr-2 chyan-2*, be worth some money, be valuable 值得　*jr-2 de-2*, be worth; be worthwhile 價值　*jya-4 jr-2*, price
	什	佶	佶	
973 10 strokes	佶	佶	值	

俞	丿	入	亼	**YU-2, to say "yes"; a surname** Usually printed 兪.
	仐	合	合	
974 9 strokes	俞	俞	俞	

219

偷	ノ	亻	亻
	亻	伶	伶
975 11 strokes	偷	偷	偷

TOU-1, to steal

偷偷的   *tou-1 tou-1 de*, stealthily, on the sly

偷看   *tou-1 kan-4*, to steal a look at; to look at surreptitiously

偷閒   *tou-1 syan-2*, to loaf, to shirk

戎	一	二	宁
	示	戎	戎
976 6 strokes			

RUNG-2, weapons of war, arms

This character is a meaning-meaning compound. The student will recognize the right half, of course, as the "lance" rad. The other part—"one" + "left" in the modern character—is supposed to be armor: "armor" + "lance" = "weapons of war, arms."

賊	丨	冂	目
	貝	貝	貝
977 13 strokes	貯	賊	賊

DZEI-2, thief; extremely

作賊   *dzwo-4 dzei-2*, to thieve, be a thief

有賊   *you-3 dzei-2*, Thief!

賊冷   *dzei-2 leng-3*, be very cold

賊

苟	一	ㄱ	ㄗノ
	屮	艹	芍
978 9 strokes	芍	苟	苟

GOU-3, if

This character used to mean "grass," and the "grass" rad. gave the meaning; the rest of the character, *jyu-4* (289, above), gave the sound. Now this character is used by sound-loan for "if."

敬	一	ㄱ	ㄗノ
	屮	芍	苟
979 13 strokes	苟ㄴ	敬ㄅ	敬

JING-4, to revere

敬重   *jing-4 jung-4*, to respect a person

敬愛   *jing-4 ai-4*, to honor

敬禮   *jing-4 li-3*, to salute; salutation, formal greeting

警	⺀	⺍	芍	JING-3, to warn
	苟	敬	敬	*Jing-3* combines meanings: "words" used to induce "reverence, caution" = "warn."
980 20 strokes	警	警	警	警告 *jing-3 gau-4*, to warn, warning 警報 *jing-3 bau-4*, danger signal (言 38)

察	﹑	丷	宀	CHA-2, to investigate
	宀	宀	宛	警察 *jing-3 cha-2*, policeman 警察局 *jing-3 cha-2 jyu-2*, police station
981 13 strokes	宛	察	察	察看 *cha-2 kan-4*, to look into (示 807)

銀	ノ	人	合	YIN-2, silver
	全	金	金ヨ	銀子 *yin-2 dz-3*, silver 銀行 *yin-2 hang-2*, bank
982 14 strokes	銀	銀	銀	定銀 *ding-4 yin-2*, deposit 银

彳	ノ	彳	彳	CHWO-4, halt. HALT rad. (162)
	彳	彳	糸	The "halt" rad. originally was a picture of a foot halted at a crossroads. Compare the form of "halt" which you have already learned (171, above). The form here is the form which can occur as an independent character.
983 7 strokes	彳			

銅	ノ	人	合	TUNG-2, brass, copper, bronze
	全	金	金	黃銅 *hwang-2 tung-2*, brass, bronze 紅銅 *hung-2 tung-2*, copper
984 14 strokes	釘	釘	銅	銅像 *tung-2 syang-4*, bronze statue (口 33) 铜

221

苦	一	十	艹	**KU-3**, be bitter
	艹	芊	苦	吃苦　　*chr-1 ku-3*, to suffer 苦處　　*ku-3 chu-4*, hardship 用苦心　*yung-4 ku-3 syin-1*, "put your back" 　　　　into a job, to exert yourself
985 8 strokes (9 strokes)	苦	苦		

約	乡	纟	纟	**YWE-1**, to agree
	纟	糸	糸	約會　*ywe-1 hwei-4*, to invite 條約　*tyau-2 ywe-1*, treaty 約定　*ywe-1 ding-4*, to agree to
986 9 strokes	紀	約	約	約

堂	l	⺍	⺌	**TANG-2**, hall; a measure for classes
	⺌	尚	尚	講堂　　*jyang-3 tang-2*, lecture hall 教堂　　*jyau-4 tang-2*, church 一堂中文　*yi-4 tang-2 jung-1 wen-2*, Chinese 　　　　language class
987 11 strokes	堂	堂	堂	

躬	ノ	亻	勹	**GUNG-1**, the body
	自	身	身	The "body" rad. gives the meaning in this character; *gung-1* (218, above) gives the sound. 躬親　*gung-1 chin-1*, personally, in person, 　　　oneself
988 10 strokes	身	身	躬	

窮	、	⼙	宀	**CHYUNG-2**, be poor, impoverished
	宀	穴	穷	窮苦　*chyung-2 ku-3*, be very poor 窮忙　*chyung-2 mang-2*, be busy without 　　　purpose 窮說　*chyung-2 shwo-1*, to talk nonsense
989 15 strokes	窮	窮	窮	穷

静	ニ	‡	主	JING-4, be quiet
				安静 *an-1 jing-4*, be quiet
				静電 *jing-4 dyan-4*, static electricity
	青	青	青'	静観 *jing-4 gwan-1*, contemplation
990 16 strokes	青'	静'	静	(青 198, 爭 618)

興	イ	午	臼	SYING-4, be happy; SYING-1, to begin
				高興 *gau-1 sying-4*, be happy
	臼	臼	同	興建 *sying-1 jyan-4*, to rebuild
				興業銀行 *sying-1 ye-4 yin-2 hang-2*, industrial bank
991 16 strokes	同	興	興	兴

草	一	十	艹	TSAU-3, grass
				The "grass" rad. gives the meaning; *dzau-3* (438, above) suggests the sound.
	艹	艻	苎	草地 *tsau-3 di-4*, lawn
				草帽 *tsau-3 mau-4*, straw hat
992 9 strokes (10 strokes)	苩	萛	草	草字 *tsau-3 dz-4*, cursive script

雪	一	⎜	一	SYWE-3, snow
				下雪 *sya-4 sywe-3*, It's snowing; snowfall
	示	示	雨	雪花 *sywe-3 hwa-1*, snowflake
				雪車 *sywe-3 che-1*, sled
993 11 strokes	雪	雪	雪	

鳥	ノ	イ	竹	NYAU-3, bird. BIRD rad. (196)
				The "bird" rad. is a picture of a bird.
	阜	阜	鳥	鳥叫 *nyau-3 jyau-4*, bird cries, birdsong
				鳥里 *nyau-3 li-3*, a *li* (one-third of a mile) "as the crow flies"
994 11 strokes	鳥	鳥	鳥	鸟

223

場	一	十	土	CHANG-3, field; a measure for events of various kinds; CHANG-2; a measure for spells or periods of things
				市場 shr-4 chang-3, marketplace
	圹	坦	坦	飛機場 fei-1 ji-1 chang-3, airfield
995 **12 strokes**	場	場	場	(易 686) 场

圖	丨	冂	冋	TU-2, picture, map, diagram
				圖書館 tu-2 shu-1 gwan-3, library
	冋	昷	咼	地圖 di-4 tu-2, map
				草圖 tsau-3 tu-2, rough sketch or diagram
996 **14 strokes**	咼	圖	圖	(口 33) 图

彑	乚	彑	彑	JI-4, pig's head. PIG'S HEAD rad. (58)
				The student already has learned one form of this rad. (80, above). Here, the horizontal stroke across the bottom is supposed to be the ground; the pig's head rises above it. Common variant 彐. Compare ywan-2 (p. 253).
997 **3 strokes**				

彔	乚	彑	彑	LU-4, prosperity
				The explanations we have of this character are not helpful. The student will simply have to remember that "pig's head" over "water" = lu-4 "prosperity." The character is now used only as a part of characters to give the sound.
	彐	彔	彔	
998 **8 strokes**	彔	彔		

綠	乚	幺	幺	LYU-4, be green
				草綠 tsau-3 lyu-4, grass green
	糸	絲	絲	綠豆 lyu-4 dou-4, lentils
				綠氣 lyu-4 chi-4, chlorine
999 **14 strokes**	綠	綠	綠	綠

俄	ノ	亻	亻'
1000 9 strokes	亻一	仁	仔
	俄	俄	俄

E-2; used to write foreign words

俄亥俄　　*e-2 hai-4 e-2*, Ohio

俄國　　　*e-2 gwo-2*, Russia

俄國革命　*e-2 gwo-2 ge-2 ming-4*, Russian revolution

害	丶	ヽ	宀
1001 10 strokes	宀	宀	宔
	宔	害	害

HAI-4, to harm

害病　*hai-4 bing-4*, to get sick

害怕　*hai-4 pa-4*, to get scared

害命　*hai-4 ming-4*, to murder

柬	一	亠	亓
1002 9 strokes	両	両	両
	束	束	柬

JYAN-3, to select

The character combines meanings. It is composed of "bundle" 束 (657, above) + two dots resembling the "eight" rad. (88, above). The two dots mean "to divide," and the character is explained: "to divide a bundle; therefore, 'to select.'"

練	ㄥ	纟	幺
1003 15 strokes	纟	纟	纟ㄅ
	纟罒	絆	練

LYAN-4, to practice

練習　*lyan-4 syi-2*, practice, to practice

練字　*lyan-4 dz-4*, to study Chinese characters

練實　*lyan-4 shr-2*, bamboo seeds

练

秝	ノ	彳	千
1004 10 strokes	千	禾	禾'
	禾一	秆	秝

LI-4, to set up at regular intervals; to set up and space out

The character's two "grain" rads. are intended to suggest the regular spacing of the plants in a field of grain.

225

麻	一	厂	厂	**LI-4, to pass through** In rural China, the main routes of passage across the countryside are roads or paths on the dikes that crisscross the paddies. It is perhaps for this reason that the "slope" rad. is in *li-4* "to pass through," while the two "grain" rads. suggest the paddy.
	厂	厈	厈	
1005 **12 strokes**	厤	厤	麻	

曆	一	厂	厂	**LI-4, to calculate the course of heavenly bodies as they pass through the Zodiac; to make a calendar; to calculate** 陽曆 *yang-2 li-4*, solar calendar 陰曆 *yin-1 li-4*, lunar calendar
	厈	厤	厤	
1006 **16 strokes**	曆	曆	曆	历

歷	一	厂	厂	**LI-4, to pass through** Compare 1005, above. The character is re-clarified with the "toe" rad. 歷史 *li-4 shr-3*, history 經歷 *jing-1 li-4*, experience, to experience
	厤	厤	厤	
1007 **16 strokes**	歷	歷	歷	历

私	丿	厶	千	**SZ-1, private** 私事 *sz-1 shr-4*, personal affair 私立 *sz-1 li-4*, privately run (like a private school or hospital) 自私 *dz-4 sz-1*, be selfish
	千	禾	私	
1008 **7 strokes**	私			

斗	丶	二	二	**DOU-3, unit of volume equal to 316 cubic inches, usually translated as "peck." PECK rad. (68)** *Dou-3* is a picture of the old scoop or measure which was used to measure out "pecks."
	斗			
1009 **4 strokes**				

科	`丶`	`二`	`千`	**KE-1**, category
	`千`	`禾`	`禾`	科學 *ke-1 sywe-2*, science
1010 9 strokes	`禾^一`	`禾^二`	`科`	科長 *ke-1 jang-3*, department chief (in a government office) 中文科 *jung-1 wen-2 ke-1*, Chinese literature department

痛	`丶`	`二`	`广`	**TUNG-4**, to ache
	`广`	`疒`	`疒`	頭痛 *tou-2 tung-4*, to have a headache
1011 12 strokes	`疒`	`病`	`痛`	痛苦 *tung-4 ku-3*, be unhappy 痛快 *tung-4 kwai-4*, be happy (甬 715)

堯	`一`	`十`	`土`	**YAU-2**, be high
	`圭`	`圭圭`	`圭圭`	It may help the student to remember this character if he thinks of it as "earth piled on earth" to suggest "high." The character is most often seen as the name of the Emperor Yao (reigned 2357–2255 B.C.), a Chinese "culture hero."
1012 12 strokes	`堯`	`堯`		堯

燒	`丶`	`丷`	`少`	**SHAU-1**, to burn
	`火`	`火⁺`	`火土`	燒飯 *shau-1 fan-4*, to cook a meal
1013 16 strokes	`燒`	`燒`	`燒`	發燒 *fa-1 shau-1*, to have a fever 燒開水 *shau-1 kai-1 shwei-3*, to boil water 燒

曉	`丨`	`冂`	`日`	**SYAU-3**, be clear; dawn; to understand
	`日⁺`	`日±`	`日圭`	曉得 *syau-3 de-2*, to know, to know of
1014 16 strokes	`曉`	`曉`	`曉`	曉示 *syau-3 shr-4*, to proclaim 曉了 *syau-2 lyau-3*, to understand 曉

227

	一	十	才	**JYAN-3**, to look into
檢	木	朴	松	檢查　*jyan-3 cha-2*, to examine 檢察官　*jyan-3 cha-2 gwan-1*, district attorney 檢校　*jyan-3 jyau-4*, to investigate
1015 17 strokes	槍	檢	檢	检

	一	十	艹	**YAU-4**, medicine
藥	芀	首	菹	吃藥　*chr-1 yau-4*, to take medicine 藥房　*yau-4 fang-2*, drugstore 西藥　*syi-1 yau-4*, Western (non-Chinese) medicine
1016 18 strokes (19 strokes)	蕬	藥	藥	(白 231, 幺 25)　药

	二	于	王	**CHYOU-2**, ball
球	王`	圲	玨	打球　*da-3 chyou-2*, to play ball 球場　*chyou-2 chang-3*, ball field 地球　*di-4 chyou-2*, the earth
1017 11 strokes	珏	球	球	

	丨	门	門	**YWAN-2**, garden, park
園	冑	肁	肁	公園　*gung-1 ywan-2*, public park 花園　*hwa-1 ywan-2*, flower garden 園丁　*ywan-2 ding-1*, gardener
1018 13 strokes	園	園		(土 86, 口 33)　园

	丨	卜	上	**SYI-1**, crockery dish
盧	广	卢	虍	The "flask" rad. is in this character for meaning; the significance of the "tiger" rad. is uncertain. The Chinese were fond of making dishes in animal shapes, so a *syi-1* may once have been a tiger-shaped crockery dish; thus, the "tiger" rad. helps with the meaning.
1019 13 strokes	虘	盧	盧	(豆 453)

228

戲	⺊	广	庐
	虘	虘	盧
1020 **17 strokes**	戲	戲	戲	戏

SYI-4, (theater) play

Popular variant 戯.

京戲　*jing-1 syi-4*, Peking opera

聽戲　*ting-1 syi-4*, to attend a play

戲院　*syi-4 ywan-4*, theater

拉	一	十	扌
	扩	扩	拉
1021 **8 strokes**	拉	拉	

LA-1, to pull; used for foreign words

拉手　*la-1 shou-3*, to shake hands; to hold hands

拉皮條　*la-1 pi-2 tyau-2*, to pimp, to act as a procurer

拉丁　*la-1 ding-1*, Latin

隻	ノ	亻	仁
	佳	佳	隹
1022 **10 strokes**	隻	隻		只

JR-1; a measure for animals, birds, boats

一隻鳥　*yi-4 jr-1 nyau-3*, a bird

一隻船　*yi-4 jr-1 chwan-2*, a boat

隻身　*jr-1 shen-1*, oneself; alone

雙	ノ	亻	仁
	佳	佳	隹
1023 **18 strokes**	雔	雙	雙	双

SHWANG-1, pair; even (opposite of "odd")

雙數　*shwang-1 shu-4*, even number

雙身子　*shwang-1 shen-1 dz-3*, be pregnant

雙關　*shwang-1 gwan-1*, pun, "double-entendre"

邑	丨	冂	口
	吕	吕	吕
1024 **7 strokes**	邑		

YI-4, city. CITY rad. (163)

The student already has learned the form of "city" which occurs as a part of characters (136, above). The form here is the independent form of the rad.

集木	ノ	イ	亻	JI-2, to get together 集子 *ji-2 dz-3*, collection of writings 集會 *ji-2 hwei-4*, to gather, to assemble 集中 *ji-2 jung-1*, to concentrate
	仁	伴	佳	
1025 12 strokes	隹	隼	集	
疋虫	⁊	ア	⼇	DAN-4, egg 下蛋 *sya-4 dan-4*, to lay an egg 壞蛋 *hwai-4 dan-4*, a "bad egg" (that is, a bad person) 蛋白石 *dan-4 bai-2 shr-2*, opal
	疋	足	延	
1026 11 strokes	蛋	蛋	蛋	
誠	二	言	言	CHENG-2, be sincere 誠實 *cheng-2 shr-2*, be sincere, be honest 誠心 *cheng-2 syin-1*, be honest 誠意 *cheng-2 yi-4*, be honest, be sincere
	訂	訂	訴	
1027 13 strokes (14 strokes)	誠	誠	誠	诚
趣	一	十	土	CHYU-4, be interesting, be pleasant 有興趣 *you-3 sying-4 chyu-4*, be interested in 有趣 *you-3 chyu-4*, be interesting 趣味 *chyu-4 wei-4*, interest
	丰	走	赳	
1028 15 strokes	趄	趣	趣	(耳 201)
耒	ノ	二	三	LEI-3, plow. PLOW rad. (127) The character is a picture. Note that it appears to include the "tree" rad. The extra horizontal strokes are supposed to represent the blades of the plow.
	丰	耒	耒	
1029 6 strokes				

1030 9 strokes

FU-4, back; to carry on the back; negative; to turn one's back on, be ungrateful

Distinguish *fu-4* from *pin-2* "poor" 貧 (p. 254). Variant 負.

負號 *fu-4 hau-4*, minus sign

負約 *fu-4 ywe-1*, to break an agreement

1031 16 strokes

LAI-4, to rely on; to repudiate

賴婚 *lai-4 hwun-1*, to break an engagement

賴學 *lai-4 sywe-2*, to cut classes

賴皮 *lai-4 pi-2*, person with no honor, no sense of shame

1032 19 strokes

LAN-3, be lazy

偷懶 *tou-1 lan-3*, to shirk, be lazy

懶几 *lan-2 ji-3*, book holder, reader's book support

懶洋洋 *lan-3 yang-2 yang-2*, not in any hurry (about doing something)

1033 10 strokes

SYI-1, "big belly"; used as a sound-loan

The "big" rad. at the bottom gives the meaning of this character. The rest of the character, "claws" + "coil," once gave the sound. *Syi-1* now is used as a sound-loan for various words: who? what? why? the name of an old Tartar tribe; etc.

1034 21 strokes

JI-1, chicken

Syi-1 (1033, above) is supposed to give the sound in this character; the "bird" rad. gives the meaning.

公鷄 *gung-1 ji-1*, rooster

鷄蛋 *ji-1 dan-4*, egg

(鳥 994)

計	丶	亠	亠	**JI-4**, to calculate, to reckon
				定計　　*ding-4 ji-4*, to devise a plan
	言	言	言	計算　　*ji-4 swan-4*, to compute
				計算機　*ji-4 swan-4 ji-1*, computer, calculator
1035 9 strokes	言	計	計	計

枼	一	十	廿	**YE-4**, foliage
				Ye-4 is a picture of a tree; the strokes at the top represent its foliage.
	廿	世	世	
1036 9 strokes	芽	芽	枼	

葉	一	十	艹	**YE-4**, leaf; generation; a surname
				This is the same word as 1036, above. The character is reclarified with the "grass" rad. This form is the form in common use today; 1036, above, is seldom seen.
	艹	芒	苎	
				葉片　*ye-4 pyan-4*, leaf
1037 12 strokes (13 strokes)	苫	苫	葉	叶

劃	フ	㇇	ヨ	**HWA-4**, to mark; to cut, to engrave
				計劃　*ji-4 hwa-4*, to plan, plan
	肀	聿	書	劃分　*hwa-4 fen-1*, to cut apart; to dissociate
				劃定　*hwa-4 ding-4*, to determine, to delimit (e.g., boundaries)
1038 14 strokes	畫	畫	劃	划

團	丨	冂	冂	**TWAN-2**, corps, club; a measure for round things
				團體　*twan-2 ti-3*, organization
	同	同	車	團結　*twan-2 jye-2*, to unite
				一團絲　*yi-4 twan-2 sz-1*, ball of silk
1039 14 strokes	團	團	團	团

享	丶	二	亠
1040 8 strokes	亩	亩	亨
	亨	享	

SYANG-3, to offer a sacrifice; to receive

The character is a picture of "a dish on which cooked food was offered as a sacrifice; the lid is on." This character is very much like the "flask" rad. 豆 (453, above).

享受 *syang-3 shou-4*, to receive

孰	丶	二	亩
1041 11 strokes	亨	亨	享
	乳	孰	孰

SHU-2, cooked, be done; who? which?

The basic meaning of this character is "be cooked, be done." The meaning "who? which?" occurs by sound-loan.

孰與 *shu-2 yu-3*, why? what need to?

孰誰 *shu-2 shei-2*, who? whom?

熟	二	亩	亨
1042 15 strokes	享	乳	孰
	孰	熟	熟

SHU-2, cooked, be done; be ripe; be very familiar with (also pronounced SHOU-2)

This character and 1041, above, originally stood for the same word; the character is reclarified here with "fire dots."

熟貨 *shou-2 hwo-4*, manufactured goods (opposite of raw materials)

熟鐵 *shou-2 tye-3*, wrought iron

油	丶	冫	氵
1043 8 strokes	沪	油	油
	油	油	

YOU-2, oil

石油 *shr-2 you-2*, petroleum

牛油 *nyou-2 you-2*, butter

汽油 *chi-4 you-2*, gasoline

香	丿	二	千
1044 9 strokes	禾	禾	禾
	香	香	香

SYANG-1, be fragrant; incense, scent.
SCENT rad. (186)

Syang-1 originally had "grain" over "sweet" and was a meaning-meaning compound. Now the "sweet" rad. has been changed to the "sun" rad.

香水 *syang-1 shwei-3*, perfume

233

齊	亠	亠	亣	**CHI-2**, to line up, to arrange; be even, be uniform. LINE-UP rad. (210) This rad. is supposed to be a picture of neatly arranged hairpins in a lady's coiffure. 齊集 *chi-2 ji-2*, to assemble
	亣	亣	亣	
1045 14 strokes	㳄	齊	齊	齐

濟	丶	冫	氵	**JI-4**, to help out; to complete 經濟 *jing-1 ji-4*, economy; be economical 經濟學 *jing-1 ji-4 sywe-2*, economics 經濟學家 *jing-1 ji-4 sywe-2 jya-1*, economist
	汸	汸	洆	
1046 17 strokes	漖	濟	濟	济

較	一	冂	曰	**JYAU-3**, to compare (also pronounced **JYAU-4**) 比較 *bi-2 jyau-3*, to compare 較量 *jyau-4 lyang-4*, to compare, to match; to contrast 較然 *jyau-4 ran-2*, be clear, be evident
	車	車	車	
1047 13 strokes	車	較	較	较

壯	レ	丩	爿	**JWANG-4**, be strong 壯丁 *jwang-4 ding-1*, able-bodied man; man subject to the draft 壯年 *jwang-4 nyan-2*, the prime of life 壯心 *jwang-4 syin-1*, resolute
	爿	壯	壯	
1048 7 strokes	壯			壯

裝	丩	爿	壯	**JWANG-1**, to load up 行裝 *sying-2 jwang-1*, baggage 裝運 *jwang-1 yun-4*, to load up and transport 裝門面 *jwang-1 men-2 myan-4*, be pretentious
	壯	裝	裝	
1049 13 strokes	裝	裝	裝	裝

慣	丶	忄	忄	GWAN-4, be used to
	忄	忄口	忄毋	習慣　syi-2 gwan-4, habits
				慣性　gwan-4 sying-4, inertia
				慣賊　gwan-4 dzei-2, thief with several arrests
1050 14 strokes	忄毋	慣	慣	惯

輕	一	冂	亘	CHING-1, be light (in weight)
	車	車一	車亿	輕重　ching-1 jung-4, weight
				輕氣　ching-1 chi-4, hydrogen
				輕工業　ching-1 gung-1 ye-4, light industry
1051 14 strokes	輕	輕	輕	轻

器	丶	口	口	CHI-4, dish, implement
	口口	吅	吴	機器　ji-1 chi-4, machine, engine
				鐵器　tye-3 chi-4, hardware, iron tools
				銀器　yin-2 chi-4, silverware
1052 16 strokes	哭	哭	器	

架	丆	力	加	JYA-4, frame; a measure for airplanes
	加口	加	加	架子　jya-4 dz-3, frame
				書架　shu-1 jya-4, bookshelf
				一架飛機　yi-2 jya-4 fei-1 ji-1, an airplane
1053 9 strokes	架	架	架	

基	一	十	卄	JI-1, base
	甘	其	其	基本　ji-1 ben-3, basic
				基地　ji-1 di-4, base (military)
				基法　ji-1 fa-3, "the basic operations" (addition, subtraction, multiplication, division)
1054 11 strokes	其	基	基	

洛	丶	冫	氵
	氵	氵	氵
1055 9 strokes	浐	洛	洛

LWO-4; the name of a river; a surname; used to write foreign words

洛洛 *lwo-4 lwo-4*, be clear and bright (said of flowing water)

洛陽 *lwo-4 yang-2*, Loyang (famous ancient capital of China)

落	一	十	艹
	艹	艹	艹
1056 12 strokes	茓	茨	落

LWO-4, to fall, to come down

落下來 *lwo-4 sya-4 lai-2*, to fall (leaves)

降落 *jyang-4 lwo-4*, to land (airplanes)

落第 *lwo-4 di-4*, to fail an exam

志	一	十	士
	士	志	志
1057 7 strokes	志		

JR-4, will, volition

壯志 *jwang-4 jr-4*, be determined, be resolute

志向 *jr-4 syang-4*, one's intention, aspiration

志願 *jr-4 ywan-4*, ambitions, "heart's desire"

誌	丶	亠	言
	言	言	言
1058 14 strokes	計	誌	誌

JR-4, to remember; to record, record

雜誌 *dza-2 jr-4*, magazine

誌喜 *jr-4 syi-3*, to express one's joy

誌

聯	一	刀	月
	耳	耵	耵丝
1059 17 strokes	聯	聯	聯

LYAN-2, to unite

聯合國 *lyan-2 he-2 gwo-2*, United Nations

聯想 *lyan-2 syang-3*, association of ideas (psychological term)

聯貫 *lyan-2 gwan-4*, to string together

(幺 25)

联

穌

1060
16 strokes

SU-1, to revive

Su-1 is supposed to suggest "to revive" by means of suggesting "a good meal": "fish" + "grain" = "a good meal."

(魚 558, 禾 65)

稣

蘇

1061
19 strokes
(20 strokes)

SU-1, Soochow; used to write foreign words

Originally this character, like 1060, above, meant "to revive" and was 1060 reclarified with the "grass" rad.

蘇聯 *su-1 lyan-2*, USSR

苏

司

1062
5 strokes

SZ-1, to control; company

公司 *gung-1 sz-1*, company, corporation

司機 *sz-1 ji-1*, chauffeur, driver

司令 *sz-1 ling-4*, (military) commander

REMAINING CHARACTERS

of the "1,020 List" and the "2,000 List"

和	HE-2, and, with; to make peace; HWO-4, to mix; HWO; a verb-suffix: "comfortably"	破	PWO-4, be broken
章	JANG-1, chapter, section, paragraph; a measure	須	SYU-1, must; be necessary 须
初	CHU-1, the beginning, the first	川	CHWAN-1, river. RIVER rad. (47). Compare 442, above.
段	DWAN-4, paragraph, section, passage; a measure	順	SHWUN-4, to move with; to agree with; favorable; prosperous 顺
辭	TSZ-2, word or expression; to decline; to resign, to fire 辞	訓	SYUN-4, to give advice 训
疲	PI-2, be worn out	煩	FAN-2, to pester, to annoy 烦
波	BWO-1, wave; to flow	絕邑	JYWE-2, to break off; (before a negative) very 绝
坡	PWO-1, slope, bank	暖	NWAN-3, be warm
婆	PWO-2, old woman; mother-in-law; stepmother	援	YWAN-2, to pull along; to give a hand to, to aid

緩	HWAN-3, be slack; to goof off; be late 缓	似	SZ-4, to resemble (also pronounced *shr*-4 in some constructions)
啦	LA; a sentence-final particle ＝了＋啊	罪	DZWEI-4, crime; suffering, to suffer
倒	DAU-4, on the contrary	野	YE-3, be wild, uncivilized
舒	SHU-1, to relax, to stretch out	印	YIN-4, to print
責	DZE-2, responsibility 责	功	GUNG-1, achievement; effectiveness; hard work
積	JI-2, to accumulate 积	攻	GUNG-1, to attack
績	JI-1, to join threads; to finish; accomplishment 绩	貢	GUNG-4, tax, to tax; contribution; to announce 贡
債	JAI-4, to owe money, debt 债	項	SYANG-4, nape of the neck; a measure for articles in documents or for items 项
轉	JWAN-3, to turn 转	散	SAN-4, to scatter, to disperse
確	CHYWE-4, be true, be definite 确	繼	JI-4, to continue, to succeed to 继
吹	CHWEI-1, to blow	斷	DWAN-4, to break into segments; stop (doing something); to decide a law case 断

240

續	SYU-4, to add to, to prolong; to follow 续	岸	AN-4, high cliff, high river-bank
讀	DU-2, to recite; to study 读	奸	JYAN-1, be crafty, be treacherous
贖	SHU-2, to redeem, to ransom; to atone for 赎	訂	DING-4, to investigate; to decide; to revise for publication 订
致	JR-4, to send; to cause	釘	DING-1, nail 钉
肝	GAN-1, the liver	頂	DING-3, top of the head; to carry on the head; be lofty; to oppose; very 顶
幹	GAN-4, to do 干	若	RWO-4, if
旱	HAN-4, drought	偶	OU-3, be accidental; be even (numbers); image (of a person); spouse
桿	GAN-1, pole; GAN-3; a measure for rifles, pistols, spears	遇	YU-4, to run into
稈	GAN-3, grain stalk; straw	列	LYE-4, line, rank, to line up, to rank; each; a measure for trains
趕	GAN-3, to rush after, to rush at; to chase off; by the time that . . . 赶	例	LI-4, example
刊	KAN-1, to carve, to engrave. Printed 刊.	烈	LYE-4, to blaze; be brilliant or famous

241

列衣	LYE-4, to split	隣	LIN-2, neighbor
劇	JYU-4, stage play; be severe, be intense 剧	憐	LYAN-2, to pity 怜
祕	MI-4, be secret, be private	眼	YAN-3, eye; hole; a measure for glances, wells, and musical beats
密	MI-4, be secluded; be deep; be secret, be mysterious; be still	班	BAN-1; a measure for classes (students), squads, and trips (flights, trains, etc.); shift, troupe
蜜	MI-4, honey	小	SYIN-1. HEART rad. (61). Compare 70, above. This form occurs only as a part of characters.
退	TWEI-4, to back off; to give back; to fade	添	TYAN-1, to add on
腿	TWEI-3, leg, thigh	犭	CHYWAN-3. DOG rad. (94). Compare 541, above. This form occurs only as a part of characters
餓	E-4, be hungry 饿	猜	TSAI-1, to guess
掛	GWA-4, to hang	倉	TSANG-1, granary 仓
待	DAI-4, to deal with; to wait for	蒼	TSANG-1, sky; be sky blue; be pale; be gray; lush vegetation 苍
玄	SYWAN-2, be dark; be abstruse; be absurd. DARK rad. (95)	槍	CHYANG-1, spear; pistol, rifle 枪

搶	CHYANG-3, to rob, to snatch 抢	碼	MA-3, to lay in neat piles; yard (of cloth); a counter or marker 码
瘡	CHWANG-1, sore, abcess, ulcer 疮	豈	CHI-3, How can it be that . . . ? 岂
創	CHWANG-4, to begin; CHWANG-1, to wound 创	碗	WAN-3, bowl
養	YANG-3, to support (one's dependents); to nourish 养	強	CHYANG-2, be strong; might; CHYANG-3, to force, to compel; JYANG-4, be stubborn
指	JR-3, to point	盜	DAU-4, to rob, robber
脂	JR-1, animal fat, lard, ointment; cosmetics; wealth	狗	GOU-3, dog
增	DZENG-1, to add to	磅	BANG-4, a pound (weight; unit of English money); to weigh
贈	DZENG-2, to give a present, to present 赠	況	KWANG-4, even more so
層	TSENG-2, story (of a building) 层	村	TSWUN-1, village
媽	MA-1, mama, "ma"; woman servant, nurse 妈	材	TSAI-2, material; ability, "genius"; coffin
罵	MA-4, to scold; to curse 骂	財	TSAI-2, wealth 财

脑	NAU-3, brain 脑	輸	SHU-1, to lose (as in gambling). Printed 輸. 输
弄	NUNG-4, to do; to handle; to make	猪	JU-1, pig
獸	SHOU-4, animal 兽	煮	JU-3, to boil, to cook up
牀	CHWANG-2, bed	著	JU-4, to spread out, to display, be displayed; to author
店	DYAN-4, store, inn	暑	SHU-3, summer; summer heat
碎	SWEI-4, be smashed, be in bits and pieces	绪	SYU-4, end of a thread; clue; to tie together; succession; dynasty; profession 绪
醉	DZWEI-4, be drunk	赌	DU-3, gamble, to bet 赌
虧	KWEI-1, to lose, to fail; fortunately, happily 亏	屠	TU-2, to butcher
醒	SYING-3, to wake up	竟	JING-4, to end; in the end, after all
腥	SYING-1, smell (of fish or raw meat)	境	JING-3, a field's edge; borders; region; circumstances
牌	PAI-2, placard	镜	JING-4, mirror 镜

物	WU-4, thing, object	筒	TUNG-2, TUNG-3, tube, large cylinder
討	TAU-3, to ask for; to marry (be a groom); to discuss　讨	鹵	LU-3, natural salt. SALT rad. (197)　卤
罰	FA-2, to punish　罚	喊	HAN-3, to yell
驚	JING-1, to scare　惊	感	GAN-3, to feel (emotionally); to move (emotionally); to appreciate
濕	SHR-1, be wet　湿	鹹	SYAN-2, be salty　咸
顯	SYAN-3, be visible; to show; be noteworthy　显	关	JYWAN-3, roll; rolled rice dumpling
暗	AN-4, be dark	卷	JYWAN-4, roll, scroll; section or chapter
窗	CHWANG-1, window	捲	JYWAN-3, to roll up　卷
泥	NI-2, mud	倦	JYWAN-4, be tired, be weak
毀	HWEI-3, to break apart; to destroy	圈	CHYWAN-1, circle; to encircle; JYWAN-1, to imprison; JYWAN-4, pen, a fold (e.g., of sheep)
洞	DUNG-4, cave, hole	券	CHYWAN-4, bond, deed, contract, diploma

拳	CHYWAN-2, fist; to tuck in; a measure for punches (with the fist)	傘	SAN-3, umbrella 伞
勝	SHENG-4, to conquer 胜	詩	SHR-1, poem, a *shih* poem, poetry 诗
騰	TENG-2, to make room for; to ride up on; TENG-1, to steam 腾	持	CHR-2, to support; to grasp, to hold; to manage; to restrain
滕	TENG-2; a surname	拔	BA-2, to pull up, to pull out
藤	TENG-2, climbing plant, vine; rattan, cane	髮	FA-3, hair 发
膝	SYI-1, knee	監	JYAN-1, to supervise; prison 监
漆	CHI-1, to paint, to varnish, paint	鹽	YAN-2, salt 盐
夢	MENG-4, dream 梦	藍	LAN-2, be blue (color) 蓝
賀	HE-4, send a present with congratulations; to congratulate 贺	籃	LAN-2, basket (usually with a curved handle); "basket" in basketball 篮
晴	CHING-2, clear sky	覽	LAN-3, to look at 览
睛	JING-1, pupil of the eye	播	BWO-1, to spread, to scatter

翻羽	FAN-1, to flip; to translate; to search through; to change one's attitude; to reprint; to go over (a hill)	途	TU-2, road; trip; career
擇	DZE-2, to pick out　择	農	NUNG-2, farming　农
澤	DZE-2, marsh; to dampen; to enrich; to favor　泽	濃	NUNG-2, be heavy, be thick, be strong in flavor; be intense (as one's interest can be)　浓
譯	YI-4, to explain, to interpret, to translate　译	扁	BYAN-3, door-plaque; sign-board; be flat
釋	SHR-4, to loosen up; to explain　释	遍	BYAN-4, to go around; be ubiquitous; a turn, a time
漸	JYAN-4, gradually　渐	編	BYAN-1, to weave, to braid; to classify; to compile　编
符	FU-2, symbol; written charm or incantation; to agree with	偏	PYAN-1, to lean to one side; be partial; on the side, secondary
附	FU-4, to attach	篇	PYAN-1, article, essay; a measure for articles, essays
腐	FU-3, to decay	騙	PYAN-4, to fool, to cheat　骗
它	TA-1, it	旗	CHI-2, flag
引	YIN-3, to lead, to draw out	揮	HWEI-1, to wave; to sprinkle; to wipe away　挥

247

勞	LAU-2, hard work 劳	儉	JYAN-3, be thrifty, be frugal 俭
撈	LAU-1, to drag for, to fish for; to make money improperly 捞	簽	CHYAN-1, to sign (formally); lots (as in "draw lots"); label 签
榮	RUNG-2, to flourish, be glorious 荣	驗	YAN-4, to try out, to examine 验
營	YING-2, camp; battalion; to manage 营	麗	LI-4, be beautiful 丽
弱	RWO-4, be weak	福	FU-2, good luck
妻	CHI-1, wife	副	FU-4, assistant
贊	DZAN-4, to approve 赞	富	FU-4, be rich, abundant
讚	DZAN-4, to praise, to eulogize 讚	朝	JAU-1, morning; CHAU-2, dynasty; imperial; reign; to face; to visit a superior
鑽	DZWAN-3, to bore into; DZWAN-1, to worm into; DZWAN-4, to bore into; drill 钻	潮	CHAU-2, tide; be damp
潛	CHYAN-2, to lie under water; to ford; be hidden	廟	MYAU-4, temple 庙
蠶	TSAN-2, silkworm; sericulture 蚕	碰	PENG-4, to touch; to run into

248

舞	WU-3, dance	恭	GUNG-1, be respectful
桃	TAU-2, peach	烘	HUNG-1, to warm or dry something over a fire
逃	TAU-2, to run away	巷	SYANG-4, crooked side street, lane
挑	TYAU-1, carrying pole (with bucket or basket on each end); to carry; TYAU-3, to probe	港	GANG-3, small stream; port, lagoon
壁	BI-4, wall, screen	哄	HUNG-3, to coax, to deceive; HUNG-1, to make a noise
避	BI-4, to flee from	居	JYU-1, to reside
劈	PI-1, to split; PI-3, to pull apart with the hands; to divide	鋸	JYU-4, saw, to saw 锯
招	JAU-1, to beckon to; to invite; to recruit; to tease; to pass a disease to; to confess	雇	GU-4, to hire
超	CHAU-1, to catch up to; to surpass	顧	GU-4, to look after, to take care of; to take into consideration 顾
針	JEN-1, needle, pin 针	娘	NYANG-2, mother
供	GUNG-1, to supply; GUNG-4, to offer in worship, offering; to testify, testimony	議	YI-4, to discuss 议

渴	KE-3, be thirsty	搬	BAN-1, to lift (a heavy object) palms up (not above the head); to transport
季	JI-4, season (of the year)	盤	PAN-2, plate, tub, dish; to coil up; to move; to sell; price; a measure for games 盘
委	WEI-3, to appoint; to abandon; really	職	JR-2, to oversee 职
秀	SYOU-4, grain in the ear; to flourish; be elegant; be accomplished	能心	TAI-4, attitude, manner 态
繡	SYU-4, to embroider 绣	環	HWAN-2, to encircle; ring, bracelet 环
誘	YOU-4, to lead on, to mislead 诱	質	JR-4, to pawn; pledge; JR-2, disposition; substance; to confront 质
透	TOU-4, to go through	之	JR-1; a particle similar to 的; him, her, it, them
陣	JEN-4; a measure for windstorms or rainstorms 阵	乏	FA-2, be exhausted; be feeble in ability; low (said of a fire)
雲	YUN-2, cloud 云	羣	CHYUN-2, herd
料	LYAU-4, material	盡	JIN-4, to exhaust 尽
般	BAN-1, to transport; to distribute; to classify, classification, category	達	DA-2, to reach 达

250

遊	YOU-2, to travel around	歐	OU-1, to vomit; used in writing foreign words; Europe 欧
游	YOU-2, to swim; to travel; to saunter; section of a river	倡	CHANG-4, to get something started; to advocate
競	JING-4, to quarrel 竞	擔	DAN-1, to carry with a pole on your shoulder (between two persons) 担
育	YU-4, to give birth to; to bring up; to nourish	膽	DAN-3, gall bladder; courage, inside of a thermos bottle 胆
依	YI-1, to agree with; to forgive; according to	缶	FOU-3, crock. CROCK rad. (121)
益	YI-4, profit. Printed 益.	灌	GWAN-4, to sprinkle; to irrigate; to record (on tape or disc); to assemble
眾	JUNG-4, crowd 众	罐	GWAN-4, jar, can
品	PIN-3, goods; quality; rank; personality; to judge the quality; to sample	權	CHYWAN-2, (political) power 权
區	CHYU-1, be small; to distinguish between; region, district 区	尾	WEI-3, tail
驅	CHYU-1, to rush, to chase, to urge 驱	皇	HWANG-2, emperor; be imperial
嘔	OU-3, to vomit; OU; a sentence-final particle of warning or caution 呕	蝗	HWANG-2, locust

251

帝	DI-4, emperor; supreme ruler	勇	YUNG-3, be brave
蹄	TI-1, hoof	守	SHOU-3, to guard
評	PING-2, to judge, to umpire, to criticize; review　评	抗	KANG-4, to resist, to oppose
響	SYANG-3, sound, to sound　响	骯	ANG-1, be dirty　肮
批	PI-1, to comment on, comment, annotation; to mark (an exam); batch; wholesale	坑	KENG-1, pit, shallow hole; to cheat somebody
屁	PI-4, gas (in the stomach); to fart; be stupid	擊	JI-1, to hit　击
敵	DI-2, enemy　敌	繫	SYI-4, to tie together; to haul up or let down on a rope; remember　系
滴	DI-1, drop, to drip	獨	DU-2, alone　独
摘	JAI-1, to pick (flowers, fruit); to criticize	燭	JU-2, candle; to illumine　烛
厭	YAN-4, to detest; be fed up with　厌	偉	WEI-3, be great　伟
壓	YA-1, to push down　压	違	WEI-2, to go against, to disobey　违

却	CHYWE-4, but, however	週	JOU-1, to revolve, circle, revolution
流	LYOU-2, to flow; to go astray; be prevalent; a current; a measure for (social) class (of a person)	綢	CHOU-2, to bind; to plan; thin silk 绸
荒	HWANG-1, be deserted, be desolate; be reckless; excessive; famine	綱	GANG-1, leading line of a net; general principle; to regulate 纲
慌	HWANG-1, be nervous	崗	GANG-1, ridge; GANG-3 岗
謊	HWANG-3, a lie; to overcharge 谎	網	WANG-3, net 网
緣	YWAN-2, along; be bound to (do something) 缘	調	TYAU-2, to harmonize; to incite; DYAU-4, tune; to transfer 调
則	DZE-2, and then . . . 则	族	DZU-2, race, tribe
側	TSE-4, side; to lean aside; to side with someone; secondary 侧	胃	WEI-4, stomach
測	TSE-4, to estimate, to guess 测	謂	WEI-4, to talk about; to call; to say 谓
廁	TSE-4, toilet 厕	資	DZ-1, fee, capital, resources; talent; to aid 资
周	JOU-1, circle, revolution, to go around, be ubiquitous, everywhere	姿	DZ-1, posture, carriage

253

格	GE-2, ruled line or space (on paper); category; compartment	榨	JA-4, to press out (as oil or sugar), press for extracting oil, sugar
錐 锥	JWEI-1, awl; to make holes with an awl	始	SHR-3, to begin
堆	DWEI-1, to pile, pile; crowd	頓 顿	DWUN-4, to pause (in reading); to prepare; DWUN-1, to pause (in writing a character.)
維 维	WEI-2, to maintain, to hold together	純 纯	CHWUN-2, be pure (said of objects)
某	MOU-3, a certain . . .	領 领	LING-3, to lead
煤	MEI-2, coal	鈴 铃	LING-2, small bell
謀 谋	MOU-2, to find (a job); to plot, plot	導 导	DAU-3, to lead
礦 矿	KWANG-4, mine (for minerals)	份	FEN-4, share, portion; a measure for portions
炸	JA-4, to set off, blast	貧 贫	PIN-2, be poor, be insufficient
詐 诈	JA-4, to pretend, to swindle, to deceive; to get information by pretending to know it	盆	PEN-2, basin, bowl
窄	JAI-3, be narrow	盼	PAN-4, to gaze at, to long for

鼓	GU-3, drum, to drum. DRUM rad. (207)	輩	BEI-4, a generation; kind or class; the sign of the plural　輩
製	JR-4, to make, to manufacture　制	糧	LYANG-2, provisions (food)　粮
損	SWUN-3, be cruel, be sarcastic; to damage; loss　损	揚	YANG-2, to lift up; to throw into the air; to winnow; to display; to publish; to praise　扬
效	SYAU-4, effect; to imitate; to devote	楊	YANG-2, poplar, aspen　杨
咬	YAU-3, to bite; to incriminate an innocent person with false testimony; to bark	腸	CHANG-2, intestine; sausage　肠
准	JWUN-3, to permit	傷	SHANG-1, wound, to wound　伤
隊	DWEI-4, squadron; team; file (of people); a measure for formations　队	湯	TANG-1, soup; a surname　汤
敗	BAI-4, defeat　败	燙	TANG-4, be scalding hot, to scald, to heat up; to iron; to get a permanent　烫
匪	FEI-3, bandit or rebel; to act or talk in a way suggestive of moral irresponsibility	丈	JANG-4, ten Chinese feet (equivalent to 144 inches); wife's parents; husband
悲	BEI-1, be sad, be grieved	仗	JANG-4, war, battle
排	PAI-2, to arrange	悔	HWEI-3, to repent; to turn away from

匀	YUN-2, be evenly distributed; to spare (space, time, money)	兵	BING-1, soldier
均	JYUN-1, be equal, be fair	際	JI-4, boundary; occasion; at the time that . . . 际
律	LYU-4, law	彈	DAN-4, a bullet; TAN-2, to hurl; to pluck (a musical instrument); to flick 弹
技	JI-4, skill	戰	JAN-4, war 战
術	SHU-4, craft, art, profession; device 术	僅	JIN-3, barely 仅
述	SHU-4, to tell a story; to transmit	勤	CHIN-2, be diligent; be frequent
序	SYU-4, introduction (to a book)	擴	KWO-4, to expand 扩
朿	TSZ-4, thorn. Distinguish *tsz-4* from "bundle" 束 (657, above)	州	JOU-1, administrative region; state (of the U.S.)
刺	TSZ-4, thorn; splinter, fishbone; to stab, to pierce; to murder; be "thorny," unpleasant	洲	JOU-1, continent (large land mass)
策	TSE-4, plan, policy	酬州	CHOU-2, to pledge with wine; to repay
棗	DZAU-3, jujube; date (fruit, tree) 枣	亞	YA-4, be ugly; used to write foreign words (sometimes pronounced YA-3)

256

啞	YA-3, be hoarse; be dumb or mute 啞	掃	SAU-4, broom; SAU-3, to sweep 扫
惡	E-4, be evil; be fierce; WU-4, to consider evil, to hate 恶	略	LYWE-4, to omit; be simple, be rough; sketch, plan
壺	HU-2, kettle, jug 壶	阻	DZU-3, to block
妨	FANG-2, to hinder	粗	TSU-1, be coarse (not fine)
紡	FANG-3, to spin, to reel; silk 纺	失	SHR-1, to lose
訪	FANG-3, to look for; to dig up (the news); to visit 访	缺	CHYWE-1, to lack
防	FANG-2, to guard against	孫	SWUN-1, grandson; a surname 孙
侵	CHIN-1, to move in on, to encroach	宣	SYWAN-1, proclaim
浸	JIN-4, to soak, to immerse	涉	SHE-4, to ford; to pass through; be connected with
帚	JOU-3, broom	終	JUNG-1, end. Usually written 终. 终
婦	FU-4, wife, woman 妇	混	HWUN-4, to mix up; to fool around; HWUN-3, to mix

棍	GWUN-4, stick, club; bad guy	剩	SHENG-4, to have left, be left over
階	JYE-1, step (on a stairway); rank, class 阶	互	HU-4, mutually; each other
揩	KAI-1, to rub	陳	CHEN-2, be properly aged (wine); be stale; to display; to state; a surname 陈
及	JI-2, to reach, together with; and; a verb-ending: "be able to"	標	BYAU-1, target; to quote a price; to bid (commercially); sign 标
級	JI-2, level, class, grade; a measure for levels, classes, or grades 级	飄	PYAU-1, to float (in the air or on the water) 飘
吸	SYI-1, to inhale, to soak up	寅	YIN-2, to respect; the third "earthly branch"
伯	BWO-2, father's elder brother; earl, count	演	YAN-3, to act in (a play); to put on a show
迫	PWO-4, to oppress, to persecute, be in difficulties	阜	FU-4, mound. MOUND rad. (170). This is the independent form; compare 76, above.
拍	PAI-1, to pat, to clap; to bounce; to take (a picture); to send (a telegram); to fawn on; beat (in music)	轟	HUNG-1, to drive off; to bombard; boom! boom! 轰
恨	HEN-4, to hate	欺	CHI-1, to cheat
乘	CHENG-4, to ride	廠	CHANG-3, factory 厂

258

滅	MYE-4, to extinguish, to go out (a fire, lights); to wipe out 灭	紗	SHA-1, gauze, sheer cloth 纱
獲	HWO-4, to grab 获	妙	MYAU-4, be slender, be graceful, be beautiful; be marvelous, be clever
祝	JU-4, to wish, to pray	秒	MYAU-3, beard of grain; smallest part; a measure for seconds (of time or angles)
源	YWAN-2, spring (of water), source	佈	BU-4, to lay out; to inform
秩	JR-4, order, arrangement	災	DZAI-1, disaster
節	JYE-2, joint; tempo; festival; section; to restrain, restraint 节	肥	FEI-2, be fat; be fertile (soil); be loose, be baggy; fertilizer
漢	HAN-4, the Han (Chinese) race; man 汉	井	JING-3, well; mineshaft
抄	CHAU-1, to copy; to confiscate; to parboil	耕	GENG-1, to plow, to till
吵	CHAU-3, to quarrel; to make noise, to disturb with noise	朱	JU-1, bright red; a surname
炒	CHAU-3, to fry (in oil, stirring all the time)	珠	JU-1, pearl
沙	SHA-1, sand, gravel; to sound gravelly, be hoarse	域	YU-4, boundary; to keep within bounds

259

括	KWO-4, to embrace, to include	网	WANG-3, net. NET rad. (122). Compare 446 and 637, above. This form is used only as a part of characters.
蒙	MENG-3, Mongolia; MENG-2, be stupid; to cover	深	SHEN-1, be deep
藏	DZANG-4, stash, treasure; Tibet	探	TAN-4, to lean out; to search out
臟	DZANG-4, viscera, entrails 脏	罩	JAU-4, cover; bamboo basket used to catch fish
森	SEN-1, forest; to inspire awe	掉	DYAU-4, to fall, to let fall; to lose; to fade; to remove (a stain)
梁	LYANG-2, horizontal beam, bridge, top-handle, ridge; a surname	島	DAU-3, island 岛
粱	LYANG-2, common millet; canary seed	彎	WAN-1, to bend, bend 弯
畜	SYU-4, to store up; to breed or raise animals; CHU-4, domestic animal	灣	WAN-1, curving shore; bay 湾
蓄	SYU-4, to store up; to breed or raise	蠻	MAN-2, barbarians to the south of China; be barbarous 蛮
抽	CHOU-1, to draw out; to smoke (tobacco); to levy; to whip; to shrink; to conscript	斧	FU-3, axe, hatchet
袖	SYOU-4, sleeve	孔	KUNG-3, small hole; Confucius; a surname

260

恢	HWEI-1, to extend, be great	尊	DZWUN-1, respect; "your" (polite); measure for Buddhist statues and for cannons (artillery)
盛	SHENG-4, be abundant; be cordial; be completely . . .	遵	DZWUN-1, to obey, to comply with
斯	SZ-1, be genteel; used to write foreign words; a surname	採	TSAI-3, to pick, to pick out, to gather
撕	SZ-1, to tear up	衝	CHUNG-1, to crash through; thoroughfare; CHUNG-4, to face; be strong; be tactless 冲
佛	FWO-2, Buddha	腫	JUNG-3, to swell up
犯	FAN-4, to commit an offense; be afflicted with; criminal	納	NA-4, to pay in 纳
刷	SHWA-1, brush, to brush; to give someone the brush-off; to cut class	抵	DI-3, to take the place of; to push against, to resist
做	DZWO-4, to make; to be; to act as	忠	JUNG-1, be loyal
搖	YAU-2, to shake, to rock, to swing to and fro	串	CHWAN-4, a string of things (such as cash), to string together; to thread your way through
謠	YAU-2, folk song, ballad; rumor 谣	患	HWAN-4, to suffer; calamity
遙	YAU-2, be far off; be long	配	PEI-4, to match up, go well with, to mate (said of animals)

鬲	GE-4, cauldron. CAULDRON rad. (193). Also read LI-4.	矩	JYU-3, carpenter's square; standard, rule, custom
獻 獻	SYAN-4, to give	拒	JYU-4, to refuse
軌 轨	GWEI-3, rut; orbit; rule, law; axle	距	JYU-4, be separated from, be distant from
韭	JYOU-3, leeks. LEEKS rad. (179). Distinguish from the "wrong" rad. 非 (654, above).	繁	FAN-2, be complicated, be numerous
耐	NAI-4, to endure, to bear	兼	JYAN-1, to put together
克	KE-4, to conquer; gram	歉	CHYAN-3, to eat without getting enough; to lack
寧 宁	NING-2, be peaceful; to prefer to; Nanking	嫌	SYAN-2, to dislike; to suspect
奪 夺	DWO-2, to take by force, to fight over	賺 赚	JWAN-4, to make money; profit
征	JENG-1, to attack	繳 缴	JYAU-1, to make a payment
症	JENG-4, disease	鞭	BYAN-1, whip; firecracker
嚴 严	YAN-2, be airtight, be strict; a surname	具	JYU-4, tool; to write out; a measure for dead bodies and machines

俱	JYU-1, be complete; every	廳	TING-1, hall, room; department of a provincial government 厅
珍	JEN-1, precious object; be precious	栽	DZAI-1, to plant; to fall down; to lose face due to failure
疹	JEN-3, measles	載	DZAI-4, to carry, to contain a load; to record; DZAI-3, a year 载
診	JEN-3, JEN-1, to examine medically 诊	裁	TSAI-2, to cut out (a pattern); to reduce, to lay off employees; to decide
趁	CHEN-4, to chase; to turn to one's own use; according to	截	JYE-2, to cut in two; to intercept; a measure for segments
衰	SHWAI-1, to get weak	承	CHENG-2, to inherit; to manage; to admit
畝	MU-3, Chinese acre (mou): 733⅓ square yards 亩	姻	YIN-1, bride; marriage connections
款	KWAN-3, sum of money; article (in treaty, contract); inscription; to entertain	托	TWO-1, to carry on the palm
誤	WU-4, be late, be too late for; by mistake 误	託	TWO-1, to entrust, to ask someone to do a job for you 讬
庭	TING-2, hall, courtyard; the imperial court; family	歸	GWEI-1, to go or come back (to where the person belongs) 归
挺	TING-3, be straight and stiff; to hold on to; fairly; a measure for machine guns	疑	YI-2, to mistrust

礙	AI-4, to get in the way 碍	繩	SHENG-2, string 绳
詞	TSZ-2, a *tz'u* poem 词	蠅	YING-2, fly (insect) 蝇
捕	BU-3, to seize, to arrest	甲	JYA-3, armor
補	BU-3, to patch up, to fill in 补	匣	SYA-2, small box
簿	BU-4, notebook, ledger	藝	YI-4, craft, art, trade 艺
薄	BWO-2, BAU-2, be thin, be weak	販	FAN-4, to peddle, to deal in 贩
博	BWO-2, be broad or comprehensive (in knowledge); of all kinds; gamble	板	BAN-3, board; printing plate; a measure for editions; be "wooden" (lifeless)
移	YI-2, to shift	版	BAN-3, printing block; edition
鼠	SHU-3, mouse, rat. MOUSE rad. (208)	隶	DAI-4, to grab, to catch hold of. GRAB rad. (171)
龜	GWEI-1, tortoise. TORTOISE rad. (213) 龟	康	KANG-1, be serene; Sikang
黽	MIN-3, toad. TOAD rad. (205) 黾	糠	KANG-1, be dry and pulpy; chaff

264

黹	JR-3, to embroider. EMBROI-DER rad. (204)	擾	RAU-3, to annoy 扰
庚	GENG-1, the evening star; the seventh "heavenly stem"	豸	CHR-4, snake. SNAKE rad. (153)
莊	JWANG-1, be serene; hamlet; store; dealer (cards); a surname 庄	苗	MYAU-2, sprout; jet of flame; vein of ore; progeny; Miao people; vaccine
智	JR-4, wisdom, learning	描	MYAU-2, to trace over
穩	WEN-3, be steady; definitely, "You can depend on it." 稳	貓	MAU-2, MYAU-2, cat
隱	YIN-3, to hide 隐	巧	CHYAU-3, be ingenious; be timely, opportune
含	HAN-2, to hold something in your mouth; to contain	墨	MWO-4, ink, be inky
錄	LU-4, to record 录	遷	CHYAN-1, to shift 迁
肅	SU-4, to command respect, to respect; Kansu	寶	BAU-3, be precious; "your" (polite) 宝
憂	YOU-1, to be grieved, be worried 忧	瓦	WA-3, tile, earthenware; to roof, to tile. TILE rad. (98)
優	YOU-1, to excel; actor 优	餅	BING-3, cakes; round, flat pastries with or without filling 饼

265

併	BING-4, be on a level with; all	視	SHR-4, to look, to look at 視
拼	PIN-1, to put together; to fight furiously	飽	BAU-3, be full, to have had enough to eat 饱
瓶	PING-2, bottle, vase	抱	BAU-4, to wrap in one's arms, to embrace; to hold, to carry; to adopt (a point of view, a child)
梅	MEI-2, plum	袍	PAU-2, long gown or robe
卯	MAU-3, the fourth "earthly branch"	泡	PAU-4, to soak; to pester; be together; bubble, blister; light bulb; PAU-1, be fluffy
柳	LYOU-3, willow	砲	PAU-4, cannon; artillery; a shot from a gun
哈	HA-1, ha! ha!; to blow	暴	BAU-4, be violent, be fierce; to lay out in the sun
恰	CHYA-4, be exact, be appropriate	爆	BAU-4, to explode; to boil, to fry quickly in very hot oil
屈	CHYU-1, to bend; be wronged; to submit unwillingly; injustice	丰	FENG-1, be pretty, be graceful, elegant. The character is a picture of a blossoming flower.
帥	SHWAI-4, leader, commander; SHWO-4, to lead 帅	豐	FENG-1, abundant, fruitful, luxuriant 丰
師	SHR-1, specialist, teacher; (army) division 师	逢	FENG-2, to meet with; to happen; whenever

266

縫	FENG-2, to sew, to mend (usually by hand); FENG-4, seam; crack 缝	爬	PA-2, to crawl, to creep; to climb
鋒	FENG-1, sharp point; the tip of a bayonet or lance 锋	陪	PEI-2, to keep someone company; with
蜂	FENG-1, bees, hornets, wasps	賠	PEI-2, to pay damages; to lose money (in business) 赔
邦	BANG-1, nation	伴	BAN-4, to keep someone company, companion
綁	BANG-3, to bind, to tie; to kidnap 绑	胖	PANG-4, be fat
捧	PENG-3, to hold something in your cupped two hands; a measure for two handfuls; praise; support, be a patron	幣	BI-4, currency, coin; silk; gifts 币
棒	BANG-4, bat, nightstick; be terrific (Peking dialect)	撇	PYE-1, to abandon; to skim something off the surface of a liquid; PYE-3, to throw
罷	BA-4, to cease, to quit; BA-1; a sentence-final particle that is also written 吧 (277, above) 罢	撥	BWO-1, to move (as with a fingertip); to set, to adjust; to transfer; subtotal, part 拨
擺	BAI-3, to swing; pendulum; to display; to put in order; to put 摆	潑	PWO-1, to throw liquid out of a container; to spill; be shrewish 泼
爪	JAU-3, claws. CLAWS rad. (87). Compare 338, above. This is the independent form.	廢	FEI-4, to abolish, to discard; crippled, useless 废
爸	BA-4, papa, pa, father	摩	MA-1, to smooth out with the hand; MWO-2; used to write foreign words

磨	MWO-2, to rub; to grind, to sharpen; to dawdle; to pester; MWO-4, to mill, to grind; millstone	搭	DA-1, to lay across; to build (for temporary use); to travel by; to add, "plus"
魔	MWO-2, evil spirit, demon	塔	TA-3, pagoda, tower
墓	MU-4, tomb	端	DWAN-1, to raise up, to hold level in front of you; be upright; tip
幕	MU-4, stage curtain; a measure for acts of a play; screen	喘	CHWAN-3, to pant
摸	MWO-1, to feel with the hand; to grope for; to sneak in or out	抬	TAI-2, to carry (between two or more people); to raise the price
鼎	DING-3, tripod, sacrificial vessel, a *ting*. TRIPOD rad. (206)	胎	TAI-1, the pregnant womb
噴	PEN-1, to spurt, to puff, to spray; PEN-4, puff 喷	痰	TAN-2, phlegm, spit
墳	FEN-2, grave, tomb 坟	毯	TAN-3, rug
憤	FEN-4, zeal, ardor; be exasperated with; be very angry 愤	倘	TANG-3, if
浮	FU-2, to float; be flighty; insubstantial; excess; FU-4, to swim	躺	TANG-3, to lie down
俘	FU-2, to take prisoner; to capture military equipment	趟	TANG-4; a measure for trips or visits; column, row

梯	TI-1, ladder, stairs	驢	LYU-2, donkey 驴
剃	TI-4, to shave	慮	LYU-4, be anxious; to plan 虑
吐	TU-3, TU-4, to spit out, to vomit	攔	LAN-2, to stop someone from doing something; to enclose; to separate 拦
肚	DU-4, belly; DU-3, tripe	欄	LAN-2, railing; (newspaper) column or section 栏
狼	LANG-2, wolf	爛	LAN-4, be tender (from cooking); be soggy; be rotten or infected; to glisten 烂
浪	LANG-4, breakers, waves; be undisciplined, be reckless	鐮	LYAN-2, scythe, sickle 镰
龍	LUNG-2, dragon. DRAGON rad. (212) 龙	簾	LYAN-2, hanging screen; curtain, drape 帘
聾	LUNG-2, be deaf 聋	溝	GOU-1, gutter, ditch; to connect 沟
臘	LA-4, winter sacrifice (in the twelfth month) 腊	購	GOU-4, to buy 购
獵	LYE-4, hunt, to hunt 猎	搞	GAU-3, to do, to make; to manage; to get; to purge
爐	LU-2, fire pan, stove; brazier; censer 炉	稿	GAU-3, draft of a speech or article; manuscript

膏	GAU-1, ointment; fat, grease; be oily, rich, sleek	跨	KWA-4, to carry something hanging at your side
估	GU-1, to appraise, to estimate	墾	KEN-3, to open new land to cultivate 垦
姑	GU-1, unmarried girl; father's or husband's sister; temporarily; be lenient	懇	KEN-3, to beseech; earnestly 恳
枯	KU-1, dried wood; be withered, be dried out	喉	HOU-2, throat
攴	PU-3, to knock. KNOCK rad. (66). Compare 384, above.	猴	HOU-2, monkey
敲	CHYAU-1, to rap on; to blackmail; to gyp	漿	JYANG-3, to starch; thick fluid 浆
鍋	GWO-1, pot, pan; bowl (of a pipe) 锅	奬	JYANG-3, prize, reward 奖
禍	HWO-4, calamity 祸	醬	JYANG-4, sauce, (food) paste 酱
窩	WO-1, small hole; nest or burrow; to harbor; to bend 窝	嫁	JYA-4, to get married (be a bride); give (a daughter) in marriage
誇	KWA-1, to praise; to boast 夸	稼	JYA-4, husbandry; grain; to sow
垮	KWA-3, to collapse	頸	JING-3, neck, throat 颈

270

勁	JING-4, be strong, strength 劲	盾	DWUN-4, SHWUN-3, shield. 矛盾 *mau-2 dwun-4* and *mau-2 shwun-3*, contradiction
煎	JYAN-4, to fry; be anxious	澆	JYAU-1, to sprinkle; to wet down; to trickle; to insinuate yourself 浇
剪	JYAN-3, scissors; to cut with scissors	饒	RAU-2, to let somebody get away with something; to give away 饶
箭	JYAN-4, arrow	繞	RAU-4, to wind something around another thing; to go around; detour 绕
夾	JYA-1, to press (between two things, like chopsticks, tongs), to squeeze 夹	橋	CHYAU-2, bridge 桥
狹	SYA-2, be narrow 狭	驕	JYAU-1, high-spirited horse; "get on your high horse," be arrogant 骄
挾	SYE-2, to press, to pinch; to carry under the arm 挟	娶	CHYU-3, to marry (be a groom)
戒	JYE-4, to guard against; to warn against; be cautious	聚	JYU-4, to get together, to assemble
械	SYE-4, weapons; shackles or fetters	削	SYAU-1, to shave off, to peel (with a knife). Printed 削.
焦	JYAU-1, to burn; to scorch or roast	銷	SYAU-1, to melt (metal); to destroy; expenses 销
瞧	CHYAU-2, to look at	揃	SHAU-1, to pick up, to pick out

271

稍	SHAU-1, soldier's ration; a little bit	註	JU-4, to annotate
鎖	SWO-3, to lock, to chain up, lock; to do a lock-stitch 锁	植	JR-2, plant, to plant, to establish. Usually written 植.
欣	SYIN-1, joy	置	JR-4, buy. Often written 置.
掀	SYAN-1, to lift to one side; to raise up; to open; to whisk away	振	JEN-4, to shake, to shake up; to call back
刑	SYING-2, law; to punish, punishment	震	JEN-4, thunderclap; to shake; to get pregnant
型	SYING-2, earthen mold for casting; law	晨	CHEN-2, dawn; morning
媳	SYI-2, daughter-in-law	唇	CHWUN-2, lips
熄	SYI-2, to put out (a fire)	帳	JANG-4, awning, tent; bill, account; to plan 帐
箱	SYANG-1, box	脹	JANG-1, debt, account; account book, ledger 胀
霜	SHWANG-1, frost	徵	JENG-1, evidence; to examine evidence; to summon to court; to recruit or levy 征
柱	JU-4, pillar; to prop up, to support	懲	CHENG-2, to punish; to repress, to restrain 惩

微	WEI-1, be tiny, be small, be slight. Distinguish from *jeng-1* 徵 (previous page).	帖	TYE-1, to submit; be smooth; TYE-3, card, note; TYE-4, model calligraphy book
掌	JANG-3, palm of the hand; paw; to handle; to take in the hand	貼	TYE-1, to paste something on; to pay; close to; settled 贴
賞	SHANG-3, to reward; to enjoy 赏	徹	CHE-4, to penetrate; to understand; be ubiquitous; all 彻
棧	JAN-4, gallery, covered passage; shed, shop 栈	撤	CHE-4, to take away
殘	TSAN-2, to cut to pieces, to murder, murderer, bandit 残	撒	SA-3, to scatter; SA-1, to release. Distinguish from *che-4* "to take away" (above).
鎮	JEN-4, rural market town 镇	臭	CHOU-4, to stink; be conceited
愼	SHEN-4, be attentive, be careful. Often written 慎.	嗅	SYOU-4, to sniff, to smell
顚	DYAN-1, top of the head; top; to take a header, to tumble 颠	壽	SHOU-4, long life 寿
塡	TYAN-2, to fill, to stuff full	籌	CHOU-2, tally, ticket; plan, to plan 筹
沾	JAN-1, to moisten; to receive benefits; be infected by	鑄	JU-4, to cast metal; to model 铸
粘	JAN-1, to paste, to glue; NYAN-2, be sticky	牲	SHENG-1, cattle; sacrificial animal

273

甥	SHENG-1, sister's children	髒	DZANG-1, be dirty 脏
審	SHEN-3, to investigate judicially; to try 审	宿	SU-4, to lodge; old, in the past; SYOU-3, night (Peking dialect)
嬸	SHEN-3, wife of father's or husband's younger brother 婶	縮	SU-4, to coil up, to bind fast; to draw in, to shorten; SWO-1, to draw in, to 缩 shrink
率	SHWAI-4, to lead, be led; generally; LYU-4; a suffix: "rate"	搜	SOU-1, to investigate
摔	SHWAI-3, SHWAI-1, to throw down	瘦	SOU-4, be emaciated
牽	CHYAN-1, to drag, to drag into 牵	嫂	SAU-3, older brother's wife
糟	DZAU-1, be rotten, be ready to fall apart	唉	AI-1, Alas! That's too bad!
遭	DZAU-1, to revolve, turn or revolution; to meet with; chance	挨	AI-1, to push, to crowd against; to delay
澡	DZAU-3, to bathe	呀	YA-1; a sentence-final particle of surprise or admiration
操	TSAU-1, to take hold of, to take charge of	鴉	YA-1, crow, raven 鸦
葬	DZANG-4, to bury	芽	YA-2, bud, sprout

秧	YANG-1, rice shoot, sprout	勾	GOU-1, hook
映	YING-4, be bright	什	SHR-2, ten; file of ten soldiers; SHE-2; first syllable in *she-2 ma*, what?
紋 紋	WEN-2, embroidery	仇	CHOU-2, enemy; to hate
蚊	WEN-2, mosquito	汁	JR-1, juice, gravy
枉	WANG-3, be crooked, be unjust; to treat unjustly; be in vain	扔	RENG-1, to throw; to throw away
旺	WANG-4, be bright, be glorious	冊	TSE-4, booklet, album; to appoint
筐	KWANG-1, basket (usually without a handle); a measure for basketfuls	仙	SYAN-1, a Taoist "immortal"; hermit
狂	KWANG-3, be reckless, be wild	瓜	GWA-1, melon. MELON rad. (97)
乙	YI-3, twist; the second "heavenly stem." TWIST rad. (5). This is the independent form; compare 5, above.	幼	YOU-4, immature
叉	CHA-1, fork; CHA-2, block up; CHA-3, to spread (usually, one's legs)	奶	NAI-3, milk
刁	DYAU-1, be wicked	污	WU-1, stagnant water; foul

275

池	CHR-2, moat, pond	朵	DWO-3; a measure for flowers
妄	WANG-4, be phony	伙	HWO-3, utensils; furniture
冰	BING-1, ice	伍	WU-3, five (used in documents for 五); file of five men; company
扣	KOU-4, to detain; to deduct; to invert (cup, bowl, etc.); to latch; a measure for a ten percent discount	伏	FU-2, to lie face down; to surrender; to admit; ten-day period in July–August
灰	HWEI-1, ashes, dust; be ash-colored, gray	沈	CHEN-2, be heavy; to sink
匠	JYANG-4, mechanic, workman	牢	LAU-2, pen for cattle; prison; firmly, securely
尖	JYAN-1, be sharp	灶	DZAU-4, kitchen stove
劣	LYE-4, be vile	玖	JYOU-3, nine (used in documents for 九)
帆	FAN-1, sail	址	JR-3, foundation; boundary
兇	SYUNG-1, be severe, be fierce, be stern; be strong (liquor or tobacco)	赤	CHR-4, be bright red. RED rad. (155)
企	CHI-4, to stand on tiptoe; to expect	抖	DOU-3, to tremble, to shiver

276

扶	FU-2, to hang onto (for support); to give support to	忌	JI-4, to abstain from; taboo
丑	CHOU-3, clown; the second "earthly branch." Printed 丑.	尿	NYAU-4, SWEI-1, urine; NYAU-4, to piss
扭	NYOU-3, to twist, to wring; to swing the hips when walking	吼	HOU-3, HOU-4, roar (of animals)
投	TOU-2, to drop; to move to; to surrender; to project; to fit in with	妥	TWO-3, be safe, be reliable
抛	PAU-2, to throw away	吞	TWUN-1, to swallow; to embezzle
折	JE-2, to snap off; to fold; to pay as collateral; discount; SHE-2, be broken; to lose money; JE-1, to spill	肘	JOU-3, elbow, wrist, forearm
抓	JWA-1, to scratch; to grab; to arrest; to draft someone (also pronounced JAU-1)	伸	SHEN-1, to stretch out (a part of the body)
杏	SYING-4, apricot	佃	DYAN-4, to till; to hunt; farmer
邪	SYE-2, be evil, be unorthodox	皂	DZAU-4, be black. 肥皂 fei-2 dzau-4, soap
否	FOU-3, not; to deny	妒	DU-4, be jealous
即	JI-2, at once; precisely; even. Printed 即.	妖	YAU-1, be weird; be bewitching

277

姊	DZ-3, older sister (also pronounced JYE-3)	枕	JEN-3, to lay one's head on
肩	JYAN-1, shoulder	杯	BEI-1, cup, glass, goblet or other small vessel to drink from; a measure for these
衫	SHAN-1, shirt, garment for upper part of body; robe, gown	松	SUNG-1, pine tree
炊	CHWEI-1, to cook	析	SYI-1, to split wood; to divide up; to explain
武	WU-3, military, martial	奈	NAI-4, but; how; endure
坦	TAN-3, be level	孤	GU-1, fatherless; solitary
臥	WO-4, to lie prone (usually said of animals); to sleep. Printed 臥.	叔	SHU-1, father's younger brother; husband's younger brother
協 协	SYE-2, be united in; to help	呼	HU-1, to breathe out; to call out; to snore
抹	MWO-3, to wipe clean, to wipe out; to wipe on, to smear on	刮	GWA-1, to scrape, to pare; to take advantage of, to exploit
拖	TWO-1, to drag	股	GU-3; a measure for puffs, whiffs, skeins, bands, gangs, surges, and shares of stock
拆	CHAI-1, to take apart	兔	TU-4, rabbit

延	YAN-2, to delay, to protract, to lengthen; to invite	疫	YI-4, pestilence, epidemic
叁	SAN-1, three (used in documents for 三)	毒	DU-2, be poisonous; be malicious; poison; bad drugs
糾	JYOU-1, to collect; confederacy; to investigate; to correct 纠	挖	WA-1, to dig; to hire away (from a competitor)
柒	CHI-1, seven (used in documents for 七)	拴	SHWAN-1, to fasten one thing to another
染	RAN-3, to dye; to form bad habits; to catch (a disease)	砍	KAN-3, to chop, to slash; to hit with a thrown object
津	JIN-1, ford or ferry; Tientsin	耍	SHWA-3, to play with, to juggle
室	SHR-4, a room	柔	ROU-2, be soft, be gentle or mild
突	TU-2, to stick out; to break through; to offend; sudden	屎	SHR-3, shit, feces; secretion
迹	JI-1, footprint; trace of; to search out or run down, to track	屍	SHR-1, corpse, carcass
迷	MI-2, to get lost; to get dirt in your eye; to develop an (unreasonable) passion for; fan, "bug"	眉	MEI-2, eyebrow
施	SHR-1, to spread, to spray; to give as charity; to put into effect (laws, etc.)	虐	NYWE-4, be cruel

279

咱	DZAN-2, DZA-2, I. 咱們 dza-2 men-2, we (you and I, the speaker and person spoken to)	姨	YI-2, mother's sister; wife's sister
炭	TAN-4, charcoal, coal	娃	WA-2, baby, child; pretty girl
卸	SYE-4, to unload; to unhitch; to get rid of	姪	JR-2, brother's child
缸	GANG-1, cistern, vat, crock	怒	NU-4, anger, passion, rage
威	WEI-1, to threaten; to inspire awe	浴	YU-4, to bathe
怨	YWAN-4, to hate; to criticize	宮	GUNG-1, palace, temple, college, dwelling
肺	FEI-4, lungs	悟	WU-4, to wake up; to notice
勉	MYAN-3, to exert yourself; to urge	凍	DUNG-4, to freeze; be cold, be freezing; jelly 冻
促	TSU-2, to rush, be rushed; to urge	訊	SYUN-4, to admonish someone; to make a judicial investigation 讯
侮	WU-3, insult, to insult, to demean	疾	JI-2, be sick; to consider "sick," to hate; be rushed
追	JWEI-1, to chase; to investigate	疼	TENG-2, to ache; to dote on

280

庫	HU-4, armory, granary, treasury 庫	栗	LI-4, chestnut
座	DZWO-4; a measure for buildings, mountains, cities, clocks, tombs	捌	BA-1, eight (used in documents for 八)
扇	SHAN-4, a fan; a measure for windows	捉	JWO-1, to catch, to capture
祥	SYANG-2, happiness; service for dead parents	捐	JYWAN-1, to contribute; to solicit contributions
羞	SYOU-1, to blush; to make someone blush; shame	挽	WAN-3, to pull back; to restore
素	SU-4, be elemental; be simple or plain; element	核	HE-2, pit, fruitstone; nucleus; to check up on
索	SWO-3, rope; to tie up; to demand; rule	桂	GWEI-4, cassia, cinnamon; Kwangsi; a surname
恥	CHR-3, to feel ashamed, shame	鬯	CHANG-4, mixed wine, sacrificial wine. MIXED WINE rad. (192)
埋	MAI-3, to bury	套	TAU-4, to wrap in; to harness or hitch up; covering; a measure for sets, suits of clothes
速	SU-4, speed	辱	RU-4, to disgrace, disgrace, insult
逐	JU-2, to chase	桑	SANG-1, mulberry tree

柴	CHAI-2, firewood	癸	GWEI-3, the tenth "heavenly stem"
閃 閃 闪	SHAN-3, to flash; to dodge; lightning	徒	TU-2, disciple; bum; be in vain; be empty, be bare
哪	NA-3, NEI-3, which one? whichever; NA; a sentence-final particle: 啊, or 呢 + 啊	剝	BWO-1, to peel
恩	EN-1, grace, mercy	娛	YU-2, to amuse
爹	DYE-1, papa, daddy	液	YE-4, juices, sap
翁	WENG-1, old man; title of respect	淚	LEI-4, tears, to weep
耗	HAU-4, to waste; to keep deadlocked. 耗子 hau-4 dz-3, mouse, rat	淋	LIN-2, to pour on, to drench; LIN-4, to strain, to filter
秤	CHENG-4, steelyard; weight used with a steelyard	淹	YAN-1, to submerge, to flood
胸	SYUNG-1, thorax, chest	毫	HAU-2, a fine hair; one thousandth part; before 不, intensifies the negation
脈	MAI-4, pulse; blood vessel; range (of mountains)	旋	SYWAN-2, to revolve; thereupon
烏 乌	WU-1, crow; be black	啟 启	CHI-3, to begin; to announce

粒	LI-4, grain, tiny piece	晝 昼	JOU-4, daytime
執 执	JR-2, to take hold of; to manage, direct	陷	SYAN-4, to sink down (as into mud); to entrap, to capture
軟 软	RWAN-3, be soft, pliable	虛	SYU-1, be poor (in health); be empty; be unreal; be humble
堅 坚	JYAN-1, be firm, be strong	荷	HE-2, lotus
掘	JYWE-2, to dig	閉 闭	BI-4, to close; to stop up
授	SHOU-4, to give, to confer; to transmit	蛇	SHE-2, snake
捨 舍	SHE-3, to give as charity; to part with	貪 贪	TAN-1, be greedy for, be avaricious
梳	SHU-4, comb, to comb	彩	TSAI-3, be ornamented; be good luck
桶	TUNG-3, a (six-pint) bucket; tub, cask	釣 钓	DYAU-4, to go fishing, to catch with hook and line
麥 麦	MAI-4, wheat. WHEAT rad. (199)	斜	SYE-2, to slant, to cause to slant
爽	SHWANG-3, be lively; be agreeable	敍	SYU-4, to chat, to chat about; rank, to rank

283

笨	BEN-4, be stupid, be clumsy	渡	DU-4, to ferry across; to spend (some time)
笛	DI-2, flute, whistle	湊	TSOU-4, to crowd, to form a crowd, to get together
甜	TYAN-2, be sweet	渣	JA-1, sediment, refuse; fragment
梨	LI-2, pear	湧	YUNG-3, to bubble up; to flow rapidly
脱	TWO-1, to take off (one's clothes)	寒	HAN-2, be cold, be wintry
脚	JYAU-3, foot; kick; JYWE-2, role (in a play)	割	GE-1, to cut
售	SHOU-4, to sell	冤	YWAN-1, to cheat, to get cheated, cheat; rival; be a waste of time
偽	WEI-4, be fake. Usually printed 僞. 伪	惰	DWO-4, be lazy
健	JYAN-4, to strengthen, be strong; be regular	愉	YU-2, be happy
偵	JEN-1, spy, to spy. 侦	惱	NAU-3, be angry, be mad at 恼
猛	MENG-3, be fierce, be violent; be potent (as medicine); suddenly	棄	CHI-4, to throw away

裕	YU-4, be abundant, be generous; to enrich	握	WO-4, to hold fast
善	SHAN-4, be good; be good at	插	CHA-1, to stick in, to insert
貳	ER-4, be double; two (used for 二 in documents) 贰	捏	NYE-1, to hold tight (between the thumb and other fingers), to pinch; to mold with the fingers
琴	CHIN-2, an ancient Chinese musical instrument, like the zither: a *ch'in*	椒	JYAU-1, pepper
壹	YI-1, one (used for 一 in documents)	棉	MYAN-2, cotton-padded; cotton
逼	BI-1, to press, to crowd; to annoy	硬	YING-4, be hard, be stiff, be stubborn
堤	TI-2, dike, dam	雄	SYUNG-2, male (of lions, chickens); be ambitious; be strong
惑	HWO-4, to mislead, to doubt	尋	SYUN-2, to look for 寻
粟	SU-4, millet, maize; rent (paid in grain)	粥	JOU-1, congee (rice gruel, millet gruel)
喪	SANG-1, to mourn parents; SANG-4, to lose; be lost (to die) 丧	紫	DZ-3, be purple, purple color
揀	JYAN-3, to choose 拣	菌	JYUN-4, mushroom; mildew, mold

喂	WEI-4, to feed (child or animal); "hello" (on the phone); Hi!	黍	SHU-3, glutinous millet. MILLET rad. (202)
悶	MEN-4, be stuffy; be bored; MEN-1, be stuffy; be muffled; to steep 闷	腔	CHYANG-1, hollow space; cavity; tune or intonation; cadenza
晶	JING-1, be clear	傲	AU-4, be arrogant
跌	DYE-2, to stumble and fall; to drop (in price)	貸	DAI-4, to lend at interest; to borrow; to forgive 贷
嵌	CHYAN-1, deep valley; to fall into; to inlay	堡	BAU-3, walled village; stronghold; -burg
飲	YIN-3, to drink; YIN-4, to water animals 饮	貿	MAU-4, to barter 贸
筋	JIN-1, tendon; vein (as seen from outside); nerve; plant fiber	猶	YOU-2, to be like; and, yet, still 犹
筍	SWUN-3, bamboo shoot	絨	RUNG-2, wool, floss, down, sponge, velvet 绒
程	CHENG-2; a measure for periods of time; awhile; journey; a standard	絡	LWO-4, LAU-4, to fall; to result; to occur 络
稀	SYI-1, be sparse, thin, infrequent	滑	HWA-2, be slippery; be untrustworthy; to slide
犁	LI-2, plow, to plow	塗	TU-2, to daub; to erase; to make a mess of 涂

溜	LYOU-1, to glide; to coast; to sneak; to watch; to sauté; LYOU-4, to walk; line; a current	隔	GE-2, partition, to partition; be separated from; every other
塞	SAI-4, strategic pass; SAI-1, to stop up; stopper or cork	虜	LU-3, to capture, captive 虏
煉	LYAN-4, to boil down; to refine, to purify 炼	暈	YUN-4, halo; be sick (motion sickness) 晕
匯	HWEI-4, to remit 汇	睜	JENG-1, to open your eyes
雷	LEI-2, thunder	盟	MENG-2, solemn declaration before the gods; oath; covenant; Mongol league
頑	WAN-2, be stupid; be stubborn; be mischievous 顽	歇	SYE-1, to rest; to stop
塘	TANG-2, pond, tank; embankment	爺	YE-2, grandfather; father 爷
肆	SZ-4, four (used for 四 in documents)	飾	SHR-4, ornament, to ornament 饰
禁	JIN-4, prohibit	筷	KWAI-4, chopsticks
碑	BEI-1, memorial tablet, monument, gravestone	愁	CHOU-2, be worried; be depressed; to worry about
疊	DYE-2 to fold; to repeat 迭	腰	YAU-1, waist; small of the back; kidney

287

催	TSWEI-1, to urge, to press	豪	HAU-2, be brave
舅	JYOU-4, maternal uncle; wife's brother	慘	TSAN-3, be tragic; be cruel; be "bad news" (students' slang) 慘
躲	DWO-3, to dodge; to hide from, to hide	瘟	WEN-1, epidemic
龠	YWE-4, flute. FLUTE rad. (214)	瘋	FENG-1, be insane; to act wild 疯
剿	JYAU-3, to attack; to plagiarize	塵	CHEN-2, dust, dirt; the non-spiritual world 尘
滾	GWUN-3, to roll; to roil, to boil	魂	HWUN-2, soul
漲	JANG-3, to rise (said of a river or price); JANG-4, to swell; to rise 漲	墊	DYAN-4, to fill up 垫
漏	LOU-4, to leak	酸	SWAN-1, acid; to taste sour; be pedantic
寡	GWA-3, be few, be alone; to lessen	誓	SHR-4, oath
辣	LA-4, be hot, be peppery; be harsh; to get burned by peppery food	磁	TSZ-2, magnetic; porcelain, china
遮	JE-1, to cover, to shade	凳	DENG-4, stool, bench

288

屢	LYU-3, repeatedly, time after time 屢	潔	JYE-2, be clean, be pure, be clear 洁
蒜	SWAN-4, garlic	潤	RWUN-4, to wet; be sleek; to enrich; to adorn 润
蓋	GAI-4, lid; bug's or turtle's shell; to put a lid on; to build; to mark with a "chop" (seal or stamp) 盖	諒	LYANG-4, to suppose; to forgive; to sympathize with 谅
蒸	JENG-1, to steam something	廚	CHU-2, kitchen
嗽	SOU-4, to cough	慶	CHING-4, good luck, blessings; to reward 庆
夥	HWO-3, to collaborate; be partners; band, partnership 伙	褲	KU-4, trousers 裤
蝕	SHR-3, to nibble; eclipse 蚀	穀	GU-3, grain, corn 谷
熏	SYUN-1, distinguished service; award for such service	輛	LYANG-4; a measure for vehicles 辆
鼻	BI-2, nose. BIG NOSE rad. (209). Called "big nose" to distinguish it from 515, above.	輪	LWUN-2, wheel; to revolve; be someone's turn 轮
銜	SYAN-2, bit; to hold in the mouth; gag 衔	豎	SHU-4, to set upright; be vertical; vertical stroke (in calligraphy) 竖
嫩	NEN-4, NWUN-4, be tender; be inexperienced; be light (in color)	賢	SYAN-2, be virtuous; to esteem

遲	CHR-2, be late 迟	膚	FU-1, skin 肤
醋	TSU-4, vinegar	齒	CHR-3, teeth; age. TEETH rad. (211) 齿
歎	TAN-4, to sigh	瞎	SYA-1, be blind, to go blind, blindly; be tangled up
撞	JWANG-4, to hit, to collide, to conflict. Also read CHWANG-2.	閱	YWE-4, to examine; to read carefully; to pass through 阅
榣	GAI-4, in general	蝦	SYA-1, shrimp 虾
撲	PU-1, to pounce on; to put on with a powder puff 扑	踪	DZUNG-1, footprint, trace
樁	JWANG-1, stake or post; a measure for affairs 桩	踢	TI-1, to kick
橫	HENG-2, be horizontal; to set horizontally; horizontal stroke (in writing); HENG-4, rude; accidental	踏	TA-4, to step on; pedal; to step out, to stroll
厲	LI-4, be severe, be harsh 厉	遺	YI-2, to leave behind 遗
履	LYU-3, to carry out	銳	RWEI-4, be sharp 锐
慰	WEI-4, to console, to soothe	鋤	CHU-2, hoe, to hoe 锄

290

稻	DAU-4, rice plant; unhulled rice	擁	YUNG-3, to crowd; to rally to the support of; support 拥
膠	JYAU-1, be sticky; glue, sticky substance; rubber, plastic 胶	擋	DANG-3, to block 挡
皺	JOU-4, be wrinkled, to wrinkle 皱	奮	FEN-4, to rouse; be aroused 奋
激	JI-1, to force out under pressure (as water); to spray; to stir up	磚	JWAN-1, brick, tile 砖
憑	PING-2, to lean on; due to the fact that; basis; What! (exclamation of surprise) 凭	蔬	SHU-1, pulse; legumes
辨	BYAN-4, to tell apart	瞞	MAN-2, to blind; to deceive 瞒
謎	MI-2, riddle 谜	鴨	YA-1, duck 鸭
諜	DYE-2, to spy 谍	嘴	DZWEI-4, mouth, bill, spout
糕	GAU-1, cake	錫	SYI-2, tin, copper 锡
燃	RAN-2, to burn, to set on fire	錘	CHWEI-2, hammer, to hammer; weight on a steelyard 锤
融	RUNG-2, to smelt	築	JU-2, to ram down 筑

二羽 彳止止	SE-4, to taste tart; to feel rough (to the touch) 涩	薑	JYANG-1, ginger 姜
賽	SAI-4, to compete, to rival 赛	瞭	LYAU-3, to finish, to conclude; to understand; LYAU-4, to look into the distance 了
糞	FEN-4, manure, shit 粪	顆	KE-1; a measure for seeds, grains, bullets, stars, jewels 颗
臨	LIN-2, be near; to copy (a painting or calligraphy) 临	闊	KWO-4, be wealthy; be broad 阔
醜	CHOU-3, be ugly 丑	嚇	SYA-4, HE-4, to scare 吓
擦	TSA-1, to wipe; nearly	鮮	SYAN-1, be fresh; to taste delicious; SYAN-3, be rare 鲜
擠	JI-3, to crowd, be crowded; to squeeze (e.g., a pimple) 挤	儲	CHU-2, to collect 储
隸	LI-4, be attached to; to control 隶	縱	DZUNG-4, to let something go uncontrolled; vertical; even though 纵
翼	YI-4, wing	瀉	SYE-4, to leak; to have diarrhea 泻
薪	SYIN-1, firewood; salary	灑	SA-3, to sprinkle; to spill 洒
薦	JYAN-4, to recommend someone 荐	額	E-2, forehead; fixed number 额

戀	LYAN-4, to love 恋	髟須	SYU-1, whiskers, beard 须
懷	HWAI-2, bosom; to emboss-om; to carry next to the bosom; be pregnant; to harbor; to have in mind 怀	覆	FU-4, to overturn; to defeat; to reply to 复
癢	YANG-3, to itch 痒	攤	TAN-1, to spread out, to display; vendor's stand; to spread around 摊
襪	WA-4, stocking, sock 袜	櫃	GWEI-4, counter (in a store), showcase, cupboard, cabinet, wardrobe; store 柜
襖	AU-3, coat, jacket 袄	麵	MYAN-4, flour; noodle; be mushy 面
霸	BA-4, bully, tyrant, to bully, to tyrannize	戳	CHWO-1, to jab; to stand a thing up; stamp, seal
露	LU-4, dew, juice; to expose to view	曬	SHAI-4, to sun a thing; be sunny and hot 晒
靈	LING-2, be effective; be alert; spirit, soul; coffin (with the body inside) 灵	蟲	CHUNG-2, bug; worm 虫
騎	CHI-2, to sit astride; to ride (e.g., an animal or bi-cycle) 骑	壘	LEI-3, to heap up; ramparts 垒
騾	LWO-2, mule 骡	饑	JI-1, famine 饥
髟松	SUNG-1, be loose, to loosen up; be easygoing; be light (said of cakes) 松	鑲	SYANG-1, to trim or edge with something; to set, to mount (e.g., jewels) 镶

鑼	LWO-2, gong 锣	犧	SYI-1; used mainly in 犧牲 *syi-1 sheng-1*, sacrifice 牺
鑰	YAU-4, key 钥	譽	YU-4, fame; praise, to praise 誉
籍	JI-2, population record, register	纏	CHAN-2, to wrap around, to roll up; to keep bothering someone 缠
仍	RENG-2, as before, still	末	MWO-4, last part, end; dust
判	PAN-4, to separate, to judge. Printed 判.	沿	YAN-2, border, edge; to follow, to fringe; along
狀	JWANG-4, shape, appearance; condition; official document	牧	MU-4, shepherd; local judge; a surname
席	SYI-2, mat; banquet; a surname	紛	FEN-1, tangled, confusing; profuse 纷
淺	CHYAN-3, shallow, superficial; mild 浅	衛	WEI-4, to defend, to assist; guard; a surname 卫

PHONETIC SYMBOLS

(bwo, pwo, mwo, fwo)

INITIALS				
B–sy used only as initials; *j–s* used as initials or as full syllables.				

ㄅ *b*	ㄅ			ㄍ *g*	ㄑ	ㄍ		
ㄆ *p*	ㄅ ㄆ			ㄎ *k*	⁻ ㄎ			
ㄇ *m*	ˋ ㄇ			ㄏ *h*	⁻ ㄏ			
ㄈ *f*	⁻ ㄈ			ㄐ *jy-*	ㄴ ㄐ			
ㄉ *d*	ㄅ ㄉ			ㄑ *chy-*	ㄑ			
ㄊ *t*	⁻ ㄊ ㄊ			ㄒ *sy-*	⁻ ㄒ			
ㄋ *n*	ㄋ			ㄓ *j*	ㄴ ㄩ ㄓ ㄓ			
ㄌ *l*	ㄅ ㄌ			ㄔ *ch*	´ ⁄ ㄔ			
				ㄕ *sh*	ㄱ ㄱ ㄕ			

日 *r*	丨 冂 冃 日
卩 *dz*	𠃌 卩
ち *ts*	一 ち
ㄙ *s*	ㄥ ㄙ

又 *ou*	𠃌 又
马 *an*	𠃌 马
ㄣ *en*	ㄣ
尤 *ang*	一 尤
ㄥ *eng*	ㄥ
儿 *er*	丿 儿
一 *i*	一
乂 *u*	丿 乂
ㄩ *yu*	ㄴ ㄩ

FINALS

These can stand alone as syllables or can combine with initials.

Y *a*	丶 丷 Y
ㄛ *wo*	一 ㄛ
さ *e*	一 さ
历 *ai*	一 𠃌 历
㇏ *ei*	㇏
幺 *au*	㇑ 幺 幺

COMPLEX FINALS

These can stand alone as syllables or can combine with initials.

Ȳ *ya*	一 丶 丷 Ȳ

世 ye	一　二　干　世	ㄨㄟ wei	ㄨ　ㄨㄟ
万 yai	一　二　丂　万	ㄨㄢ wan	ㄨ　ㄨㄢ　ㄨㄢ
幺 yau	一　乙　幺　幺	ㄨㄣ wen	ㄨ　ㄨㄣ
又 you	一　丆　又	ㄨㄤ wang	ㄨ　ㄨ　ㄨㄤ　ㄨㄤ
弓 yan	一　丆　弓	ㄨㄥ weng	ㄨ　ㄨㄥ
ㄣ -in, yin	一　ㄣ	ㄩㄝ ywe	ㄥ　ㄩ　ㄩㄝ　ㄩㄝ　ㄩㄝ
尢 yang	一　二　干　尢	ㄩㄢ ywan	ㄩ　ㄩㄢ　ㄩㄢ
ㄥ -ing, ying	一　ㄥ	ㄩㄣ yun	ㄩ　ㄩㄣ
ㄚ wa	ノ　ㄨ　ㄨ　ㄨ　ㄚ	ㄩㄥ yung	ㄩ　ㄩㄥ
ㄨㄛ wo	ㄨ　ㄨ　ㄨㄛ		
ㄨㄞ wai	ㄨ　ㄨ　ㄨㄞ　ㄨㄞ		

Tone marks for words written in these phonetic symbols are ´, ˇ, and `, for tones 2, 3, and 4, respectively. They are written to the right of the syllable. Tone 1 is indicated by the absence of a tone mark. Neutral tones are not indicated. For usage examples, see page 298.

297

COMPARISON CHART

Characters, Symbols, and Romanization

Below are examples of the four systems for writing Chinese presented in this book. The expressions written in Yale romanization show the modified Yale style used throughout this book; normal Yale romanization uses accent marks like those used in *pinyin*, as explained on the facing page. The number after the definition is the serial number of the character in whose explanatory block the character combination appears.

Chinese character/ phonetic symbol		Modified Yale	Pinyin	Definition
女	人	nyu-3 ren-2	nǚ rén	woman (11)
大	小	da-4 syau-3	dà xiǎo	size (50)
不	好	bu-4 hau-3	bù hǎo	No good! (73)
中	國	jung-1 gwo-2	zhōng guó	China (114)
日	本	r-4 ben-3	rì běn	Japan (235)
知	道	jr-1 dau-4	zhī dào	to know (267)
句	子	jyu-4 dz-3	jù zǐ	sentence (289)
客	氣	ke-4 chi-4	kè qì	be polite (325)
學	會	sywe-2 hwei-4	xué huì	to learn (330)
旅	行	lyu-3 sying-2	lǚ xíng	to travel (954)

CONVERSION CHART

Pinyin to Yale Romanization

This conversion chart provides a quick and convenient reference for students using textbooks or other materials in which *pinyin* spellings occur. It shows only those spellings in *pinyin* that differ from those in the Yale romanization system. The tone marks for both systems are ˉ, ´, ˘, and ` for tones 1, 2, 3, and 4, respectively.

INITIALS

Pinyin	Yale
c	*ts*
(*ch* = *ch*)	
q	*ch* (before *i* or *y*)
x	*s* (before *y*)
z	*dz*
zh	*j* (except before *i* or *y*)

MEDIALS

Pinyin	Yale
-*i*-	-*y*-
-*u*-	-*w*-

FINALS

Pinyin	Yale
ao	*au*
iu	*you*
o	*wo*
ong	*ung*
ui	*wei*
un	*wun*

FULL SYLLABLES

Pinyin	Yale	Pinyin	Yale
ci	*tsz*	*ri*	*r*
ju	*jyu*	*shi*	*shr*
jun	*jyun*	*si*	*sz*
lü	*lyu*	*xu*	*syu*
nü	*nyu*	*xuan*	*sywan*
nüe	*nywe*	*xue*	*sywe*
qu	*chyu*	*xun*	*syun*
quan	*chywan*	*zhi*	*jr*
que	*chywe*	*zi*	*dz*

ALPHABETICAL INDEX

The alphabetical index includes all the characters presented in this book. The characters are alphabetized according to their pronunciation in the Yale system of romanization. A character with two or more pronunciations will appear under each pronunciation. All characters with the same Yale spellings are listed in order of ascending tone. Exceptions to this arise in the case of phonetic-series listings; here, the character that provides the key to the phonetic series appears first, followed by characters sharing that element and having the same reading. Since the tone of the key character may sometimes be numerically higher than that of a character in its group, the student should make sure, when using this index, to scan up and down a group of characters sharing the same spelling. This kind of index arrangement reflects the nature of the Chinese writing system and therefore provides a convenient visual review aid.

If a character is in the first character group, that character's series number (1–1062) is given in roman type. If a character is also a radical, its number in the sequence of 214 radicals is given in superscript. Characters in the second group are referenced by the page number (pp. 239–294) set in italic type and followed by the letter *a* or *b* to indicate whether the character appears on the left (*a*) or right (*b*) side of the page.

bi–3 匕 137[21]
bi–3 比 567[81]
bi–3 彼 877
bi–3 筆 91
bi–4 幣 p.267b
bi–4 壁 p.249a
bi–4 避 p.249a
bi–4 必 494
bi–4 畢 950
bi–4 閉 p.283b
bing–1 兵 p.256b
bing–1 冫 564[15]
bing–1 冰 p.276a
bing–3 丙 533
bing–4 病 534
bing–3 餅 p.265b
bing–4 併 p.266a
bing–4 並 653
bu–3 卜 118[25]
bu–3 捕 p.264a
bu–3 補 p.264a
bu–4 不 73
bu–4 步 668
bu–4 布 958
bu–4 佈 p.259b
bu–4 部 603
bu–4 簿 p.264a
bwo–1 剝 p.282b
bwo–1 撥 p.267b
bwo–1 播 p.246b
bwo–1 波 p.239a
bwo–2 伯 p.258a
bwo–2 博 p.264a
bwo–2 薄 p.264a
bwo–4 癶 632[105]
byan–1 邊 575
byan–3 扁 p.247b
byan–1 編 p.247b

byan–4 遍 p.247b
byan–4 便 126
byan–1 鞭 p.262b
byan–4 變 667
byan–4 辛 550
byan–4 辨 p.291a
byan–4 采 516[165]
byau–1 標 p.258b
byau–1 髟 946[190]
byau–3 表 110
byau–3 錶 111
bye–2 別 208

—C—

cha–1, cha–2, cha–3
　叉 p.275a
cha–1 插 p.285b
cha–2 察 981
cha–2 查 914
cha–2 茶 361
cha–4, cha–1, chai–1
　差 501
chai–1 拆 p.278a
chai–2 柴 p.282a
chan–3 產 626
chan–2 纏 p.294b
chang–1 昌 344
chang–4 倡 p.251b
chang–4 唱 345
chang–2 長 226[168]
chang–2 镸 889[168]
chang–2 常 368
chang–2 腸 p.255b
chang–3, chang–2
　場 995
chang–3 廠 p.258b
chang–4 鬯 p.281b[192]
chau–1 超 p.249a

抄 炒 吵 朝 潮 車 少 徹 撤 塵 沈 臣 辰 晨 陳 稱 趁

懲 成 城 誠 承 乘 秤 七 柒 妻 漆 其 欺 旗 期 奇 騎 齊 程

气 气 汽 氣 啓 豈 起 器 企 棄 侵 親 勤 琴 輕 青 情 晴 清

請 慶 抽 仇 愁 籌 綢 酬 醜 丑 臭 吃 持 池 遲 尺 恥 齒 彳

球
區
驅
屈
曲
取
娶
趣
去
羣
窮
圈
拳
券
全
泉
權
勸
犬

犭
缺
却
確

—D—

答
搭
達
打
大
呆
歹
歺
代
袋
貸
大
帶

島
道
導
盜
稻
的
德
得
登
燈
凳
等
提
笛
氐
低
底

待
戴
隶
擔
膽
單
彈
旦
但
淡
石
蛋
當
擋
黨
刀
刂
到
倒

抵 的 地 弟 第 商 滴 敵 帝 丁 釘 頂 訂 鼎 定 都 斗 抖 豆

鬥 都 賭 毒 獨 讀 度 渡 妒 肚 冬 東 凍 董 懂 動 洞 端 短

段 斷 堆 兌 對 隊 多 奪 隋 惰 朵 躲 盾 頓 顛 典 點 佃 墊

店 電 刁 弔 掉 調 釣 爹 疊 諜 跌 丟 姿 資 姊 子 字 紫

自
咱
雜
哉
栽
載
災
再
在
咱
瓚
讚
葬
髒
藏
臟
糟
遭
早

棗
澡
灶
皂
造
則
責
擇
澤
賊
怎
曾
增
贈
走
租
祖
組

導
遵
阻
族
足
宗
踪
總
縱
鑽
嘴
最
罪
醉
昨
作
ナ
左
做
坐
座

—E—
俄
餓
額
惡
恩
而
兒
尔
耳
二
貳

—F—
發

紡 訪 放 非 匪 飛 肥 肺 費 廢 分 紛 粉 份 墳 憤 糞 奮 妨 房 防

乏 罰 法 髮 翻 凡 帆 煩 繁 反 販 飯 犯 範 匚 方

復 複 覆 福 副 富 服 甫 付 符 府 腐 附 婦 父 斧 負 傅

丰 豐 蜂 逢 縫 鋒 封 風 瘋 否 缶 夫 膚 俘 浮 伏 弗 扶 复

310

gung-1 弓 218⁵⁷
gung-1 躬 988
gung-1 宮 p.280b
gung-3 廾 141⁵⁵
gung-4 共 297
gung-1, gung-4
　供 p.249a
gung-1 恭 p.249b
gwa-1 刮 p.278b
gwa-1 瓜 p.275b⁹⁷
gwa-3 寡 p.288a
gwa-4 掛 p.242a
gwai-4 夬 469
gwai-4 怪 592
gwan-4 卝 504
gwan-1 絲 505
gwan-1 關 506
gwan-1 官 407
gwan-3 管 742
gwan-3 館 408
gwan-4 貫 769
gwan-4 慣 1050
gwan-4 蕚 193
gwan-1 觀 796
gwan-4 灌 p.251b
gwan-4 罐 p.251b
gwang-1 光 748
gwang-3 廣 972
gwei-1 圭 422
gwei-4 桂 p.281b
gwei-1 歸 p.263b
gwei-1 規 795
gwei-1 龜 p.264a²¹³
gwei-3 癸 p.282b
gwei-3 軌 p.262a
gwei-3 鬼 291¹⁹⁴
gwei-4 貴 124
gwei-4 櫃 p.293b

gwo-1 鍋 p.270a
gwo-4 過 514
gwo-2 國 114
gwo-3 果 597
gwun-3 ｜ 3²
gwun-3 滾 p.288a
gwun-4 棍 p.258a

—H—

ha-1 哈 p.266a
hai-2 還 448
hai-3 海 602
hai-4 亥 250
hai-2 孩 251
hai-4 害 1001
han-2 含 p.265a
han-2 寒 p.284b
han-3 厂 154²⁷
han-3 喊 p.245b
han-4 旱 p.241a
han-4 汗 182
han-4 漢 p.259a
hang-2 航 953
hang-2 行 421¹⁴⁴
hau-2 毫 p.282b
hau-2 豪 p.288b
hau-3 好 19
hau-4 号 690
hau-2, hau-4 號 691
hau-4 耗 p.282a
he-2 何 823
he-2 河 557
he-2 荷 p.283b
he-2 合 176
he-2 和 p.239a
he-2 曷 387
he-1, he-4 喝 388
he-2 核 p.281b

貫
慣
蕚
觀
灌
罐
光
廣
圭
桂
歸
規
龜
癸
軌
鬼
貴
櫃

弓
躬
宮
廾
共
供
恭
刮
瓜
寡
掛
夬
怪
卝
絲
關
官
管
館

鍋
過
國
果
｜
滾
棍

旱
汗
漢
航
行
毫
豪
好
号
號
耗
何
河
荷
合
和
曷
喝
核

—H—

哈
還
海
亥
孩
害
含
寒
厂
喊

311

禾
嚇
賀
黑
很
恨
橫
候
喉
猴
吼
厚
後
呼
忽
壺
胡
湖
虍

虎
庫
互
戶
護
烘
哄
轟
紅
滑
華
化
花
畫
劃
話
胡
湖
虍

淮
襄
懷
壞
歡
莧
圜
環
還
緩
奐
喚
換
患
荒
慌
謊
皇
蝗

黃
揮
灰
恢
回
悔
毀
會
匯
活
火
灬
伙
夥
和
或
惑
禍
皇
蝗

隻 獲 貨 昏 婚 魂 混

沾 佔 站 展 斬 暫 戰 棧 章 掌 長 張 脹 帳 丈 仗 朝

—J—

渣 乍 榨 炸 詐 摘 窄 債 占 粘

針 參 珍 疹 診 枕 振 震 陣 徵 爭 睜 蒸 正 征 整 政 症 證

着 找 爪 爫 召 招 昭 照 着 遮 折 者 這 偵 真 鎮 亲

几 集 己 紀 忌 記 幾 機 饑 擠 濟 給 季 寄 彑 彐 技 既 繼 計
基 擊 激 績 積 迹 鷄 亼 即 吉 結 亟 極 急 疾 籍 及 級

際 今 巾 斤 近 津 筋 金 僅 緊 浸 盡 禁 進 京 景 巠 經 頸
勁 晶 睛 精 井 敬 驚 警 淨 靜 竟 境 鏡 競 周 週 州 洲 粥

315

撞 追 佳 錐 捉 桌 准 準 加 架 夾 家 嫁 稼 叚 假 甲 賈 價

尖 兼 堅 菓 艱 奸 开 戔 賤 監 肩 間 簡 儉 檢 剪 箭 煎 柬

揀 減 件 建 健 漸 薦 見 將 獎 漿 醬 江 薑 講 降 強 匠 交

較 校 教 椒 澆 焦 繳 膠 驕 剿 脚 角 叫 覺 街 階 卩 㔾

jye-2 截 *p.263b*
jye-2 潔 *p.289b*
jye-2 節 *p.259a*
jye-2, jye-1, jye-3
　　結 778
jye-3 姐 221
jye-3 姊 *p.278a*
jye-3 解 905
jye-4 介 600
jye-4 界 601
jye-4 妾 701
jye-1 接 702
jye-4 借 794
jye-4 戒 *p.271a*
jyou-1 丩 258
jyou-1 糾 *p.279a*
jyou-3 久 631
jyou-3 玖 *p.276b*
jyou-3 九 151
jyou-1, jyou-4 究 768
jyou-3 酒 364
jyou-3 韮 *p.262a*[179]
jyou-4 就 300
jyou-4 救 747
jyou-4 臼 229[134]
jyou-4 舅 *p.288a*
jyou-4 舊 356
jyu-1 居 *p.249b*
jyu-4 鋸 *p.249b*
jyu-2 局 898
jyu-3 舉 934
jyu-4 句 289
jyu-4 具 *p.262b*
jyu-1 俱 *p.263a*
jyu-4 巨 496
jyu-3 矩 *p.262b*
jyu-3 拒 *p.262b*
jyu-4 距 *p.262b*

jyu-4 虔 670
jyu-4 劇 *p.242a*
jyu-4 據 671
jyu-4 聚 *p.271b*
jyun-1 均 *p.256a*
jyun-1 軍 649
jyun-4 菌 *p.285b*
jyung-1 冂 20[13]
jywan-1 捐 *p.281b*
jywan-3 关 *p.245b*
jywan-4 卷 *p.245b*
jywan-1, jywan-4
　　圈 *p.245b*
jywan-3 捲 *p.245b*
jywan-4 倦 *p.245b*
jywe-1 夬 469
jywe-2 決 788
jywe-2 亅 13[6]
jywe-2 掘 *p.283a*
jywe-2 絕 *p.239b*
jywe-2 脚 *p.284a*
jywe-2 覺 552
jywe-2 角 904[148]

—K—

kai-1 揩 *p.258a*
kai-1 開 503
kan-1 刊 *p.241a*
kan-3 凵 464[17]
kan-3 砍 *p.279b*
kan-4 看 121
kang-1 康 *p.264b*
kang-1 糠 *p.264b*
kang-4 亢 952
kang-4 抗 *p.252b*
kau-3 丂 689
kau-3 考 942
kau-4 靠 846

亮 瞭 料 列 烈 裂 劣 獵 留 溜 流 柳 六 驢 慮 屢 履 旅 律

率 綠 略 —M— 麻 麼 摩 馬 嗎 媽 碼 罵 埋 買 賣 脈 旅 律

麥 瞞 滿 蠻 曼 慢 忙 毛 矛 貓 卯 冒 帽 貿 沒 煤 眉 每 梅

美 妹 門 們 悶 盟 猛 蒙 夢 米 迷 謎 宀 祕 密 民 皿

罟名明命某謀母畝木牧目四

末抹莫摸模墨沒宀棉免勉面麵苗描貓秒妙

莫模基幕摩磨魔

廟滅

哪內嫩能尼呢泥你疒您寧奴努怒農濃弄暖嫩

-N-
拿納那哪奶奈耐男南難惱腦鬧呢那

嗽
穌
蘇
俗
宿
縮
粟
素
訴
速
肅
松
鬆
訴
送
酸
算
蒜
瘦

要
衰
率
摔
帥
拴
雙
霜
爽
水
氵
睡
稅
說
帥
盾
順
搜
瘦

似
勢
事
士
室
市
式
試
是
誓
氏
示
礻
視
適
釋
叔
殳
書

舒
蔬
梳
輸
孰
熟
贖
暑
蜀
屬
黍
鼠
數
束
樹
術
述
豎
刷

鞋 寫 瀉 卸 械 謝 吸 奚 希 稀 析 犧 膝 西 盧 戲 席 息 媳

熄 錫 昔 惜 習 喜 洗 匕 夕 糸 係 繫 細 心 忄 小 新 薪 欣 媳

辛 信 星 腥 醒 刑 型 形 行 杏 興 幸 姓 性 修 休 羞 宿 嗅

秀 袖 戌 虛 需 須 鬚 許 續 序 敍 畜 蓄 繡 熏 尋 巽 嗅

訊 斯
訓 撕
兄 糸
凶 糸
兇 絲
胸 死
雄 似
宣 四
旋 寺
玄 巳
選 肆
學
血　–T–
雪 他
穴 她
厶 牠
私 它
司 塔
思 踏

糖 堂 倘
台 躺 趟
胎 桃 逃
抬 討 套
太 特 疼
態 滕 藤
攤 貪 彈
痰 談 毯
坦 探 歎
炭 湯 燙
梯 剃 蹄
踢 唐 塘

堤 材 財 戈 裁 采 彩 採 菜 參 慘 蠶 殘 倉 蒼 操 艸 廿 草 冊
提 題 體 替 聽 廳 庭 挺 亭 停 偷 亠 投 頭 透 擦 猜 才

村 磁 詞 辭 此 束 刺 次 圖 塗 屠 徒 突 途 土 吐 兔 通 桶
側 廁 測 策 曾 層 湊 粗 促 醋 囪 悤 聰 从 從 催 錯 存 寸

wei-4 僞 p.284a	
wei-4 胃 p.253b	
wei-4 謂 p.253b	
wen-1 㿈 924	
wen-1 溫 925	
wen-1 瘟 p.288b	
wen-2 文 360[67]	
wen-2 紋 p.275a	
wen-2 蚊 p.275a	
wen-2 聞 202	
wen-3 穩 p.265a	
wen-4 問 200	
weng-1 翁 p.282a	
wo-1 窩 p.270a	
wo-3 我 44	
wo-4 握 p.285b	
wo-4 臥 p.278a	
wu-1 屋 397	
wu-1 污 p.275b	
wu-1 烏 p.282a	
wu-2 无 60[71]	
wu-2 毋 212[80]	
wu-2 無 749	
wu-3 侮 p.280a	
wu-3 五 148	
wu-2 吾 867	
wu-3 伍 p.276b	
wu-4 悟 p.280b	
wu-3 午 594	
wu-3 武 p.278a	
wu-3 舞 p.249a	
wu-4 兀 58	
wu-4 勿 375	
wu-4 物 p.245a	
wu-4 惡 p.257a	
wu-4 戊 497	
wu-4 務 841	
wu-4 誤 p.263a	

僞 胃 謂 㿈 溫 瘟 文 紋 蚊 聞 穩 問 翁 窩 我 握 臥 屋 污

烏 无 毋 無 侮 五 吾 伍 悟 午 武 舞 兀 勿 物 惡 戊 務 誤

—Y—

ya-1 壓 p.252a	
ya-1 鴨 p.291b	
ya-2 牙 576[92]	
ya-1 呀 p.274b	
ya-1 鴉 p.274b	
ya-2 芽 p.274b	
ya-4, ya-3 亞 p.256b	
ya-3 啞 p.257a	
yan-1 淹 p.282b	
yan-1 烟 969	
yan-2 延 p.279a	
yan-2 嚴 p.262a	
yan-2 炎 672	
yan-2 鹽 p.246b	
yan-2 研 767	
yan-2 言 38[149]	
yan-3 㕣 99	
yan-2 沿 p.294b	
yan-3 广 155[53]	
yan-3 演 p.258b	
yan-3 眼 p.242b	
yan-4 彥 966	
yan-2 顏 967	
yan-4 厭 p.252a	
yan-4 驗 p.248b	
yang-1 央 278	
yang-1 秧 p.275a	
yang-2 易 686	
yang-2 揚 p.255b	
yang-2 楊 p.255b	
yang-2 陽 687	
yang-2 羊 115[123]	
yang-2 羋 475[123]	
yang-2 洋 611	
yang-3 養 p.243a	
yang-3 癢 p.293a	
yang-4 恙 561	

–Y–

广 演 眼 彥 顏 厭 驗 央 秧 易 揚 楊 陽 羊 羋 洋 養 癢 恙

壓 鴨 牙 呀 鴉 芽 亞 啞 淹 烟 延 嚴 炎 鹽 研 言 㕣 沿

you-1 優 *p.265a*
you-2 尤 298
you-2 游 *p.251a*
you-2 遊 *p.251a*
you-2 猶 *p.286b*
you-2 由 799
you-2 油 1043
you-2 郵 897
you-3 友 210
you-3 有 180
you-3 酉 363¹⁶⁴
you-4 又 85²⁹
you-4 右 573
you-4 幼 *p.275b*
you-4 誘 *p.250a*
yu-2 予 692
yu-4 預 693
yu-2 于 612
yu-2 余 613
yu-2 餘 872
yu-2 兪 974
yu-2 愉 *p.284b*
yu-2 娛 *p.282b*
yu-2 於 656
yu-2 禺 489
yu-4 遇 *p.241b*
yu-2 魚 558¹⁹⁵
yu-3 與 933
yu-4 譽 *p.294b*
yu-3 羽 781¹²⁴
yu-3 語 868
yu-3 雨 283¹⁷³
yu-4 域 *p.259b*
yu-4 浴 *p.280b*
yu-4 裕 *p.285a*
yu-4 玉 62⁹⁶

yu-4 聿 81¹²⁹
yu-4 育 *p.251a*
yun-2 勻 *p.256a*
yun-2 云 684
yun-2 雲 *p.250a*
yun-3 允 878
yun-4 暈 *p.287b*
yun-4 運 650
yung-3 擁 *p.291b*
yung-3 永 559
yung-4 用 403¹⁰¹
yung-3 甬 715
yung-3 勇 *p.252b*
yung-3 湧 *p.284b*
ywan-1 寃 *p.284b*
ywan-2 元 72
ywan-4 院 838
ywan-2 原 332
ywan-2 源 *p.259a*
ywan-4 願 334
ywan-2 援 *p.239b*
ywan-2 緣 *p.253a*
ywan-2 員 732
ywan-2 圓 733
ywan-2 袁 578
ywan-2 園 1018
ywan-3 遠 579
ywan-4 怨 *p.280a*
ywe-1 曰 82⁷³
ywe-1 約 986
ywe-4 月 178⁷⁴
ywe-4 刖 450
ywe-4 樂 894
ywe-4 越 651
ywe-4 閱 *p.290b*
ywe-4 龠 *p.288a*²¹⁴

余
餘
俞
愉
娛
於
禺
遇
魚
與
譽
羽
語
雨
域
浴
裕
玉

優
尤
游
遊
猶
由
油
郵
友
有
酉
又
右
幼
誘
予
預
于

聿
育
勻
云
雲
允
暈
運
擁
永
用
甬
勇
湧
寃
元

源
願
援
緣
員
圓
袁
園
遠
怨
曰
約
月
刖
樂
越
閱
龠
元
院
原

STROKE COUNT–STROKE ORDER
INDEX

This second index of characters is arranged by stroke count and stroke order and therefore enables the student to find, for reference or review, any character in this book whose pronunciation he or she does not know or is unsure of. The index has been organized by the stroke count–stroke order system rather than the traditional radical system because mastery of the latter requires considerable time. Mastery of the radicals is one of the goals of this book, not a skill assumed of its users, whereas the stroke count–stroke order system can be used by a student almost immediately. It is also a system that, as George Kennedy says, "appears to be widely used in China today."

In order to use the index, you should first count the number of strokes in the character under consideration. As you learn new characters and how to write them from the diagrams, the ability to count correctly the number of strokes and learn the little tricks familiar to every first year student of Chinese will come naturally. (For example, the shape ㄱ is counted as one stroke rather than two.) Characters in this index are grouped according to the total number of strokes in the character, beginning with characters having the fewest strokes (1 to 3 strokes) and concluding with those having the most strokes (18 or more). Where a discrepancy exists, count the strokes that are actually made as you write the character by hand rather than use the "official" count traditionally used in Chinese dictionaries.

You must then determine into which of the following four categories the *first stroke* in the character falls: 1) a dot, including any stroke downward to the right; 2) a horizontal stroke, including any angle that begins with a left to right horizontal; 3) a vertical stroke, including angles that begin with a vertical; or 4) a left, downward-slanting stroke, including angles that begin this way. To summarize:

1. Dot	﹨	or	﹀
2. Across	—	or	¬
3. Down	│	or	∟
4. Left	╱	or	<

All characters with the same number of strokes are subdivided into these four categories of "first strokes." Much like an alphabetical system, these categories are further ordered according to the category (dot, across, down, left) into which the *second stroke* of the character falls. For example, if one character has twelve strokes and its first and second strokes are "dots" (盜), it will appear before a character of twelve strokes of which the first is a dot and the second a horizontal stroke (童), and so on. Note that characters whose first element is the common "grass radical" ⺿ are classified in the stroke count–stroke order system as if the first stroke were a downstroke, though this differs from the writing diagrams in the text.

All of the characters appearing in *Reading and Writing Chinese* are given here, with the exception of characters that ordinarily appear in modern texts only as parts of other characters. The index does, however, include all forms of radicals.

The system of reference to characters and page numbers is explained in the introduction to the Alphabetical Index on page 301.

1-3 strokes

1-3

[丶]
、 61³
丬 564¹⁵
丷 88¹²
氵 181⁸⁵
宀 127⁴⁰
冖 37⁸
冖 47¹⁴
辶 171¹⁶²
亠 68
忄 67⁶¹
广 155⁵³
之 *p.250b*

[一]
一 8¹
二 9⁷
三 10
弋 847⁵⁴
彐 80⁵⁸
弓 218⁵⁷
于 87⁵¹
尸 329⁴⁴
弋 42⁵⁶
十 22²⁴
丂 689
匚 143²²
匚 145²³
卩 84²⁶
巳 760²⁶
阝 76¹⁷⁰;136¹⁶³
下 351
工 443⁴⁸
土 86³²
士 134³³

于 612
丁 519
七 150
寸 186⁴¹
扌 14⁶⁴
才 596
厂 154²⁷
廾 141⁵⁵
大 50³⁷
丈 *p.255b*
乙 *p.275a*⁵
叉 85²⁹
叉 *p.275a*
刁 *p.275a*
已 273⁴⁹
巳 275
巳 274
也 6
了 17
子 18³⁹
刀 102¹⁸
力 206¹⁹
刃 522
兀 58
尢 59⁴³

[丨]
丨 3²
丿 13⁶
乚 5⁵
卜 118²⁵
匕 137²¹
上 346
冂 20¹³
口 21³¹
口 33³⁰
刂 205¹⁸
巾 352⁵⁰

二 三 又 彐 弓 于 尸 弋 十 丂 匚 匚 卩 巳 阝 下 工 土 士

[丶] 、 冫 丷 氵 宀 亠 辶 亡 忄 广 之

[一] 一

于 丁 七 寸 扌 才 厂 廾 大 丈 乙 又 刁 己 巳 巳 也 了

子 刀 力 刃 兀 尢 [川] 丨 丿 乚 卜 匕 上 冂 口 口 刂 巾 也 了

5 strokes

矢 失 乍 禾 外 冬 用 包 皮 句 册 合 参 付 代 氏 仗 他

仙 白 印 犯 卯 斥 瓜 台 母 奴 幼 奶

6

[丨] 汗 污 江 他

池 尖 亥 守 安 忙 妄 交 衣 充 冰 次 兆 州 羊 主 米

[一] 艮 耒 戎 式 耳 刑 聿 圭 寺 吏 地 吉 束 老 考 西 再 臣

西 共 扣 托 灰 列 死 在 百 有 存 而 匠 至 戍 羽

光 劣 此 早 吐 吃 同 虫 曲 凸 因 回 帆 虍 肉 网 收 艸

[丨] 尖

[丿] 兒 舛 合 企 全 年 刖 朱 缶 成 先 丢 舌 竹 竼 名 多 各

[亻] 朵 危 色 伙 伍 休 伏 臼 似 份 件 任 自 向 血 丝 舟 行 奸

好 19
她 12
如 787
糸 28[120]
糸 174[120]

7 strokes

[丶]
沈 *p.276b*
決 788
沙 *p.259a*
汽 413
沒 184
完 548
究 768
牢 *p.276b*
況 *p.243b*
冷 920
辛 549[160]
言 38[149]
快 470
忘 500
序 *p.256a*
良 305
初 *p.239a*
社 797
判 *p.294a*
弟 220
兌 238
灶 *p.276b*

[一]
甬 715
弄 *p.244a*
玖 *p.276b*
形 886
戒 *p.271a*

志 1057
坑 *p.252b*
址 *p.276b*
昙 889[168]
走 434[156]
酉 363[164]
赤 *p.276b*[155]
攻 *p.240b*
均 *p.256a*
却 *p.253a*
豆 453[151]
車 412[159]
匣 *p.264b*
更 125
吾 867
孝 385
束 657
克 *p.262a*
求 746
甫 404
抖 *p.276b*
抗 *p.252b*
扶 *p.277a*
技 *p.256a*
找 508
把 468
扭 *p.277a*
抄 *p.259a*
批 *p.252a*
投 *p.277a*
抛 *p.277a*
折 *p.277a*
抓 *p.277a*
村 *p.243b*
材 *p.243b*
李 249
杏 *p.277a*
邪 *p.277a*

好 她 如 糸 糸

辛 言 快 忘 序 良 初 社 判 弟 兌 灶

7

[丶] 沈 決 沙 汽 沒 完 究 牢 況 冷

[一] 甫 弄 玖 形 戒

志 坑 址 昙 走 酉 赤 攻 均 却 豆 車 匣 吾 孝 束 克 求

甫 抖 抗 扶 技 找 把 扭 抄 批 投 抛 折 抓 村 材 李 杏 邪

低 888
兵 *p.256b*
皂 *p.277b*
身 185[158]
迎 811
近 580
狂 *p.275a*
系 860
妨 *p.257a*
妒 *p.277b*
妙 *p.259b*
妖 *p.277b*
姊 *p.278a*
努 844
災 *p.259b*
辵 983[162]

8 strokes

[丶]
注 801
法 546
河 557
泥 *p.245a*
沾 *p.273a*
油 1043
泡 *p.266b*
波 *p.239a*
沿 *p.294b*
治 866
宗 808
定 424
宜 129
官 407
空 900
姜 701
庚 *p.265a*
於 656

放 527
怪 592
性 790
怕 547
享 1040
京 299
店 *p.244a*
府 816
底 529
夜 495
育 *p.251a*
刻 507
房 393
肩 *p.278a*
衫 *p.278a*
券 *p.245b*
並 653
炒 *p.259a*
炊 *p.278a*
炎 672

[一]
隶 *p.264b*[171]
玩 93
武 *p.278a*
青 198[174]
表 110
妻 *p.248a*
取 365
幸 89
坦 *p.278a*
坡 *p.239a*
坴 675
亞 *p.256b*
戔 166
或 113
東 165
事 316

低 兵 皂 身 迎 近 狂 系 妨 妒 妙 妖 姊 努 災 辵

[丨] 注 法 河 泥 沾 油 泡 波 沿 治 宗 定 宜 官 空 姜 庚 於 **8**

放 怪 性 怕 享 京 店 府 底 夜 育 刻 房 肩 衫 券 並 炒 炊

炎 [一] 隶 玩 武 青 表 妻 取 幸 坦 坡 坴 亞 戔 或 東 事

朋 股 周 兔 忽 食 依 使 供 例 佳 阜 版 延 迫 帛 兒 的 昏

采 爸 斧 念 金 舍 命 侖 制 牧 物 知 垂 刮 季 和 委 肥 服

9 strokes

狗 欣 所 往 爬 征 彼 参 妹 姑 姐 始 紉

洋 柒 津 洞 洗 洛 活 染 派 宣 室 穿 突 客 姿 逃 迹 送 迷

9

[丨]

洲

祝 美 羗 卷 前 首 剃 炸
帝 亲 音 計 訂 施 彥 恢 恨 恰 亭 亮 疫 度 扁 軍 祕 祖 神
[一]
癸 春 毒 珍 段 型 垮 哉 城

封 嘔 韋 政 軌 要 葉 某 甚 革 巷 南 故 胡 挖 按 挑 拼 持
指 拴 拾 括 者 柬 柱 枯 相 柳 查 咸 頁 研 砍 厚 面 耐 耍

10 strokes

[丶]

保促俘俗俄侮修係段皇泉追帥盾待律很後紅

紀約姨娃姪姻怒

10

[丶] 流浪酒浸消涉浮浴

海家宮容窄害案悟悔凍准旁站這討記訊託訓

旅高衰畝症病疹疾疼疲效庫席唐座庭畜扇袖

唇 烈
捕 砲 破
振 夏 原
挾 捎 致
捌 桑 書
捉 弱 展
捐 孫 院
挺 陣 除
挽 降
挨 校
核 桂 根
桃 格 匪
套 辱

[冂]
鬥

索 髟
袍 被 恥
祥 瓶 栽
羞 拳 兼
料 粉 益
烘 烟 恐
連 速 通
逐 袁 哥
栗 配

[一]
馬 素 班
珠 彗

柴桌荒草茶剛時財閃哪唉骨蚊員哭恩盈豈

[ノ]
鬯奚爹翁殺倉途造透逢拿針釘笑氣缺耕耗

特矩乘秤租秧秫脂胸脈倍隻倦借值倒們倘

俱倡個候條息臭躬島烏射師鬼留狼狹航般徒倘

11 strokes

355

13 strokes

14 strokes

[丶]

演 *p.258b*
滴 *p.252a*
滾 *p.288a*
漸 *p.247a*
漢 *p.259a*
滿 903
漆 *p.246a*
漲 *p.288a*
漏 *p.288a*
寧 *p.262a*
蜜 *p.242a*
寬 859
寡 *p.288a*
實 770
窩 *p.270a*
察 981
辡 550
辣 *p.288a*
端 *p.268b*
齊 1045²¹⁰
遮 *p.288a*
說 240
誌 1058
語 868
認 524
誤 *p.263a*
誘 *p.250a*
旗 *p.247b*
豪 *p.288b*
膏 *p.270a*
敲 *p.270a*
慢 472
慣 1050
慘 *p.288b*
瘧 *p.288b*

14

辡
辣
端
齊
遮
說
誌
語
認
誤
誘
旗
豪
膏
敲
慢
慣
慘
瘧

[丶]

演
滴
滾
漸
漢
滿
漆
漲
漏
寧
蜜
寬
寡
實
窩
察

瘋 *p.288b*
瘦 *p.274b*
廣 972
麼 159
塵 *p.288b*
腐 *p.247a*
複 911
歉 *p.262b*
精 842
榮 *p.248a*
熄 *p.272a*

[一]

需 971
壽 *p.273b*
魂 *p.288b*
境 *p.244b*
聚 *p.271b*
墊 *p.288b*
趕 *p.241a*
截 *p.263b*
輕 1051
歌 318
遭 *p.274a*
緊 492
監 *p.246b*
酸 *p.288b*
摘 *p.252a*
摔 *p.274a*
摸 *p.268a*
誓 *p.288b*
榨 *p.254b*
槍 *p.242b*
奪 *p.262a*
磁 *p.288b*
厭 *p.252a*
凳 *p.288b*
盡 *p.250b*

瘋
瘦
廣
麼
塵
腐
複
歉
精
榮
熄

[一]

需
壽
魂
境
聚
墊

趕
截
輕
歌
遭
緊
監
酸
摘
摔
摸
誓
榨
槍
奪
磁
厭
凳
盡

15 strokes

廚 賣
廟 熱
摩 輛
廢 輪
慶 暫
廠 歐
褲 豎
遵 賢
導 遷
養 選
　　遲

[一]　醉
震　醋
髮　歎
穀　鞋
增　撞
墳　撈
趣　撕
　　趙

撒 履
撥 慰
撤 劈
撲 隨
播
鴉　[丨]
樣
椿　賞
標　幣
橫　輩
模　鬧
概　劇
確　慮
碼　膚
厲　齒
憂　墨
彈　影
層　瞎
　　暴
　　賠

賭 賤 噴 閲 數 蝦 蝗 踪 踢 踏 遺 罷 獎

銷 鋤 鋒 篇 箭 範 箱 舞 靠 稼 稿 稻 膝 膠 皺 價 儉 躺 樂

[ノ]
餘 餓 銳 鋪

16 strokes

質 盤 徹 德 徵 衝 編 練 緩 線 緣

激 憑 親 辨 辦 龍 謎 謀 諜 謂 憐 襄 懂 磨 糖 糕 鄰 燒 燈

16

[丶]
燙 澡 濃 澤

17 strokes

襄 706
應 544
禮 481
糠 p.264b
糟 p.274a
糞 p.292a
營 p.248a
燭 p.252b

[一]
霜 p.272a
環 p.250b
幫 537
聲 705
聰 379
聯 1059
戴 359
擊 p.252b
臨 p.292a
醜 p.292a
艱 371
擦 p.292a
擠 p.292a
擴 p.256b
隸 p.292a
檢 1015
壓 p.252a
翼 p.292a
隱 p.265a

[丨]
戲 1020
虧 p.244a
薄 p.264a
薪 p.292a
薦 p.292a
薑 p.292b
點 282

瞭 p.292b
熊 p.271a
顆 p.292b
賺 p.262b
購 p.269b
闊 p.292b
嚇 p.292b
雖 642
牆 850

[丿]
懇 p.270b
鍋 p.270a
龠 p.288a[214]
繁 p.262b
臉 585
膽 p.251b
鮮 p.292b
儲 p.292b
優 p.265a
獲 p.259a
縮 p.274b
績 p.240a
總 605
縱 p.292b

18 and up

[丶]
瀉 p.292b
灣 p.260b
灑 p.292b
灌 p.251b
寶 p.265b
額 p.292b
競 p.251a
顏 967
識 526

18+

醜 艱 擦 擠 擴 隸 檢 壓 翼 隱
襄 應 禮 糠 糟 糞 營 燭
[一] 霜 環 幫 聲 聰 聯 戴 擊 臨
[丨] 戲 虧 薄 薪 薦 薑 點

瞭 熊 顆 賺 購 闊 嚇 雞 牆
[丿] 懇 鍋 龠 繁 臉 膽 鮮 儲
[一] 霜 環 幫 聲 聰 聯 戴 擊 臨

優 獲 縮 績 總 縱
瞭 瞧 顆 賺 購 闊 嚇 雖 牆
[丿] 懇 鍋 龠 繁 臉 膽 鮮 儲
瀉 灣 灑 灌 寶 額 競 顏 識

RADICAL CHART II	**1** STROKE	一 [1]	丨 [2]	丶 [3]	丿 [4]	乙 [5]	凵 [(5)]	亅 [6]
See front endpapers for explanation.	**2** STROKES	二 [7]	亠 [8]	人 [9]	亻 [(9)]	儿 [10]	入 [11]	八 [12]
丷 [(12)]	八 [(12)]	冂 [13]	冖 [14]	冫 [15]	几 [16]	凵 [17]	刀 [18]	刂 [(18)]	力 [19]
勹 [20]	匕 [21]	匚 [22]	匸 [23]	十 [24]	卜 [25]	卩 [26]	卩 [(26)]	厂 [27]	厶 [28]
又 [29]	巛 [47]	辶 [162]	阝 [163]	阝 [170]	**3** STROKES	口 [30]	囗 [31]	土 [32]	士 [33]
夂 [34]	夊 [35]	夕 [36]	大 [37]	女 [38]	子 [39]	宀 [40]	寸 [41]	小 [42]	尢 [43]
尸 [44]	屮 [45]	山 [46]	巛 [47]	巛 [(47)]	巛 [47]	工 [48]	己 [49]	巾 [50]	干 [51]
幺 [52]	广 [53]	廴 [54]	廾 [55]	弋 [56]	弓 [57]	彐 [58]	彑 [(58)]	彡 [59]	彳 [60]
小 [(61)]	忄 [(61)]	扌 [64]	氵 [85]	犭 [94]	艹 [140]	辶 [162]	辶 [162]	**4** STROKES	心 [61]
小 [(61)]	忄 [(61)]	忄 [(61)]	戈 [62]	户 [63]	户 [(63)]	手 [64]	扌 [(64)]	支 [65]	攴 [66]
攵 [(66)]	文 [67]	斗 [68]	斤 [69]	方 [70]	无 [71]	旡 [(71)]	日 [72]	曰 [73]	月 [74]
木 [75]	欠 [76]	止 [77]	歹 [78]	歺 [(78)]	殳 [79]	母 [80]	比 [81]	毛 [82]	氏 [83]
气 [84]	水 [85]	氵 [(85)]	火 [86]	灬 [(86)]	爪 [87]	爫 [(87)]	父 [88]	爻 [89]	爿 [90]
片 [91]	牙 [92]	牛 [93]	牛 [(93)]	犬 [94]	犭 [(94)]	王 [96]	礻 [113]	四 [122]	罒 [122]
月 [130]	艹 [140]	辶 [162]	辶 [162]	**5** STROKES	玄 [95]	玉 [96]	王 [(96)]	瓜 [97]	瓦 [98]